CANDY GIRL MENTALITY

CANDY GIRL MENTALITY

KEYS TO TURNING BITTER MOMENTS INTO SWEET SUCCESS

LISA L. HOWZE

A WORD OF THANKS TO OUR
BULK BOOK ORDER PARTNERS

"Gifts aren't to be paid back; they're to be paid forward."

~ Cedric Crawford

We, at The Lisa Howze Experience, LLC, value the relationships that we have built over the last three decades. As such, if this book was purchased for you as a gift, we owe a debt of gratitude to our bulk book order partners, who are committed to investing in the lives of their clients, employees, and most of all, students.

Feel free to extend your words of appreciation to:

_____

Copyright ©2022-2023 by The Lisa Howze Experience, LLC

All rights reserved. Printed in the United States of America. No part of this book may be reproduced in any manner whatsoever without written permission except in the case of brief quotations embodied in critical articles and review. The opinions expressed in this publication are of the author's and do not reflect the views or the opinions of the publisher.

Some names and characteristics have been changed, some events have been compressed, and some dialogue has been recreated to protect the identity of the innocent and guilty.

Published by The Lisa Howze Experience, LLC

Cover design by University of Moguls Publishing and Design
www.universityofmoguls.com

ISBN-13: 979-8-218-12150-1

For speaking engagements and bulk book orders, visit website:
iamlisahowze.com

Linked In:
linkedin.com/in/lisahowze

Facebook:
facebook.com/lisa.howze

Instagram/Twitter:
@iamlisahowze

ENDORSEMENTS

"*Candy Girl Mentality* is a must-read for every woman whose little girl inside is still looking to heal from past hurt. As a strong advocate for teenage girls and believer in the power of sisterhood, I appreciate the level of transparency and vulnerability that Lisa demonstrates in this page-turning memoir. By sharing both her highs and lows, she amplifies the voice of many successful professional women who are free to now remove their masks and stop suffering in silence."

—Shaun Robinson
President and Founder, S.H.A.U.N. Foundation for Girls
Executive Producer, Actor, and National Primetime TV Host

"*Candy Girl Mentality* is a masterful gift to the world, chock-full of lessons and personal conviction to be successful. Every mother with a daughter, sister with a friend, teacher with a class, and anyone who thinks barriers are insurmountable should read this book."

—Lee E. Meadows, Ph.D.
Meadows Consulting

"Lisa Howze's book, *Candy Girl Mentality,* is a must read that takes you on a journey of her amazing life. From adolescence to adulthood, you are given a front row seat to witness the evolution of who she becomes. The life lessons she gains along the way are masterfully weaved throughout each chapter and provide a road map on how to pursue your purpose through the difficulties of life. Success is a journey, and *Candy Girl Mentality* is a great guide to help you navigate the trip!"

—Crisette Ellis
First Lady of Greater Grace Temple
National Sales Director, Mary Kay
Radio Talk Show Host of "We Got Issues"
on 910 AM Superstation

"*Candy Girl Mentality* is an investment that yields dividends forever. Parents who want long-term financial success for themselves and their children are encouraged to read this book and follow Lisa's example on how to manage money and wield its power."

—Gail Perry-Mason
Author of *Money Matters for Families*
Founder of Money Matters for Youth Financial Literacy Program

"*Candy Girl Mentality* is the literary embodiment of Lisa's life cycle from young entrepreneur to financial literacy champion and beyond. With the core tenets of strength, courage, and wisdom, Lisa encourages the reader to overcome obstacles along their pathway to purpose. Her practical advice will awaken the 'candy girl' in all of us as we pursue our God-given destiny."

—Kecia Williams Smith, Ph.D., CPA
Assistant Professor of Accounting

"What letter would I write to my younger self? This singular question, posed by Lisa in her book *Candy Girl Mentality: Keys to Turning Bitter Moments into Sweet Success*, invoked a myriad of thoughts, emotions, and sentiments. A real "look in the mirror" moment; you know—to thine own self be true. I had thoughts of joy, feelings of nostalgia, and a few regrets. However, answering the question and writing the letter was cathartic. As Lisa expertly drew me in, I needed to go deeper, read more, and discover what other pearls of wisdom she had. No matter where you are on this life journey, *Candy Girl Mentality* is a MUST read for everyone regardless of your age, gender, or profession. Through her own life experiences, Lisa lays bare what most may want to keep private, while encouraging and providing practical application for turning the bitter into sweet. *Candy Girl Mentality* is the type of book you can't read just once but will want to read again and again . . . well done!"

—Katrina I. Crawley, Esq.

"I continue to be inspired by Lisa Howze and the example she sets for high school and college students who greatly benefit from her guidance and varied experiences. As such, *Candy Girl Mentality* is a gift that keeps giving. It not only is a tool for leaders who are responsible for mentoring the next generation but proof for them to never give up! This book also has the power to reach adults who may be suffering the loss of a job, facing new challenges, or dealing with disappointment. *Candy Girl Mentality* will show you how to regain your confidence and get started down a new path."

—Peggy D. Dzierzawski
Retired President and Chief Executive Officer
Michigan Association of Certified Public Accountants

"*Candy Girl Mentality* is an inspiring story that gave me an even greater appreciation for Lisa Howze and the phenomenal leader she is. While working with her in Detroit city government, I watched how she masterfully leveraged her CPA background and government experience to successfully launch an initiative that helps thousands of individuals and families get the financial support they need at tax time. In addition to its long-lasting impact, the program has been recognized as a municipal best practice."

—Rose Gill
Principal, Bloomberg Associates

"When I met Lisa Howze, I instinctively knew she was a special person who supported and encouraged others to live their best life. If you are looking for something to inspire you to the next level, you will find it with *Candy Girl Mentality*. Lisa stated, 'If you want to be great in life, you must attach yourself to a cause greater than you.' It encouraged me to look within myself and refine what I want to achieve in different areas of my life, make the right decisions, and act now. I highly recommend reading her book and know it will transform and expand your goals and dreams!"

—Dubrece Miller
Staff Accountant

I dedicate this book to

the memory of my mom and dad.

Because you were, I am.

TABLE OF CONTENTS

Foreword xv
Preface xix
Introduction xxiii

SECTION I: STRENGTH 1

Chapter 1—Parental Guidance 3
Chapter 2—You Gonna Learn Today 19
Chapter 3—The Making of Candy Girl 37
Chapter 4—Go Blue: Lessons Beyond the Classroom 53
Chapter 5—The CPA Advantage: But Not Without Adversity 85
Chapter 6—P.I.M.P.-o-lo-gy 105
Chapter 7—Pain Has a Purpose 125

SECTION II: COURAGE 149

Chapter 8—That Was a Good Job 151
Chapter 9—I Didn't See That Coming! 167
Chapter 10—Politics 101: The Call, The Run, The Rise 183
Chapter 11—Let's Go Higher: Michigan House of
    Representatives 211
Chapter 12—Let's Go Even Higher: Detroit Mayoral Run 225
Chapter 13—In Over Your Head 261

SECTION III: WISDOM 281

Chapter 14—Maximize the Meantime 283
Chapter 15—No Setback…Girl, Bounce Back! 301
Chapter 16—Each One, Teach One! 317

Citations 331
Acknowledgements 335
Life Experience Elevation Pyramid (L.E.E.P.) 339
Mission 340
About the Author 341

FOREWORD

I stand in complete awe of Lisa LaShawn Howze! She is incredibly young to own the lifetime of wisdom, courage, and strength that she imparts with impassioned purpose to her readers. I remember our first meeting like yesterday. Lisa was an intern for the large commercial bank where I worked as a senior C-suite executive. I was one of few African American females in my position. As such, I believed it was extremely important to welcome young talent to our firm, share insights, and address questions they might have in hopes of them considering permanent employment with the bank.

At one of the bank's weekly networking events, I recall meeting Lisa and being very impressed with and somewhat amused by this intelligent, inquisitive, and confident young woman. When I asked about her major, she expressed an interest in "marketing." Surprised by my disapproving reaction, she quickly decided to recommit her focus to the accounting program that she had begun at the prestigious University of Michigan. Although we could not persuade her to continue to work for the bank after graduation, I was pleased to learn years later that she had a successful start to her career in public accounting. Since then, everything she has accomplished personally and professionally has been nothing short of outstanding.

Lisa's spirited attitude and strong belief in herself were evident to me from the very beginning. I sensed that this young woman was destined to explore and discover the full extent of her capabilities.

She was ready for opportunity and willing to entertain other people's ideas of success. Lisa savored a broad landscape of perspectives, tried them on for size, and leveraged the ones most suitable to help her breakthrough to the next level.

Candy Girl Mentality shows all of us why strength, courage, and wisdom are needed to overcome obstacles and elevate our lives, careers, and finances through Lisa's example. Her experiences are eye-opening, her reflections are riveting, and her authenticity is abundant. Together, they provide guidance to the novice, reinforce learnings to the more experienced, and cause the most seasoned of us to reminisce about our own timeless collection of life lessons that can and should be passed on to future generations.

As you read this masterful piece of literature, I invite you to breathe in and breathe out–in yoga fashion–the deep meditative impact of Lisa's life-learned discoveries. Enjoy a smile and outright laughter when you meet her unique humor in the valleys and high points of her journey. Share in her successes and empathize with the depth of her pain and emotions during times of setback. Finally, when you reach the part of the book that gives you an opportunity to participate in a powerful exercise, I urge you to engage wholeheartedly. While Lisa mentions how writing *Candy Girl Mentality* has been life changing for her, nothing can be more compelling than reading this book, completing the exercise, and going through the life-altering experience for yourself.

In closing, Lisa is indeed the finest example of a self-actualized person that I know. It has truly been a pleasure to have sustained a long-lasting connection and friendship with her. Like a beautiful butterfly, she has been consistent in her evolution and willingness to lift others as she climbs. With her talents and understanding of what makes one whole and happy on full display in *Candy Girl Mentality*, I am honored to have been a "fly on the wall" to witness a well-lived life. Therefore, I know without a doubt that after reading her story, you will feel the same as I do.

Warmly,

Linda D. Forte
Senior Vice President, Business Affairs and
Chief Diversity Officer, Comerica Bank (Retired)

PREFACE

I have a collection of journals that over the years have documented and captured some of my most intimate thoughts. While poring through pages of notes, I could tell the condition of my heart based on the nature of my prayers, the ambition of my goals, and sentiment of my reflections.

The entry that best caught my attention was penned on May 12, 2013—Mother's Day! In it, I accounted for how I attended two different church services that Sunday, with each having its own celebration and tribute to mothers. In writing about that experience, I said:

"I felt my emotions stir as I reflected on my mother and our times together. I tried to focus on the more tender moments; the loving, supportive moments when my mother was my biggest cheerleader. When she sat in the front-row seat of my success. When she held my hand when I felt scared or afraid, and I held her hand as she slowly drifted away from me."

I concluded the entry with a statement that suggested how rekindling memories from my past, particularly about my mom, had a way of conjuring up emotions and evoking sadness that I had not planned to feel that day. So, what did I do next? I did as I had always done. I bottled up all those melancholy feelings and kept it moving—at least until the pain I had been suppressing got triggered once again.

PREFACE

Does this sound familiar?

If you are anything like me, you know what it is like to maintain a busy lifestyle that helps you avoid dealing with life's most sensitive issues. As the saying goes, "You can run, but you cannot hide." Instead of hiding, why not seek answers to help you unlock the following questions: Who are you? Where are you? Why are you here?

Four years ago, when I started this journey to become a first-time author, I had no idea that it would turn into an adventure in self-discovery. Through my coach's example, I was inspired to actively begin the writing process by first outlining the significant emotional events that happened in my life. From there, I found that I could take the years of notes written in my journals and translate them onto the pages of the book that you now hold in your hands. Were there events that came from out of nowhere that slowed me down in the process? Absolutely! However, I could not let them stop me. The messages and lessons that I impart by telling my story are too valuable to not be shared with the world.

Furthermore, I never imagined how rewarding the writing process could be. While my original purpose for writing this book was singularly focused on you gaining the perspective you need for the life and career you want, so much more has since evolved for both you and me. By revisiting certain aspects of my life, I was fortunate to see things that I had not thought about in years through a different lens. I even developed new narratives that are now more empowering than some of the stories I had previously been telling myself. Sure, I could have played it safe by only giving you my career highlights and treating the intimate details of my story as secrets that I kept close to the vest. However, if I had taken that approach, I know I would have robbed you of a possible breakthrough of your own. I didn't want to do that at all.

Therefore, I decided instead to lean into this idea that I learned from a thought leader that says, "You cannot heal what you will not reveal." By choosing to be vulnerable and going beneath the surface, I know that my story will help someone who may have gone, is currently going, or is yet to go through a similar experience.

Finally, while the word "success" is part of the subtitle of this book, I want you to know that success is a relative term. Its meaning varies depending on who you talk to. However, in the context of what has been discussed so far, we can universally agree to define success as your ability to push past pain and persevere, go from hurt to healed, and share your own aha moments along the way.

INTRODUCTION

*I*f you could sit and have a conversation with your younger self, what would you say?

Like millions of other people in the world, chances are you have thought about this question more than once. As you get older, with every milestone birthday, there is a tendency to reflect on who you were and what you were like in your youth compared to who you are today. Granted, being young is synonymous with making mistakes, giving too many f*cks, lacking focus, and wasting time, energy, and money on people, places, and things that hold less value today than they did when you were younger.

In a pointless attempt to rewrite history, you say things like, "If I had known then what I know now, I would have done things differently." Bull***t! Who are you fooling? Even if it were possible to go back and fix some of your past mistakes, you and I both would just find something else to screw up. And, if we are being totally honest, some of us waited until we turned 40 to "show your natural a**!" as my mom would say. But that is a different story for a different book. 😉

Like me, you probably had an encounter with an adult-figure—like a parent, teacher, counselor, pastor, close relative, supervisor, older sibling, or mature friend, who tried to give you some advice, but you failed to listen. Here is the good news: There is no need to beat yourself up. If it helps, Alexander Pope said, "To err is human; to forgive, divine." Besides, you cannot change the past by rehearsing your regrets. However, you can mentor a young person and help them create a brighter future.

I may not have known a lot of things growing up. However, life has taught me many valuable lessons that I never could have learned from a textbook. If that describes you as well, do not be afraid to show your scars. Your imperfections. Your flaws. They should serve as constant reminders—not only of what you have been through but what you have overcome. When we share our downs as well as our ups, we give the next generation the freedom to fail without the shame of failure. For every young person and the young at heart, life will constantly put you to the test. Your ability to pass will be measured by how often you get back up and try again.

When I consider the opening question for myself, there is no need to travel back in time. Why? Because the younger me has never left me. She has been with me throughout this entire journey. The two of us—she and I—we—are inseparable. If, in fact, there was no "SHE," there would be no "ME!" And, in case you missed it, I DID NOT WAKE UP LIKE THIS! It took a lifetime for me to become the woman I am today, and yet, I am still evolving.

What has been the secret to my success? I have been knocked down but refused to stay down. Though passed over, I never passed up an opportunity to get better and grow stronger. Despite being told "NO" a million times, I never accepted "NO" as the final answer. Therefore, the fight that is in me is because of the fight that was in her. The enterprising mind that I have today is the result of her rising to the occasion back in the day. Depending on which arena I am in, some people call me "Lisa," others call me "Ms. Howze," while some others call me "Representative." However, my friends from high school affectionately call me "Candy Girl!" It only makes sense given all the candy sales I transacted in the back halls of Cass Technical High School, located in my hometown of Detroit, Michigan. More on that later.

In the meantime, if I could sit and have a conversation with the 17-year-old me, I would simply say, "THANK YOU!" and then hand her a letter that reads as follows:

> June 29, 2021
>
> Dear Candy Girl,
>
> You are the sh*t!
>
> I thank you for teaching me how to view certain situations in life. You never allowed anything to stop you. If you tried something one way and it did not work out, you were determined to find another way—a better way. And, eventually, you did. You never settled for "good enough." You always strived for more because you had the audacity to believe that more was possible—not only for you but for others around you as well.
>
> As an adult Black woman, I draw so much of my strength from the example you set as a teenage girl. Now the time has come for you and I to join forces and show the world what it means to have a Candy Girl Mentality!
>
> Are you up for the challenge?
>
> Of course, you are! So, let's GO!
>
> Yours truly,
>
> Lisa
> (a.k.a. "Your Future Self")

INTRODUCTION

What does it mean to have a Candy Girl Mentality?

In short, Candy Girl Mentality has nothing to do with gender and everything to do with an entrepreneurial mindset and how you respond to life's setbacks. When you think like an entrepreneur, you are unstoppable. Your persistence is unparalleled, and your focus is fierce. While being flexible, you do not let obstacles get in your way. Why? Because you firmly believe that for every problem, there is a solution. In many ways, *you* are that solution. As you think outside the box and consistently add value to the lives of people and organizations you serve, you can and will be able to name your price. Beware, however; there is a price that comes with reaching the pinnacle of your career success.

What is that price, you ask?

It usually shows up in the form of setbacks, which are those uncomfortable, unpleasant occurrences that unfortunately are a natural part of life. You cannot avoid them. You can only learn to embrace them. While the path of least resistance may appear more attractive, there is no opportunity for growth. Therefore, whether the setback is represented by the loss of a loved one or failure to get promoted on your job, you always have an opportunity to choose your response. In fact, it was Lou Holtz who said, "Life is 10 percent what happens to you and ninety percent how you respond to it." Therefore, when you have a Candy Girl Mentality, you can turn your setbacks into bounce backs, losses into wins, and bitter moments into sweet success.

Is that enough to get you excited about what lies ahead? I sure hope so.

After reading *Candy Girl Mentality*, you will understand that:

- You were created on purpose for a purpose.
- All you have is all you need to get started.
- The best education sometimes comes from lessons learned outside of the classroom.
- You can overcome disappointment and still excel in your life and career.
- Losing is not always a bad thing.
- You can be courageous in the face of great opposition.
- Elevation usually follows your decision to maximize the meantime.
- You can bounce back from setbacks.
- Mentorship is important.

In sharing my story and all the above universal principles, my hope is that you will instantly be inspired and stirred into action, knowing that dreams do come true. As I always say, "If I can do it, you can do it, too. Except, when you do it, I hope you do it even better!"

How to Get the Most Value out of Reading this Book

As you prepare to dive in, there are three things you should be aware of: 1) I have arranged the book in three sections—Strength, Courage, and Wisdom. I encourage you to keep all three attributes in mind, as they will be critical to your career advancement and financial success; 2) If you are anything like me, you loathe exercises at the end of each chapter, no matter how life-changing the author says completing them will be. Good news! I decided to spare you the trouble. However, when you reach Chapter 15, please be prepared to accept my challenge and complete the exercises described therein. I guarantee it will be a rewarding experience and more than worth your investment. No cheating by peeking ahead! 3) Finally, I want you to enjoy reading my story as much as I enjoyed writing it.

Without any further delay, let the story of *Candy Girl Mentality* begin!

SECTION I
STRENGTH

The power to push past limits

PARENTAL GUIDANCE

The captain's resonant voice permeated throughout the cabin as he announced the aircraft's descent into Detroit Metropolitan Airport. He continued, "The current temperature in Detroit is 33 degrees with overcast skies. Flight attendants, please prepare the cabin for landing. We will be arriving at the gate momentarily."

"Thirty-three degrees!" I exclaimed. I was just in Vegas where the weather was a blistering 88 degrees and sunny. What was I thinking? Michigan weather can be downright disrespectful, especially when I was returning home from a warmer climate! No matter how much I complained, the cold crisp air is exactly what I needed to awaken my sleepy head that had hardly touched a pillow in over 20 hours at that point. Let's be clear, my lack of rest was not the result of a reckless night of roulette or the persistent play of slot machines in the smokey Vegas casinos. Gambling of that nature is not my thing. I will leave that to the thrill seekers who do not mind easily parting ways with their hard-earned cash.

Instead, I had been in Vegas for a three-day personal development training event that wrapped up on Sunday night. While sleep deprived, I made my early morning flight which returned me to

Detroit just before 1 p.m. on Monday afternoon. Eyes crimson red, stomach growling from hunger, I needed to get some rest but not before getting some comfort food in my belly. As such, I was a woman on a mission.

After deplaning, I immediately made a beeline to baggage claim, retrieved my luggage, scurried up the escalator, crossed over the bridge from the terminal to the parking garage, descended a different escalator to the Ground Transportation Center where outside I was hoping to see the airport shuttle that would take me to my vehicle. Unfortunately, it was not there. The 10-minute wait felt like an eternity. However, I was relieved once I reunited with my SUV. After leaving the parking lot, I headed east on I-94 with the intent to visit one of my favorite breakfast spots in the city—New Center Eatery, located on the same boulevard as the renowned Hitsville USA Museum—the birthplace of Berry Gordy's Motown Records.

Knowing exactly what I wanted to eat, I ordered without hesitation. The server loaded up my plate with eggs over easy, crispy, savory, salmon croquettes like Momma used to make, and a side bowl of grits topped with grilled shrimp and grated cheddar cheese. I always asked for whole wheat or multigrain toast with no butter and a side of strawberry jelly. Though I had a tall glass of orange juice in front of me already, I asked the server for a cup of hot water with lemon and honey. I used this combination as an elixir to help digest all the rich food I had just devoured. Stomach full, I could immediately feel the sleep gods hovering over my head, hoping I would slip into a slumber. I could not let that happen—at least not there! So, I cashed out my check and jetted toward the exit.

It was half past three o'clock. Before I left town, I had agreed to volunteer for the city's Angel's Night campaign. However, I was in no physical condition to keep my commitment. All I could think about was getting home, taking a shower, and resting. Not only did I need to rest my body from all the travel, but I needed to rest my mind. I had a big opportunity ahead of me the next day, and I did not want to blow it!

The Big Day

I woke up the next morning with a nervous excitement. Not waiting for the alarm clock to sound, I sprung out of bed in anticipation of what the day would bring. As I got dressed, my favorite gospel songs played in the background. There is something about gospel music to help quicken my spirit and add an extra pep in my step. Before heading out the door, I took one last glance in the mirror, winked at myself, and with confidence said, "You've got this!"

Slowly pulling out of the garage, I put my foot on the brake for a moment's pause to type the location's address into my GPS. The screen read back to me, "Total Distance: 33 miles. Estimated Travel Time: 37 minutes." I looked at the clock; it was 8:45 a.m. My appointment was at 9:30 a.m. *DAMN IT! I did it again!* I underestimated the amount of time it would take to get out of the house and onto the road. To make matters worse, it was snowing, which meant I needed to strike a balance between safety and speed. I could not be late for this meeting! Hoping and praying all the way there, I pulled into the parking lot with 10 minutes to spare—not the 30 minutes that would have been ideal.

Oh, well! Who said you had to be perfect to be successful? I will be honest. I have struggled with time my whole life. It started in my youth. I don't use that as an excuse, but it has been part of my reality. The only thing was, right then, in that very moment, I needed to shake off the guilt of my chronically late past and instead be prepared for the opportunity ahead of me. Before getting out of the vehicle, I changed my shoes and said a quiet prayer. After closing the driver's door, I suddenly heard their voices.

WAIT! WHAT! WHO IS THAT?

My mom went first.

"Hold your head up. Look them in the eye and don't hold back. Let your light shine!"

Next, there was my dad.

I could hear him saying, *"Hey, darlin'! I'm proud of you. I always knew you'd do great things. Now, go in there and show them what you're made of!"*

As I approached the front entrance, I had a renewed sense of energy. I was ready to conquer the world. My confidence level was on TEN and any sense of nervousness immediately faded away. As I entered the vestibule, I looked for a sign that would direct me to the meeting room.

Ahh, this way! I thought.

Part of the way there, I was intercepted in the hallway by the gentleman with whom I had two prior meetings. We shook hands, and then he showed me into the room where 11 other people awaited my arrival. I walked around the horseshoe-like table and greeted each one of them with a firm handshake and square look in the eyes. As each person introduced themselves, I made mental notes—connecting their faces and names with many of the profiles that I had studied the previous night. Among the 12, there were two women who served on the executive leadership team. I knew that I would need to impress them, given the amount of influence they carried. I was ready!

After the introductions, I was asked to take a seat at the head of the table that allowed me to see everyone's faces. The recruiting manager, also an executive vice president, sat opposite me. He opened the interview as follows:

"Lisa. Again, welcome. Now that you have met all of us, would you mind spending the first five minutes telling us about yourself and why you believe you're best suited for this position?"

Every job candidate hates the "tell me about yourself" interview question. However, I was prepared to not make a common mistake and regurgitate everything listed on my resume in chronological order like most candidates. Instead, I said,

"Jim. That is an excellent question. The best way to get to know me is to understand what I believe. And, I have three fundamental beliefs:

1) In life, there are no such things as mistakes, accidents, or coincidences. Everything happens for a reason.
2) People and organizations do not suffer from a lack of money. Instead, they suffer from a lack of imagination and creativity.
3) If you want to become significant in life, you must first attach yourself to a cause that is much bigger than you." In other words, it's not about me because it's much bigger than me.

Where did I get these beliefs?

Life.

My parents.

My mom and dad were my first teachers. My experiences with them helped shape my character and outlook on life. Just as a pilot is entrusted to safely transport passengers from point A to B, a parent's job is to protect his or her children and provide guidance to help them grow and develop. In either scenario, there is no guarantee that the experience will be without turbulence. Mine certainly was not. As I reflect on my upbringing, it was far from perfect. However, my parents did the best they could with the information and resources they had.

So, let's dig in and find out who these amazing human beings were.

Mother's Strength

My mom was old school, which means she was very private. If there was something that she didn't want you to know, she certainly was not going to tell you. If you asked her a question that she felt was none of your business, she did not feel obligated to answer and would just ignore you. She expected that same kind of discipline from her children, particularly me, as the youngest and most impressionable. To school me, she'd say, "Just because somebody asks you a question, it does not mean you have to give them an answer." This concept was a bit confusing to me as a kid because I was also taught to tell the truth, the whole truth, and nothing but the truth. So, help me, God!

CHAPTER 1—PARENTAL GUIDANCE

I would certainly need the Lord if she knew I was writing this book and "putting her business in the streets." For some of you, this may be hard to believe. For others who grew up like I did, you know exactly what I mean. If there was such a thing as child censorship, my mom was its enforcer. Trips outside the house to a friend's or relative's house was first met by this speech, "Now, when you get over there, don't you go running off at the mouth. You keep your 'trap' shut!" That was enough to make me think twice before I let something slip. Ha!

Seriously, what was she afraid I would tell?

If I did "tell," would anyone even care?

Somehow, like my mom, you may have convinced yourself that other people's opinions matter. Let me let you in on a little secret. Come close, now. ***Those people couldn't care less about you!*** In reality, people have a hard enough time keeping up with their own sh*t to be concerned with yours.

Nevertheless, my mom's disposition remained the same. By keeping a close rein on me, at least, she thought she could secure the Pandora's box of "family secrets." She added new meaning to the phrase, "Don't let the left hand know what the right hand is doing?" As an adult, I get it: Everything is not meant for public consumption. However, my mom's strict orders to remain silent in many ways stifled my ability to speak up and speak out when it mattered most. Too often, little girls become women who continue a cycle that they learned in their youth. To keep the façade going, the outward appearance sings, "I'm happy, healthy, and worry-free." On the inside, however; you are screaming, "HELP!"—an all too familiar cry that manifests itself in different forms, which we will also discuss later.

If this describes you, then stop it! If this is or was your mom, I understand. You are not alone. Despite her mysterious nature, my mom was the Bomb.com! Her commitment to education was unwavering. I cannot think of a time when she was not available to celebrate my various accomplishments. For example, she attended my parent–teacher conferences and award ceremonies and helped me prepare for my middle school spelling bee competitions. I was a fortunate kid to have my mom involved so deeply in my schooling.

She always emphasized the importance of books over toys. Her mantra was, "Don't buy that chile [sic] no toys; get her some books." Apparently, this was her message to other parents who would shower their kids with a boatload of material gifts, ranging from name brand clothes and shoes to electronic games and toys, to Barbie dolls, etc. You name it: I didn't have it!

My mother believed in giving me what I needed versus what I wanted. Because she had lived through some very difficult times, she understood that life would make great demands of me. Therefore, she made it her business to secure my future with a solid education. If this meant drilling me with math study guides, flash cards, or multiplication charts, so be it. These exercises were part of a summer learning enrichment program designed by my mom. Originally, I dreaded the drills but later developed a love for learning that did not require my mom to get on my case about studying. Instead, I turned learning into a game. The more I "played," the stronger I became. The more I practiced, the more advanced I had gotten doing math problems in my head—a skill that I still use today.

Thanks, Mom!

While her stern exterior said one thing, her actions spoke volumes in how she expressed care and concern for others. She made a lot of sacrifices to care for me, my brothers, and her aging relatives. Personally, I felt her love each time she whipped me up a breakfast sandwich, just before I dashed out the door to go to school. I felt her love whenever she would return home from a downtown shopping spree, bearing gifts for me. "Try this on," she'd say, as we both hoped whatever it was would fit perfectly. Finally, I felt her love when she would tell me, "Lisa, you're going to be a special star!" She affirmed me. She believed in me. And, she was there for me every step of the way, until her steps got shorter.

Now that you've gotten to know my mom a little bit, let's meet Dad.

Dad's Integrity

If the words tall, dark, and handsome were grouped together in the dictionary, my dad's picture would be next to it. He stood 6 feet and 3 inches tall. A southern boy, native of South Carolina, my dad was FINE! He had a smile that would light up the world and brighten up the day of anyone who encountered him. His voice was smooth like butter. Better yet, imagine a man holding his partner close on the ballroom dance floor. After a long pause and tight embrace, he gracefully moves her across the room while the audience holds their breath in anticipation of the grand finale. When I say smooth, I mean that kind of SMOOTH! I loved to hear him call me "Darlin'!" It was a term of endearment that melted my heart without fail. Overall, my dad was a man of few words. When he did speak, it was with a southern drawl—slow and deliberate but dripping with profound pearls of wisdom. I was fortunate to be his sounding board at times. It did not always make sense to me back when I was younger, but it makes a world of sense to me today.

With only a ninth-grade education, my dad emigrated from South Carolina to Detroit, Michigan, in the 1940's to obtain work in the factories. For years, he held down two jobs—one at a Chrysler assembly plant and the other at the UniRoyal tire company. He had a penchant for being on time. He believed in earning an honest day's pay for an honest day's work. My dad had no interest in cutting corners. He believed that anything worth doing was worth doing well.

Outside of work, Dad was a charitable man with a strong commitment to his faith. As a deacon at his church, my dad believed in serving others. At least once per week, he would make his rounds to bakeries across metro Detroit to pick up day-old bread used to feed the homeless. His church also ran an "Open Door" program that not only fed the less fortunate but provided them clothing and toiletries that came from generous public donations.

Because my dad worked in the automotive industry, he was handy with tools and knew his way around a car's engine. Whenever a neighbor or friend had a problem with their vehicle, they would bring it to my dad to fix. Dressed in full Dickies coveralls, Dad would seemingly work miracles for those hopeful souls, eager to put their cars on the road again.

My dad also kept a meticulous lawn and yard, year-round. If a nearby neighbor had trouble taking care of their property during any of the four seasons, it was not uncommon to see my dad assisting them with yard maintenance and snow removal as well. He was what you would call a "good neighbor"!

The irony about my dad is that although he worked for Chrysler, he loved to drive Cadillacs. The long-stretched, luxury sedan suited a man of his stature well and reflected one of the many fruits of his labors. In his wisdom, however, he knew not to pull that golden brown Cadillac Seville into the parking lot at Chrysler. That act was frowned upon then and even so today.

When my dad was not cruising the scene with a gangsta lean in his Cadillac, he would tear up the road on the back of a Kawasaki motorcycle. Dressed in dark denim jeans, a black leather motorcycle jacket, black leather boots with silver buckles, and an imposing helmet secured tightly on his head, my dad seemed bigger than life. I had such great admiration for him as a kid. I could be outside playing with friends and if I returned to the house and saw either the golden-brown Cadillac or the Kawasaki motorcycle parked out front, my stomach would immediately fill with butterflies. When I say I was excited, you better believe, I was EXCITED!

You see, I did not grow up with my dad in our home. As such, I often found myself longing for his presence. On those random occasions when he did come for a visit, I would instantly go into "show and tell" mode. I'd pull out my recent report card, certificates of achievement, and blue ribbons to show him how smart I was. I just wanted him to be proud of me. If I were lucky, he would give me a few dollars as a way of saying keep up the good work. And, just like that, he would be gone again.

The time in between his visits seemed like an eternity. I would pester my mom about him with no intentions of letting up. I was persistent. Now, if she had done something that was especially disappointing that hurt my little feelings, she was met with a resounding outburst as I exclaimed, "I WANT MY DADDY!" as tears flooded my eyes and flowed down my cheeks.

Your Wish Is My Command

My wildest dreams came true one hot summer day in the month of June 1986. I was 12 years old at the time when I had been working with the Summer Youth Employment Program offered through the local police mini station. I met a woman named Sharon who gave me my first assignment, which was to clean up the parking lot that was littered with trash behind the department store located at Greenfield and Grand River. After successfully completing that project, I returned to the police mini station to receive my next assignment. Sharon asked me if I wanted to make some additional money. I said, "Sure. What do I need to do?"

She said that I would simply need to pass out literature door to door. She then introduced me to the leader of the entire operation. He was a fair-skinned, medium-build brother who stood about 5'10" tall. He wore a Rastafarian knit cap (in the traditional red, yellow, and green colors) that kept his extremely long dreadlocks contained. To complete his look, he also wore an African print dashiki. When he stepped forward to greet me, he said, "Hello, Lisa. I'm Mr. Maccabee."

I remember going to a big mansion-like house with lots of rooms and people everywhere. They spoke of Yahweh and the Hebrew Israelite religion. I was not well-versed in any form of religion at that point of my life. Mom seemed to only take or send me to church on Easter, Mother's Day, and Christmas. Nevertheless, Mr. Maccabee assigned a partner to me, and together we hit the streets with a stack of literature in hand. I learned to knock on doors, hand the occupant a piece of literature, and ask for donations. In exchange for my time and effort, I got paid! While I still knew little about the Hebrew Israelite faith, I was confident that Mr. Maccabee was a kind, trustworthy man who had gained the respect of me and my mom.

One day, my mom and I approached him about helping me fulfill a mission that I like to call, **"Operation: Let's Go Find My Daddy!"** Gladly, he accepted.

It was a Saturday afternoon around 1 p.m. when Mr. Maccabee picked us up in a white stretch limo that I often saw parked at the mansion. Looking especially clean, the white exterior sparkled like diamonds, while the tires glistened in the sun. As we piled into the back seat of the limo, the proud look on my mom's face signaled she would take pleasure in pulling up to my dad's eastside home in style.

Following Mom's precise directions, Mr. Maccabee pulled in front of the single-family home that had a short flight of steps leading up to the front door, facing the streets. Mr. Maccabee got out of the limousine dressed in his full African garb—Rasta cap and dashiki—and a dark pair of shades. He knocked on the door and out came my dad. Without saying too many words, Mr. Maccabee gestured toward the limo and down the steps my dad came. As he approached the rear passenger door, I rolled down the window. Straight out of a Hollywood movie, I lowered the frames on my sunshades so he could see my eyes. Then I whispered, "Daddy, it's me!"

He looked at me without saying a word, turned around, and went back into the house.

Shock?

Disbelief?

Denial?

I'm not sure what was going on in his head. In the meantime, Mr. Maccabee started the limo's engine, and we pulled off.

Days later, I learned that the conversation my dad had with the person on the other side of his front door went something like this:

"John, who was that?" Sarah, his wife, asked.

"Oh, that was a friend of mine who brought her granddaughter by to say hello."

"Mm-hmm!" she replied under her breath.

When my dad went to bed that night, he could not get a moment's rest. He tossed and turned non-stop, as the movie reel of the day's events continued to play in his mind and weigh on his conscience. The following morning, he confessed to his wife that he had fathered a child outside of their marriage. Sarah, whom everyone affectionately called "Fatty" did not scream, yell, or pitch a fit. Instead, she simply asked, "What does the child need?" With compassion, she declared, "I guess we'll have to take her school shopping."

Lessons

By the world's standards, my conception could have easily been viewed as a mistake, which could not be further from the truth.

Considering I had no say in who my parents would be, I can only credit that responsibility to an authority much greater and more knowledgeable than me. Through careful orchestration, two imperfect people were brought together to help fulfill a perfect plan. Therefore, when I came into this world kicking and screaming on August 5, 1973, it was not by accident; it was by design. I know without a doubt that I am here for a reason, which is evident by the series of events that transpired in the above scenario.

At a critical time in my adolescent life, my parents, through their actions, taught me valuable lessons steeped in courage, integrity, and forgiveness. For example, it was not easy for my mom to set aside her pride and make that trip to the eastside, but for my sake, she did it. Likewise, it was not easy for my dad to tell the truth about his affair, but for my sake, he did it. Lastly, my bonus mom did not have to accept me as his child, but for my sake, she did. Thankfully, their sacrifices made it possible for me to freely have an open relationship with my father—just in time for my 13th birthday.

Let's Ride

In the remaining pages of this book, you will gradually witness how the perfect plan unfolds and appreciate all the people who played a pivotal role in my progress, including Mama Fatty.

So, fasten your seat belt and get ready for the ride!

CHAPTER 2

YOU GONNA LEARN TODAY

"Wash yo hands and go in der and take off dem germy a** clothes!"

Those were just a few directives Momma called out to me and my four older brothers when we were growing up. She did not play about keeping her house clean and germ-free. She had a strong affinity for Roman Cleanser, also known as Clorox, and ammonia. These formulas were known to disinfect and kill germs on sight. When you came in the house, you knew better to wash your hands before touching her refrigerator or a pot on the stove. If you violated any one of these rules, you were guaranteed a good cursing out or side-eye look that only a mother could give. Last, but not least, street clothes were restricted beyond a certain point. Momma believed that once you had been outside—whether riding the bus from school or playing with friends in the front yard—your clothes had become contaminated. To sit on her sofa or even the edge of her bed while wearing those "germy" clothes was a big NO-NO! Therefore, we pretty much had to strip our clothes at the front door and immediately go take a bath.

Sound familiar?

For those of us who lived through the global pandemic of 2020, let me just tell you something: The Center for Disease Control and Prevention (CDC) had nothing on my momma!

Why do I share this funny little story with you?

One, to let you know again that my mother was "no joke," and two, to confess that in my adult life, I find myself repeating the very things I heard her say when I was a kid. Proudly, I have adopted her values for cleanliness and education. Truth be told, there are certain things you just never forget.

What about you? Are there certain things you say or do that make you ask, "Have I become my mom?" or "Have I become my dad?" Here is one way to find out. If you were in the audience at one of my speaking engagements and I asked, "By a show of hands, how many of you have ever heard these words growing up: 'Go to school, get good grades, so you can get a good job!'?" I bet you a pack of Watermelon Now & Later's and a stick of Double Mint chewing gum all hands would go up, including yours. My next question would be, "Have you ever told your children or someone else's child the same thing?" If so, then guess what? You are no different.

Furthermore, this guidance on education has been passed down from generation to generation as the universal formula for success. While it is true that more education can result in earning more money over your lifetime, the formula is not foolproof. What do I mean? Have you ever known anyone to go to college, get their degree, but not be able to find a job in their field of study? Fortunately, the formula has worked for me, but I

Classroom learning by itself is not enough.

will tell you that classroom learning by itself is not enough. Why? In school, we are trained to work for money, but no one bothered to teach us *how to make money work for us*. Trust me, if there had been a Personal Money Management 101 or Fundamentals of Wealth Building 201 course offered in high school or college, I would have gladly taken it. Since that was not the case, money hardships in my family proved to be a more formidable teacher. In effect, I learned by studying my environment, processing things I saw and heard about money, and unfortunately, through negative experiences. Let's dive in and see what I mean.

If you grew up anything like me, you know what I mean when I say we were "poor." Don't get me wrong. Mama kept us clean. We just didn't have a lot of things like some other families. Unlike my great nieces and nephews today, for example, I did not have my own bedroom. In fact, until about age 14, I shared a bed with my mother. It's a wonder she let me stay that long, considering how many times I wet the sheets and stained the mattress as a kid. In the summertime, she and I would lie in bed dressed in as little as possible, while fanning ourselves with an old newspaper to try and beat back the heat. There was no air conditioning unit in the window nor central air flowing through our home. All we had instead was a stationary fan that seemed to only blow hot air.

Furthermore, the heat had a way of driving out the roaches and mice from their secret hiding places. When bug spray and other contraptions did not kill or help to contain these pests, a good ole fashion smack with one of my mother's high-heeled shoes always did the trick. *SPLAT!* As for the mice, there were mouse traps placed near open vents, around the baseboards in the kitchen, and sometimes on the countertops. Let me tell you, the kitchen was no place to wander in the middle of the night for a cup of water, lest you forget the traps were set and ready to spring into action. Lo and behold, it seemed like my brothers took turns getting their big toes caught in one of those traps. *OUCH!* That was no fun.

Do you wanna know what was even less fun for me? Going to bed on an empty stomach. You see, at the beginning of the month, the refrigerator and cabinets were filled with groceries. Mind you, a lot of the stuff came from government programs designed for women with infants and children. For example, there were staples like the big block of cheese, the off-brand-named powdered milk that came with instructions to "just add water," and the puffs cereal that came in a sealed plastic bag but no box. With the government food stamps that Mom also received, she was able to purchase our favorite Banquet® oven-fried chicken, TV dinners, and pot pies, which required minimum preparation. However, when the pot of neck bones, green beans and potatoes, black-eyed peas, and cornbread that she cooked ran out toward the end of the month, we usually resorted to Vienna sausages, potted meat sandwiches, and fried bologna.

One day, I remember telling my mom that I was hungry, to which she replied, "You betta take yo' can in der and open a can of soup!" In my whiny voice, I said, "But I don't want no soup!" referring to what I thought were the two most boring choices of all soups: chicken noodle and tomato. Do you think my mother was bothered by my pickiness? Absolutely not! She was not moved like some parents are today, who let their kids tell them what foods they will or will not eat. She simply said, "I guess you must not be hungry then!" As a result, I just cried my hungry little butt to sleep!

As I grew older, I watched how my mom managed credit. She had a Lerner department store credit card, where she shopped for my school clothes and other accessories. I always loved when she came home with bags filled with goodies just for me. She was an expert when it came to shopping off-season and taking advantage of the seasonal markdowns, which helped to stretch her money. When she was not using cash or credit to complete her purchases, she would simply put the items in layaway, making small payments over time until she paid off the balance. In the meantime, if she hit the lottery, there was a good chance that she could get the items out much sooner.

For my mom, the lottery was her go-to source for supplementing her meager income. If not the lottery, she always looked to get a windfall from a lawsuit of some sort. I often heard her say, "I've got my lawsuit in," to reassure my brothers and me that money was on the way. The only settlement I remember her receiving was for $6,000, when she unfortunately broke her ankle after slipping on some ice in the mall parking lot one winter.

While she recuperated in the hospital, can you imagine my brothers caring for me in her absence? Picture them getting me ready for school. One scooped my wooly afro up into a ponytail on top of my head, while another one tied red and yellow ribbons around it. It certainly was something to behold, but they pulled it off. Nevertheless, when my mother returned home, I was most impressed by the envelope filled with cash that she showed me before depositing it all into a bank account. The memory of her saving that large sum of money always stuck out in my mind.

At six years old, I may have been small, but I was very observant. In fact, I watched everything my mom did; she could not get much of anything past me. If I wasn't somewhere with my eyes wide open, taking mental notes, I was listening within earshot of her conversations, picking up more insights that way as well.

For example, I can recall several phone conversations my mother had with my grandmother. They usually went something like this:

> "Hey, Ma! I dreamed of fish last night. What does that play for?"
>
> My grandmother replied, "In the *Three Wise Men,* fish play fo' 1-0-6,"
>
> "What about the Kansas City Kitty?" my mom asked.

In an instant, my grandmother set the phone down to go search for her Kansas City Kitty.

What were they referring to by these strange names?

The *Three Wise Men* and *Kansas City Kitty* were the names of two out of three of the most prominent tools, known as dream books, used to translate dreams into lottery numbers. The third book in the trilogy was called the *Red Devil.* I don't know about you, but the idea of consulting the devil, no matter what color he (or she) is, does not sit well with my spirit. Regardless of how I felt, playing numbers was their thing. A good dream and as much as an itch in the palm of my mother's hand had her convinced that money was coming in an express overnight package with her name on it!

Make no mistake, their numbers game was fierce! At their disposal, they had an arsenal of tools they used to increase their chances of picking a winning number, including dream books, lottery tip sheets, and something called the "run down." The run down was their secret weapon that required a level of mastery that surpassed that of any skilled number cruncher. Since this was a family affair, one of my uncles oversaw this part of the numbers game operation. No one could do the run down quite like him. What was it?

The run down was a systematic approach to predicting when a 3-digit number may "fall" again based on the historical sequence of numbers that had "fallen" in the past. Given my fascination with numbers and being a young mathematician of sorts, my uncle tried to explain the run down to me, but my mind could not grasp the concept. I, therefore, just left it alone and could only wish that my mom would do the same. No such luck!

Before lottery became legal in many states including Michigan, there were so-called "street numbers." Though illegal, you must applaud the genius of the creators of the numbers game who pumped what some have estimated as hundreds of millions of dollars annually into the United States economy. The game became popular among people who were just scraping by to make ends meet. The idea of making a bet for 10 cents and turning it into $54 was quite appealing. My mom invested in this program regularly. When I was somewhere between four and six years old, I remember her calling her numbers in over the phone at night. She'd rattle off a three-digit number preceded by a city's name. For example, "Pontiac: 3-5-7" or "Detroit: 6-4-2". This was a combination of the racetrack's location and the order in which the horses finished the race to determine the winning numbers that evening.

The person on the other end of the phone was her very own "numbers man." He was also considered a runner for whoever was paying him to take bets from customers like my mom. Whether she won or lost, it did not matter to him. He took his commission off the top.

Other times, she played her numbers on credit with a man at the local diner, who would come from behind the counter to take her "order." Obviously, my mom had a good reputation for settling her debts, otherwise the privilege of credit would not have been extended. However, this was risky business because she was counting on playing a winning number that would provide the money that she needed to settle the debt.

As states started to realize how much money was being circulated in the numbers game, they had to get in on the action. As such, the Michigan Lottery was established in 1972 (one year before I was born) under the guise of supporting school children via a state education fund. In 1977 and 1981, the Daily 3 and Daily 4 games were added, and my mom was a regular participant, along with several of my aunts and uncles. Their wagers alone were enough to ensure no child in Detroit Public Schools ever had to go without a textbook. My mom easily played $20-$40 worth of lottery numbers per day. As a kid, I did not see the logic in her gambling; I only saw waste.

Today, as a finance professional, I wonder how much money my mom could have earned in her lifetime if she had invested money in the stock market instead of "throwing it away" in the lottery. If only someone had run down those numbers to her. But who? My mom wasn't exactly born into the Rockefeller family. Instead, she was raised by a homemaker and factory worker whose own gambling habits caused instability in the family and separation amongst my mom and her eleven siblings.

Furthermore, by growing up in the middle of the Great Depression, which happened to be caused by the stock market crash of 1929, I can only imagine that my mom grew up believing that investing in stocks was a sure way to lose your money. Not to mention, this period was marked by high unemployment, food insecurity, children not being in school, and low aspirations for a college education since there were no jobs. As such, the focus of that era was pure survival. As a product of her environment, she could not afford to take any "unnecessary risks," right?

Nevertheless, when I begged my mom to stop playing the lottery and get a "real job," her reply was always, "I'm going downtown tomorrow." Somehow, going downtown translated into the place where she would go to handle business and by virtue get this illusory job. Well, "tomorrow" never seemed to come. While playing the lottery and other forms of gambling continued for generations with my elders and other family members, I made up my mind at a young age that the numbers game was not for me!

Do you remember when I said I was always watching and listening? Well, this applied to my brothers, too. It was a quality they wish I never had because if there was something I saw or heard them doing that I felt Mom should know, I was spilling all the beans! Ha! However, in the story that follows, they set an example for me that I admired and wanted to follow.

During the harsh Detroit winters in the early 1980s, it was not uncommon to get 6 to 12 inches of snowfall. I always saw it as the perfect time to build a snowman or make snow angels in the front yard. However, my brothers saw it as the ideal scenario to make some dough, moolah, money. Dressed in thermal underwear and multiple pairs of tube socks, they wrapped their feet with plastic bags to help insulate them against the dampness that would inevitably get inside their boots.

In pairs of two, they went from house to house asking neighbors if they could shovel their snow. Elderly women like our homebound next-door neighbor were ones they knew would welcome the help. After several hours of being out in the snow, they would come in the house to thaw out and get some of Mom's homemade chicken noodle soup–not the canned stuff she offered me. Nevertheless, when they spread their money on the table, collectively, they had about $150, which was a big deal for a bunch of teenage boys.

Impressed by what they had done, I decided the next time it snowed, I would skip the snow angels and venture out instead to try and make some money of my own. Mind you, I was probably seven or eight years old, 4 feet tall, and could not have weighed more than 100 pounds in a wet snowsuit. Did I let any of that stop me? Nope!

Fully armored with layers of long johns, denim jeans, thermal socks, and snow boots, I zipped my coat and grabbed a black skull cap to pull down low over my eyes. My goal was to look like a boy as much as possible, in hopes that my neighbors would let me work as well. With shovel in hand, I proceeded down the street and knocked on the door of the first house that I saw needed help. When the person on the other side of the door saw me standing there, I knew I looked like a small fry in their eyes. However, in the deepest voice I could muster, I asked, "Can I shovel your snow?" Unexpectedly, the big belly black man peering back at me shouted, "No! You cannot shovel my snow! Gon' get out of here, little girl!"

Rats! My cover was blown. So much for my impersonation-of-a-boy routine. Dragging my shovel behind me, I returned home feeling defeated. Although I had been dealt a disappointing blow, it never stopped me from believing that I, too, could make a buck just like my brothers. I just needed to figure out how.

In the middle of the summer of 1982, we were forced to leave that neighborhood because our landlord decided he did not want us there anymore. Would you believe we were kicked out onto the harsh streets of Detroit for the second time in two years? As a matter of fact, I had not even reached my ninth birthday. Can I just tell you this? Eviction is a b**** that I would not wish upon any family! Once was enough, but twice? This time, it was awfully embarrassing to have all our belongings scattered on the curb at the intersection of a major thoroughfare on Detroit's westside. The weather did not help either. It was a blazing hot 80 degrees, but the humidity made it feel more like 105 degrees, especially under the sting of the slow and consistent stares coming from gawkers who passed by in their rusted out hooupties.

Frightened by all this, my eyes welled with tears that rolled down my cheeks like hot springs. Can you imagine hearing them sizzle once they finally reached the scorched pavement? Think about the sound a splash of water makes when dropped into a hot skillet. That's how hot it was to me. Standing in that heat, I got burning mad! As one scary thought after another entered my mind, I cried uncontrollably. My brothers tried everything they could to console me, but nothing seemed to work.

With each passing hour, I felt abandoned and alone, although they were standing there with me. "*Where is Mom?*" I wondered. She was off somewhere trying to figure it out. My little brain could not process it all at the time. It was way too much for an eight-year-old to bear. I can now only imagine how my mother must have felt, as this was not the repeat performance that she had hoped for either. To make matters worse, my 70-year-old grandmother who had been living with us was displaced and needed a new home, too.

Time out! I'm sure you are wondering how we got into this predicament in the first place, right? Was Mom not paying the rent on time? Could she not afford it? Were there warning signs? If so, did she ignore them? Or did she fail to decide only to let someone else decide for her? All of these are valid questions, but here's the real deal. My mom had been advocating for what was right. In fact, she could have been a poster child for landlord-tenant rights. The two-family flat where we lived had numerous code violations, including an illegal electric meter set up. My mom had taken photos that showed how one unit was stealing electricity from another unit: ours. She complained to the landlord nonstop, but he chose not to do a damn thing about it! As a result, she withheld rent. In turn, that old, mean, and nasty landlord put my mother, her five children, and my grandmother out on the streets.

DAMN! That was cold.

That evening, we ended up at Aunt Marilyn's house. While there was some relief, I was still crying, as my hair wildly covered my head. She looked at me and said, "Chile, when was the last time yo' momma did something to yo' head?" In between sulks, I tried to explain to her how my mom normally combed my hair—a pageboy and four interconnected braids. As country as it sounded, it worked for my mom who didn't have to deal with pigtails and barrettes for at least 17 years before I came on the scene in a sea

CHAPTER 2—YOU GONNA LEARN TODAY

of boys. Aunt Marilyn did the best she could to recreate the style I described. Bless her heart!

As I cried myself to sleep that night, I prayed for things to get better. I asked to be rescued and bring an end to this all too confusing chapter in my life. The very next day, my mother called Aunt Marilyn's house and told her that one of my uncles was willing to take us in to live with him and his family. For 10 months, we made our home in his basement, which was nicely finished and large enough to accommodate all of us until we found permanent housing. My grandmother, however, continued to live with Aunt Marilyn.

When I started fourth grade in the fall, my mom kept me enrolled at the same school I attended before the eviction. However, instead of walking a few blocks to school, my uncle's house was at least 5 miles or a 10- to 15-minute car ride away. It easily took an hour to get there on two city buses, an option I took once by myself and completed the transfer, too. As a nine-year-old, that would be unheard of today, not to mention unsafe. Hell, it wasn't safe back then!

No matter which method of transportation I used, I arrived at school late almost every single day. In my homeroom class, the teacher would have covered a lesson on 3-digit multiplication and long division. She might as well have been speaking a foreign language. Given my tardiness, I had no clue what was going on nor how to tackle the problems. The best solution I could offer was to put my head on the desk and stay out of the teacher's way. Since there was no reasonable way for her to stop teaching the other students to give me specialized attention, I simply checked out.

After a while, the strain of the commute back and forth took a toll on my mom and me. Eventually, she pulled me out of that school, and I started to be bussed to Gompers' Elementary School in the district where my uncle lived. Situated in the middle of nowhere, it was the first time that I attended a school with white kids who appeared to be just as poor, if not poorer than me. Just when I started to get settled in at that school, it was time to move again, and there were only about four weeks left in the school year. Therefore, in May 1983, with the assistance of my mother's oldest brother, we moved out of my other uncle's basement into a four-bedroom home in a new neighborhood that was only a stone's throw away from where we had been living.

During this period of transition, I had attended three different schools for 4th grade alone. The neighborhood school I attended for 5th grade brought the total number of elementary schools I attended up to five. As you can see, the evictions created a lot of instability in my life and disrupted the continuity of my education. It's a wonder I made it! Without understanding my backstory, someone could have easily looked at my primary school transcript, seen all the school transfers, and assumed that I was a troubled kid with low to no expectation for success. Nah, Son! I was not going out like that! As a matter of fact, over the summer, one of my older brothers helped me with my math, including complex multiplication and division problems. Therefore, by the time I reached 5th grade, math was a breeze.

Then, what came next was a game changer!

Paradigm Shift

In the new neighborhood, there was a girl who lived in the corner house across the street from us. Let's say her name was Diana Dawson. We were both in 5th grade but attended different schools.

Diana came from a two-parent household and had three younger brothers. Her father was White, and her mother was Black. Diana and I frequently played basketball or volleyball together in her backyard. On occasion, I would be invited inside her house to play video games. On the other hand, Diana's parents were too strict to allow her to cross the street, let alone visit inside anybody else's house.

One summer, Diana set up a lemonade stand in front of her house. The going rate for a cold glass of America's most refreshing soft drink was about 25 cents. Neighbors and passers-by alike supported Diana's venture, including me. Not only did I think this was a neat thing she had done, I was impressed by her success and decided that if Diana could do it, "I could do it, too!" Only if I did it, it had to be bigger and better, which meant providing a variety of treats to appeal to more than one craving.

Therefore, I also offered Kool-Aid®, popsicles, penny candy, and freshly-popped popcorn—not the kind that you pop in the microwave. My popcorn was made the old-fashioned way—on top of the stove. In my mother's cast iron pot that for me seemed to weigh a ton, I heated enough cooking oil to coat the bottom of the pot before adding the popcorn kernels. Afterwards, I covered the pot and waited to hear the magical eruption occur on the inside, as I vigorously shuffled the pot back and forth. Once that sucker got going, all you could hear was *pop-pop-pop-pop-pop!* Next, I filled lunch-size, brown paper bags with these white clouds of joy. For the finish, I topped them off with a generous amount of hot, melted butter that caused the outside of the bag to look like a greasy, hot mess. Yes, that's just the way some people liked it! Ha! In fact, if the bag didn't show signs of butter, they would have questioned whether it was good.

In addition to perfecting the popcorn, I had become a meteorologist of sorts at the young age of 10. Literally, I would watch the nightly news to see what the weather forecast would be on the days of my sales. If it were going to be hot and sunny the next day, I knew that I would sell a lot of lemonade. However, if it was going to be cloudy and rainy with temperatures in the 60s, then I knew it was going to be a slow day if I made anything at all.

Profit maximization was certainly my goal. I remember a neighborhood kid paying me a dollar for a sandwich bag filled with an assortment of penny candy, including Jolly Ranchers® and regular and fruit-flavored Tootsie Rolls®. After he had taken his candy home, surprisingly, he returned with his purchase in hand and a grimace on his face. Noticing that he was visibly upset, I asked, "What seems to be the problem?" He exclaimed, "You said this was penny candy; there are only 33 pieces in here!" I quipped, "Yea, it is penny candy—three penny candy! How do you expect me to make a profit?" Seemed like a good answer at the time. However, in retrospect, if I had made customer service part of my goal, I would have thrown in a complimentary bag of popcorn or cup of lemonade and thanked him for being a loyal, committed customer. Oh well, you live and learn.

From this business venture, I earned enough money to buy the name-brand clothes that my mom could not afford. You should have seen me! I wore my new Levi's blue jeans, Adidas T-shirt, and all-white tennis shoes with great pride. The moral of the story is, if you want something badly enough, you will figure out an honest way to make it happen. Here's the thing, though, I did not wait until I was forty years old to get this understanding. I have been thinking like this ever since I was 10 years old. At that young age, I proved to myself that the lack of money in my family was never going to be an excuse to hold me back from what I wanted out of life.

Therefore, as I conclude this chapter, the three keys to breaking the cycle of poverty off the lives of children who grow up in families like mine, include education, exposure, and entrepreneurship. My mom had the first "E" covered when she made sure I stayed committed to my education, despite the hiccup of multiple school changes along the way. However, it took the hardship of being evicted the second time to bring us to the new neighborhood where I was exposed to entrepreneurship, which only expanded my view of what was possible.

Finally, as we prepare to go into the next chapter to see more of my entrepreneurial mindset at work, I am reminded of a rhetorical question that my mom used to always ask me. It was, "Why do you think I had you?" Well, if you keep reading, "You gonna learn today!"

[*In my Kevin Hart voice.] 😊

CHAPTER 3

THE MAKING OF CANDY GIRL

🎵 *"It takes two to make a thing go right!
It takes two to make it outta sight!"* 🎵

Rob Base and DJ EZ Rock introduced "It Takes Two" to my classmates and me during the fall semester of our sophomore year at Cass Technical High School. The song was an instant hit in 1988 and still draws people to the dance floor today. While sitting in third hour biology class, we could hear the thunderous sounds of the song's baseline from the 3rd floor. If you are wondering where the loud music was coming from, picture a souped-up white pick-up truck in which it was customary during that era to see wrapped in an elaborate airbrushed design that regularly parked outside of our school. Perhaps it was someone's older brother or cousin behind the steering wheel; I'm not sure. However, I do know that our teacher, Mr. Masters, did not care for the "noise." It suited us just fine since class seemed to go by a bit faster as we bobbed our heads to the beat.

Let me take a step back to tell you about my beloved high school alma mater. Cass Tech, or Cass, for short, is notorious for producing graduates whose names read like Who's Who in America. For example, you're probably familiar with platinum recording artist and rapper Big Sean, actress Shaun Robinson who hosts *90-Day Fiancé* and *90-Day Bares All* on The Learning Channel (TLC), and legendary singer and actress Diana Ross. In addition to these greats, you can travel almost anywhere in the world and meet someone who is connected to this inner-city, college preparatory high school. In fact, Cass has been recognized nationally by the U.S. Department of Education as a School of Excellence, with a 97% graduation rate.

In my case, I am a proud graduate of the Cass Tech Class of 1991, which produced some of the finest accountants, attorneys, doctors, engineers, composers, educators, creative directors, public servants, and professional athletes you'd ever want to meet. Individually and collectively, we made magic happen in the dimly-lit hallways of an eight-story building that **was** located at 2421 Second Avenue— just a stone's throw away from the central business district in downtown Detroit. As we walk down memory lane, I will recount my steps as an honor student turned young entrepreneur and high school leader. In the process, you will witness the making of Candy Girl and begin to see firsthand the Candy Girl Mentality at work.

Are you ready?

Entering sophomore year, I had a 3.83 GPA. It ticked me off that I got a "B" in a stupid drafting class that kept me from being an all-A student my freshman year. Although I was disappointed, I knew I had bigger hills to climb in the years ahead. Because Cass is a college preparatory high school, choosing a curriculum is like choosing a major in college based on career interest. For example,

CHAPTER 3—THE MAKING OF CANDY GIRL

if you wanted to become a doctor, you were likely to study the sciences within the Chem-Bio curriculum. Likewise, if you wanted to become a singer or dancer, you studied within the Performing Arts curriculum, and so on. I chose business because I always had an enterprising mind. The lemonade stand I had when I was only 10 years old is a case in point.

While I had an early appetite for business and entrepreneurship, Ms. Stevenson, who happened to be my favorite teacher, helped to guide me through Accounting 101 and 102. One day during the school's career day program, a banker visited our classroom and asked, "So, students, what do you want to be when you grow up?" One of my classmates eagerly raised her hand and then answered, "A CPA." I didn't know exactly what a CPA was, but it sounded good to me. From that point forward, I decided that I wanted to be a CPA, too.

It was also during the fall semester of 10th grade that I was exposed to Junior Achievement, an after-school program that teaches youth in grades K-12 about economics, leadership, and entrepreneurship. My Junior Achievement (JA) class met on Thursday nights, which meant I missed several episodes of The Cosby Show. Big sacrifice, right? Not really. Choosing JA over The Huxtables, I can firmly say that I made the right choice because that organization and its teachings literally changed my life. I'll explain.

In my JA class, the volunteer instructor assigned students to smaller groups and asked us to choose a fundraising project. My group chose to sell M&M's, in which we equally divided a case of 60 individual boxes of peanut M&M's. For some reason, I ended up with the larger box and used it to carry my share of M&Ms to sell at school the next day. Granted, I could have easily put the candy

STRENGTH

in my book bag and sold it once I got to school. However, with the larger box in hand, I sold out before the city bus let me off at school that morning. Instead of throwing away the empty box, I decided to store it in the bottom of my locker.

Whenever I opened my locker, a classmate standing nearby would see the box and ask in a very curious tone, "Lisa, you got M&M's?" I'd say, "No, but I can get you some." Afterwards, I'd close the locker and go about my day. Upon returning to my locker another time, a different classmate standing nearby would see the empty box sitting there, and just like the first classmate, ask with excitement in their voice, "Oooh, Lisa, you got M&M's?" With a mischievous smile on my face, I replied, "No, but I can get you some!" This unintentional torture of my classmates went on for about two weeks, as I drew more interest in this empty box of candy.

Finally, one Saturday morning, I decided to make good on my promise to my classmates by visiting the wholesale candy store in my neighborhood. When I stepped inside Leddy's Wholesale Candy on Grand River near Greenfield, I thought I had died and gone to candy heaven. Think Willy Wonka, but only a fraction of the size. There was candy from wall to wall and from floor to ceiling, but I did not let that distract me. I came in there for one thing and one thing only—to buy a case of peanut M&M's. A full case of 60 boxes cost $15.00 or 25 cents each. I only had $13.00. Do you think I let that stop me? Of course, not! I asked Mr. Leddy if he could take out the extra eight boxes and sell me the rest based on what I could afford. He agreed, and I was on my way.

I was so proud of what I had done: I could not wait to get home to show and tell my mother. However, when I arrived, I found her disheveled and in a somber mood. It was clear to me that she was in

CHAPTER 3—THE MAKING OF CANDY GIRL

no condition to get excited about my new venture. So, I just quietly went to my room without saying a mumbling word.

When I went to school on Monday, I sold all 52 boxes @ 50 cents each. At the end of the day, I went behind one of the stalls in the girls' bathroom to count the money I had shoved into my purse. It added up to $26. I said to myself, "Hmm! I started out with 13 and ended up with 26. That sounds like good math to me. I think I'll do it again!"

That afternoon, I returned to the candy store and doubled my investment, while also adding Reese's Peanut Butter Cups to the sales mix. I knew for sure that the movie-sized version that came four to a pack would be a big hit with all the students at Cass—not just my classmates. Remember, Cass had eight floors and up to 3,000 students running around the building, trying to get to class. While I sold the M&M's for 50 cents, the Reese's Cups, which only cost me 50 cents, sold for one dollar. Either way, I was going to double my money and make a fifty percent profit.

Like before, I took the candy to school the following day and sold out by 5th hour. Just as I had planned, I doubled my money again; this time from $26 to $52. Naturally, I wanted to keep expanding my reach and growing my profits at the same time. Therefore, I reinvested all my cash once again. On Day 3, my goal was to leave school empty-handed, except for having a purse full of cash. To make this happen, I needed to increase capacity by investing in a larger tote bag and recruiting a couple of classmates to help me sell. Mind you, these weren't just any classmates. The two girls that agreed to help were good friends of mine from middle school. I trusted them, and with their assistance, I managed to sell out on Days 3, 4, and 5–grossing over $400 in sales on Friday alone.

To think, I went into the week with only $13 to my name! Pretty impressive for a 15-year-old, huh?

Whereas I would have loved for my girls to continue selling candy with me, they made it clear, "Lisa, you our girl and all, but we can't keep this up. We need to get to class!" While I respected their position, I still needed to move this product! Therefore, I found two replacements whose names we will call Errol Shepherd and Daphne Taylor. Both were studying in the business curriculum as well. When this dynamic duo joined my budding candy enterprise, it was at a critical time when cravings for in-class snacks were on the rise. Over time, they helped me understand that M&M's and Reese's Cups by themselves were not enough to satisfy everyone's sweet tooth.

As students demanded more variety, I had to deliver by adding the following fan favorites to the product mix: Snickers, Twix, KitKat, Skor, Mars, Pay Day, Almond Joy, Mounds, Skittles, Starburst, Twizzlers, Sour Patch Kids, and Now & Laters. You should have heard how I used to rattle off that list of candy with rapid-fire speed. It was a blast! But do you think it stopped there? Of course not! They insisted that I sell potato chips, too. So, I did; including Better Made brand potato chips–a Detroit hometown favorite that I offered in three varieties–plain, barbecue, and Red Hot!

You know what came next, right? To help them wash it all down, they wanted me to supply them with something to quench their thirst. Therefore, I added Hi-C drink boxes and 12-ounce cans of Faygo pop–another Detroit favorite, which some folks call "soda." It's pop people! But I digress. Ha! I was a full-blown, walking vending machine. I promise; if I had one more year in high school, they would have asked me to strap a microwave to my back and

CHAPTER 3—THE MAKING OF CANDY GIRL

sell hot sandwiches. It was definitely "cray-cray," but I loved every minute of it!

One of my good friends and faithful supporters, Terry Esper, who is now Dr. Terry Esper, will always be remembered for helping me coin the following call and response routine: He'd say, "Lisa, WHATCHU GOT?" to which I responded, "WHATCHU NEED?!" To this day, we laugh hysterically about those good ole days. All jokes aside, I was about that life when it came to my candy business. For instance, I was very meticulous about the quantities of each candy variety that I ordered. For example, I knew that peanut M&Ms sold more than the plain ones. Whereas another one of my friends liked caramel Twix and Sour Patch Kids, someone else was fond of Pay Days and Skittles. Whatever combination made them happy, I was sure to have it because I aimed to please. Given my daily sales volume, Mr. Leddy started delivering my candy order directly to my house instead of having me come into the store to pick it up. How was that for customer service? Being a teenage boss chick was not too shabby either! Ha!

The best hours of the school day to sell the most candy were between 1st and 5th hour. That's when students were most hungry or just needed to get their sugar "fix". No place was off limits in terms of where and when a sale could go down. Whether we were in class, the cafeteria, a stairwell, or outside the stalls in the girls' bathroom, it didn't matter to me. If you were not fortunate to have a class with me, the best time to catch me was in between classes. It was crazy because if you didn't know any better, you would have thought a fight had broken out in the middle of the hallway based on the way students hovered around me to get their sugar fix before the tardy bell rang. At the center of it all, there I was crouching like a tiger in a deep squat, while dishin' candy and clockin' dollars left and right. It would not be a stretch to say that in those 10 minutes between classes, I alone made $10-15 in sales, which was equivalent to a rate of $60-90 per hour. I usually collected my money from Errol and Daphne before I left school to go to my co-op job. Errol just "loved it" whenever I stopped by Ms. Rose's 5th hour yearbook class. His boys would see me coming and be like, "Aye-yo, 'E,' here come yo' pimp!" While Errol hated that characterization, I got an absolute kick out of it!

I was always good at stacking my money. It didn't take very long to save my first $700 in cold hard cash. Excited to share my good fortune with my older brother who is closest to me in age, I remember taking the big wad of money out of my purse and dropping it at his feet. I said to him, "Go ahead. Count it!" His eyes lit up and a big grin crept across his face as he began to realize how profitable my candy business had become. After counting it, he couldn't deny what he held in his hands. At that moment, he was certain that his little sister was onto something!

He was correct in his assessment, as I was beginning to cement my reputation as "The One and Only 'Candy Girl'" at Cass Technical High School. Unfortunately, there were those in the school administration that wanted to stop my flow. Even though some teachers bought candy from me as much as the students, the administrators were a different story. Their job was to enforce the rules, right? While sitting in my accounting class, an announcement came over the P.A. system that said, "Students: While we appreciate your entrepreneurial endeavors, we ask that you cease and desist from all solicitations in and around school property." When I heard those words, I immediately knew the message was intended for me and my crew. However, I let it go in one ear and right out the other.

Do you think for one second that I was going to let some ominous voice in the main office interfere with my cash flow? Heck, No! My goals were simple: keep selling candy, keep making money, and avoid getting caught! Regrettably, my candy had been confiscated once or twice by the Math and English department heads. Here's the crazy thing: whenever they took my candy and locked it away in their offices, they always gave it back to me at the end of the school day. Who does that? My guess is that they didn't really want to punish me, which I appreciate. Perhaps their end game was to persuade me to be more careful-next time. (Wink, wink.) Therefore, I chilled out for a couple of days, to let the heat die down. Then, when I felt the coast was clear, I was back on the "Block," ready to make another killing!

I reached a point at which I started making about $300 in weekly profit. Before anyone starts to wonder, "Lisa, did you pay taxes on any of that money?" Let me assure you that the income I generated after expenses was not enough to trigger a tax filing for me or my mom, for that matter. Besides, there were only so many school/sales days in a calendar year. Since I was on solid ground with the Uncle Sam, the only people I had to worry about cutting into my profits were Errol and Daphne. They both wanted a bigger piece of the action.

Get this, I was already paying them, but I guess it was not enough according to their standards. Would you believe they threatened to go on strike if I didn't agree to give them a raise? At first, I was like, "Bump it. I'm not givin' them nuthin! I'll keep all the profits for myself!" After a couple of days flying solo, I realized that I was more profitable with their help than I was without it. Therefore, I came to my senses and conceded to their wishes. As a 17-year-old, I had gotten an early lesson in labor negotiations. Ha!

You're probably wondering, "Lisa, what did you do with all the money?" That's a great question. As a high school student, I was doing at least five out of the seven* things you can do with money. In fact, whenever I'm talking with an audience of high school students or adults about financial concepts and personal money management, it is clear to them that I first knew how to earn it, which was evident by my candy sales. Second, I knew how to grow it by reinvesting the profits to make more money. After that, I spent some, gave some away, and saved the rest. To paint a picture of what that looked like, check out the short stories that follow:

As the Candy Girl, I had an image to uphold, which meant I needed to invest in my wardrobe and make sure my hair was always on point. I never really liked to go shopping at the mall unless it was totally necessary. I preferred boutique shopping because it allowed me to find unique pieces like this golden-brown and black three-piece pantsuit that came with an opened-front duster. Oh, I thought I was super fly in that number! Let me tell you!

My signature hairstyle was created on and for my 17th birthday. I went to a salon in downtown Detroit, where the stylist gave me a "baaad" asymmetrical haircut, allowing the hair on the left side of my face to partially cover my left eye. Likewise, my hair on the right side was short enough to create pencil curls. To finish the look, I had my stylist crimp the words "Sexy at 17!" in the back of

---

* The seven (7) steps to building wealth and effectively managing money as prescribed herein are as follows: 1) Earn it; 2) Share it; 3) Save it; 4) Invest it; 5) Protect it; 6) Enjoy it; and 7) Master it!

my hair. You couldn't tell me nothing! Although, my supervisor at work thought it said, "Sex at 17," as the "y" in "sexy" wore off over time. Boy was I embarrassed! We laugh about it today, though. 😊

Whereas I did not do a whole lot of extravagant shopping, there was that one trip to the Somerset Collection, a high-end shopping mall located in a northern suburb of Detroit. I bought a Coach designer handbag that over time developed a sway in the leather from all the money I shoved into it. I also bought a pair of Gucci gym shoes—not the all-leather ones but the ones with canvas and leather combined. What did I do that for? Those Gucci gym shoes did not sit well with some of my classmates. One of them, who shall remain nameless, said, "Aww, hell naw! Lisa got Guccis now?! I'm not gonna keep buying candy from her so she can get rich!" True to form, he stopped buying candy for a while. But guess what? After a few days went by, he started buying candy from me again. Turns out his temporary bout of jealousy was not strong enough to overcome his craving for sugar. Besides, where else was he going to go?

In addition to spending money on a few selfish pleasures, I was able to pay for all my senior class outings, graduation photos, prom, my senior trip, and other extracurricular activities. This was a big relief for my mom who did not have to carry that burden based on her limited funds. In fact, I was able to give her money from time to time, whether for groceries or to pay certain other household bills. It felt good to help because my mom was like my unofficial business partner anyway. A true "ride or die" indeed, she really came through for me when I was in a pinch. For example, one day, I ran out of drinks by the end of 4th hour, and my classmates were heated–literally and figuratively.

What could I do to stop them from dying of thirst for at least the next hour? I called home and asked my mom if she would bring me the extra case of Faygo that was in the freezer. Without hesitation, she got dressed, placed the 24 cans of ice-cold pop into a duffle bag, and carried them on a 45-minute city bus ride to my school. After a seamless exchange at the front entrance of the building—right outside the main office, no less—I was back in business! Fifteen minutes later, I was sold out...again! Mom saved the day! As I look back on that experience, I must admit that was a real "gangsta" move on my mom's part. If nothing else, it damn sure was BOSSY! Thanks, Mom! 😊

Finally, here is my favorite and most impactful story of them all. Do you remember the $700 I told you about earlier? It was at that point that I decided I would stop saving my money at home and take time to open a bank account instead. Since I worked at Manufacturers Bank as a co-op student, it was convenient for me to open not just one, but two accounts: a traditional savings account that earned interest at a rate of 5% per year, and a time deposit account that was paying around 7.5% in annual interest. Those rates have been unheard of for quite some time, but the way inflation is set up right now, we may reach those levels again. Who knows!

In the meantime, let me break down how big of a deal it was for me to exercise this act of financial awareness and really independence. You've heard people talk about the importance of having multiple streams of income, right? Well, as a teenager, I was ahead of the game. Think about it: While minimum wage was $3.35 per hour, I was earning $5.20 per hour at my co-op job, making approximately $300 in weekly profits from my candy sales, and receiving interest income from my savings–at a minimum

CHAPTER 3—THE MAKING OF CANDY GIRL

annual rate of 5%. In its simplest form, my money was making money! None of my teachers taught me to do this. So, where did I get the idea?

I am certain Junior Achievement played a role, and perhaps the Urban Bankers Forum meetings I used to attend after school. Maybe it came from watching my mother sock away that extra $6,000 she won in a lawsuit after her slip and fall accident when I was in first grade. Shoot, maybe I just wanted the security that comes with having money in the bank. The way I figured it, if I had money in the bank, I would never be broke! At the end of the day, what I was doing was not normal when compared to my peers.

The way I figured it, if I had money in the bank, I would never be broke!

Some of them came from two-parent households, received weekly allowances, never had to take the bus to school, and wore nice clothes on a regular basis. I was just the opposite, which meant I had to work hard, while working smarter for every dollar I got. Ultimately, I had saved more than $4,000 by the time I graduated from high school. This money came in handy once I got to college, too. More on that in a bit.

Some ask, "Lisa, did you have any competition?" No, not really. Two other students tried to copycat what I was doing, but they couldn't keep up with how vast my candy operation had grown. Eventually, they just died on the vine. However, would you believe that one of them had the audacity to say to me, "Lisa, the only reason people like you is because you sell candy." Based on how my bank account was set up, if that were true, I'd say that was not a bad position to be in.

STRENGTH

More important than being liked, my classmates trusted me to handle the money, which is why I was elected treasurer of our senior class. In addition, I was vice president of Business Professionals of America (BPA), a student-centered organization that allowed me to compete, develop leadership skills, and aspire to a career in accounting. What I learned through BPA complemented my studies in the business curriculum at Cass. Furthermore, I was a member of the National Honor Society (NHS) and the Junior Office Training Society (JOTS), which helped me get my co-op job at the bank. I guess you could say I was a well-rounded student who had the respect of both my classmates and "many" of my teachers.

Why not all my teachers? Well, there was one teacher who was not totally "sold" on Lisa Howze. I was not so fond of her either. In fact, I had done everything in my power for five semesters since the start of 10th grade to avoid taking a class with her, as she taught business management and business law. She wore long, colorful muumuu-like dresses and had a habit of visiting other teachers' classrooms that I had been taking. She always referenced her age, saying that she was "65 and holding!" The truth is, she was in her forties. It took a while before I finally figured out her game. She enjoyed the flattery coming from those who would say in disbelief, "No! You can't be. You look good for your age!" Leave it to me to burst her bubble.

By second semester of senior year, I could no longer escape death's door. My luck had run out, and I ended up having to take the business management course with that disciplinarian of a teacher who went by the name Dr. G.—short for Dr. De Lois Gibson. She was no-nonsense and a stickler for classroom rules and decorum. One day, we had an untimely encounter in the hallway outside her classroom. Prior to that rude awakening, I had just finished conducting candy sales in the back stairwell. Rushing to get to her class, which was no more than 100 feet away, the tardy bell rang, and I found myself on the wrong side of the door. Because I was late, she refused to accept my homework assignment.

While an appeal was within my rights, there was nothing my mom could do to reverse Dr. G's position. For the first time in my high school career, I felt defeated. The words she said to me when I first enrolled in her class played over and over again in my head: "Lisa. You may have all your other teachers fooled, but you're not fooling me." Can you believe that? I guess she meant what she said because she was not gonna let me get away with a DAMN thang, including turning in a late homework assignment, not that day or any other day for that matter!

I could have easily dubbed her "the teacher from hell" as a result of that incident, but it turns out that Dr. G. was a godsend. How so? Well, it was almost time to graduate, and I had just participated in a program in which I had applied for an internship as an underwriter with an insurance company. When I was unsuccessful at getting the job, I went to Dr. G. sounding pitiful. The conversation that followed literally changed my life. She said to me, "Well, Lisa. What do you want to be when you grow up?" I said, "A CPA," just like my classmate did in 10th grade. Dr. G. replied, "Then you need to talk to someone who is a CPA." That's when she picked up the phone and made a call to a gentleman named Roger Short.

At that time, Mr. Short was the Auditor General for the City of Detroit. He was a CPA who started his career in public accounting at Arthur Andersen, one of the Big Eight accounting firms at the time. I went to meet with Mr. Short and, as a result, he connected me with the folks at Arthur Andersen's Detroit office. There I was, a 17-year-old girl, meeting with the office managing partner and recruitment manager for a multinational firm that had offices in every major U.S. market and abroad. From that day forward, my eyes were set on starting my career in public accounting with Arthur Andersen. That seed would have never been planted were it not for Dr. G. She was the type of educator that every student needs—especially students like me. In her, I found a teacher who was unwilling to accept my bull***t and raised the level of expectation from and for me. Some would view her approach as hardcore, but the teachers who are the hardest seem to have the greatest impact. Dr. G was one of those kinds of teachers.

In closing, they say what doesn't kill you will only make you stronger. While I was used to making money and getting good grades, Dr. G. was helping me build character. For that reason, she is just as much responsible for "The Making of Candy Girl" as anyone else.

GO BLUE: LESSONS BEYOND THE CLASSROOM

*F*emale. (*Check.*)

Black. (*Check.*)

Low-income family. (*Check.*)

Lower expectancy rate of graduation. (Wait. Hold up!)

Based on these attributes, when I entered the University of Michigan in the fall of 1991, I clearly fit the profile of a first-generation college student (FGS). However, it's a good thing nobody told me about that last part, especially since I had no desire to live down to someone else's low expectations of me. For that matter, the idea of not finishing what I started never entered my mind. Granted, I did not come from a family of college graduates. My older siblings could not talk to me about studying for exams or managing the challenges of campus life. My parents were not equipped to navigate the system of higher education and all that came along with it. In many ways, the odds were stacked against me. I'm just glad I didn't get the memo. Instead, I came into the university with my blinders on. My goals were simple and straightforward: 1) Get accepted into the Michigan Business School during sophomore year; 2) land a job in public accounting with Arthur Andersen; and 3) graduate in four years, not six.

Was it easy?

Of course not.

Nothing about my life leading up to this point had been easy. However, resilience and resourcefulness had always been my best friends. They had been carrying me all along, and there was no way they were going to abandon me on this leg of my journey. Therefore, I am grateful that I did not become a statistic. You know, a young person who went to college, never completed their degree, but has a boatload of debt and no job to help pay for it.

Backstory on College Selection

Would you believe that Michigan was not my first choice? Okay, Wolverine Nation! Before you jump down my throat and throw me out of the M Den, allow me to explain. In the late '80s and early '90s, racial tension was once again pervasive on the Ann Arbor campus of U of M. Black students felt compelled to stage sit-ins and speak out in protest against discriminatory practices that affected their education. When I heard the stories on the evening news, it was a big turnoff. Therefore, when recruiters from Michigan visited Cass for "on-the-spot" admissions, I opted not to meet with them. Instead, I met with Michigan State University, got accepted, and declared that I'd be going to E. Lansing in the fall. However, after several failed attempts to visit the MSU campus, I had a change of heart and decided to become a Wolverine after all.

To think, I was "this close" to becoming a Spartan. SOMEBODY HELP ME! (Ha!)

To be honest, if mom had gone along with my plans, I would have attended one of the Historically Black Colleges and Universities (HBCUs). The representatives from North Carolina A & T University and Florida A & M University, who visited my classes during senior year, made a lasting impression. Both schools promoted their strong business programs and talked about the personal advantages I'd gain as a Black student indoctrinated into the HBCU culture. Unfortunately, none of that mattered because my mom and uncle felt "it don't take all dat" to go to school and get an education. In other words, the South was too far away from home, and 'nobody was coming down there to see my black a**!'

In fact, it would have suited my uncle just fine if I had gone just 15 to 20 minutes up the road to the U of M Dearborn campus. In my mind, if I were going to have the full Wolverine experience, I needed to be in Ann Arbor! PERIODT!

Move-in Day

Ann Arbor is an interesting place. Once we arrived on campus, it was clear that the squirrels ruled the town. Instead of them yielding to us, we yielded to them. In fact, one squirrel stopped in the middle of the intersection in front of my dad's '86 Dodge Caravan, rose on his hind legs, and stared us down, as if to say, "I dare you to hit me!" While tempting, we knew better. My second observation was the deafening surround sound of hip-hop music coming from nearby cars. As a kid from the inner city of Detroit, I was used to seeing *brothas* gripping the steering wheel of a midnight blue '78 Cutlass that had diamond sparkles in the paint, white-wall tires with 20-inch rims, and a trunk stuffed with a sub-woofer that kicked out all-time favorites like "It Takes Two" by Rob Base and DJ EZ Rock, or "Booming Systems" by LL Cool J. Ironically, the scene was quite different on this sunny afternoon in Ann Arbor. Upon closer examination, I realized these lovers of hip-hop music were Asian kids who drove late model Nissans, Mercedes Benzes, and BMWs. It was obvious they came from wealthy families. Finally, the students on foot acted as if they had bumpers on their butts. Like the squirrels, you would've thought they were invincible given how they crossed the streets from every direction. At one point, Dad slammed on his brakes to avoid hitting one of them. Wouldn't that have been something?

However, without incident, we finally pulled in front of South Quadrangle, an eight-story red brick dormitory that was home to first-year students and athletes, namely basketball and football players. While my dad and I unloaded my things, Mom remained seated in the van. When we reached my room on the 6th floor of Bush House, one of my roommates, who was from a small town in Ohio, had already arrived, built a loft, and unpacked all her things. She looked as if she had been there for months. Our other roommate, who was from the local Ann Arbor area, had not arrived yet. In her absence, I decided to take the bottom bunk. My Ohio roommate and I greeted each other, and her dad shook hands with my dad. It was a cordial encounter, but I knew our living arrangement was going to take getting used to, considering I had never shared the same space with a White girl, let alone two.

After securing all my things in the room, I followed Dad outside to the van to prepare for final goodbyes. Mom was sitting right where we left her. She never bothered to come inside. Apparently, her mind was preoccupied with other thoughts. In a whisper, before

CHAPTER 4—GO BLUE: LESSONS BEYOND THE CLASSROOM

Dad pulled away from the curb, Mom asked me if she could "hold something."

WTF! You're hitting me up for money? DAMN! If I'm not mistaken, I'm the one who is about to be a broke college student, right?

None of what I was thinking seemed to matter to her. As far as she was concerned, my three-year adventure in high school as the "Candy Queen Pin" meant I had money to give. Without Dad knowing, I quietly handed over a $100 bill and then watched them slowly pull away. No hugs or kisses goodbye. No "call me later when you get settled." Nothing! I stood there filled with emptiness. It was a very lonely feeling.

Then reality set in. South Quad was my new home, and anything I had previously known would become a distant part of my memory. While turning to re-enter my dorm, over my left shoulder, I caught a glimpse of something that helped to boost my spirits. The Michigan School of Business, or as I affectionately called it, "B-School", was situated on the other side of the Law Quad and was immeasurably taller than all the other buildings in the area. With its peak nearly touching the clouds, B-School had become my new focus and motivation. Nothing was going to keep me from reaching my destiny. No family drama. No unpleasant memories from the past. Nothing! As far as I was concerned, I was a "no-limit soldier" with marching orders to not stop until the mission had been accomplished.

After getting settled into my room, I called one of my Cass Tech classmates who also started at U of M with me. It was time to gather at the Diag, where we'd learn the Michigan fight song, "Hail to the Victors!" As we walked up South University, we saw him–a mystical figure that stood about 6'9" and wore black-rimmed sunglasses. He was like a modern-day Pied Piper with a trail of people following him closely. Soon after, I learned that this man, myth, and legend was none other than Juwan Howard–a member of the Fab Five.

If you followed Michigan Men's Basketball between 1991 and 1993, this period marked the height of the Fab Five Era. When these five young men—Chris Webber, Jalen Rose, Juwan Howard, Jimmy King, and Ray Jackson—stepped foot on campus in Ann Arbor, they changed Michigan basketball forever. Many people watched and admired their style of play and athleticism from afar, but as a season ticket holder during my freshman year, I had the extreme fortune to witness their greatness up close and personal. When they walked onto the gym floor at Crisler Arena, the energy in the building skyrocketed, as the entire student section went wild with excitement. At the top of my lungs, I joined in screaming, "Go Blue!"

The whole experience was surreal. *Somebody, pinch me.* "I go to Michigan! I go to Michigan!"

Freshman Year/Making the Transition

My naiveté as a first-gen student revealed itself when I received a notice from the University of Michigan, Office of Financial Aid stating that I owed $4,000 toward my tuition. WHAT!

How could this be? I wondered.

Then it dawned on me. In high school, my guidance counselor instructed me to, "Just put zeros on everything!" when I asked for assistance in completing the FAFSA (federal application for

CHAPTER 4—GO BLUE: LESSONS BEYOND THE CLASSROOM

student aid) form. Totally confused, I left the office and returned home with the application in hand. As I started to pore over the form again, I read where it asked about "Assets." I thought to myself, I know Ms. Wimberley said to put zeros on everything, but I do have some money in the bank, including savings and my time deposit account. I didn't want to be dishonest, so I declared what I had in each of those accounts. My mom signed the form, and we submitted it from there.

Well, my "honesty is the best policy" attitude did not take me very far in this case. While many of my friends from Cass received refunds from their financial aid packages and others qualified for food stamps, I was facing a big fat tuition bill from the financial aid office. DAMN! While it hurt to shell out $4,000, the good news was that I still had the money and thankfully did not blow it on something stupid over the summer. As I share this story 30 years later, I realize that "my financial information" should have never been considered in the application for aid. So, technically, U of M owes me some money. I'm just saying!

In addition to this financial aid faux pas, I did not have any scholarships outside of the Michigan Merit Scholarship. You would have thought I'd have scholarships up the wazoo considering that I graduated 7th in my class and in the top three percent of all graduating seniors in the Detroit Public School System. Unfortunately, I made the mistake of thinking that because I had good grades, "they" were going to just "give" me scholarship money. Boy, was I wrong! I learned the hard way, with scholarships and in life, no one just gives you anything. You must apply yourself. Therefore, the main reason I did not have any additional scholarships is because I never applied. I just didn't know any better, and neither did my parents.

The math courses in college were much more difficult than the ones that I had taken in high school. For example, calculus, or Math 115, kicked my natural black behind that first semester. I was fortunate enough to make it out of there with a "C." Thankfully, my degree program only required me to take one math course.

At the start of the semester, however, I had a rude awakening, literally, when my two roommates flung open the door to our dorm room, drunk off their behinds. It was 11 p.m. on a Thursday night and I had class the following morning at 9 a.m. It didn't matter to them, as they insisted, "Come party with us, Lisa!" While they were laughing and falling all over each other, I was like: "WTH! Who parties on a Thursday night? Don't you know I have class in the morning?" Besides, the idea of mid-week drunkenness was not my thing. While I didn't like it, I had to get used to waking up the next morning to vomit in the hallways, elevators, and laundry room. It made me very watchful of where I stepped. Eww!

Just so you know that I was not a total stick in the mud, I did my fair share of partying, too. When it came to Black Greek fraternity parties, you could most certainly find me at a party with the Nupes or men of Kappa Alpha Psi Fraternity, Inc. Yo, baby!

Making New Friends

Raquel lived two doors down from me. She was an African American girl from the suburbs of Chicago, by way of South Bend, Indiana. She was highly intelligent, heavily opinionated, and hopelessly confused. Why the latter description? She was a Dallas Cowboys fan, loved Notre Dame Fighting Irish football, and obsessed over Coach Bobby Knight and the Indiana Hoosiers Men's basketball team. Don't get me wrong: to this day, she is a die-hard Michigan fan who bleeds blue, but whenever we played the Irish in football or the Hoosiers in basketball, she could become exceptionally obnoxious. While neither one of us held Michigan football season tickets, we had become accustomed to watching the games on Saturday afternoons in the 5th floor student lounge along with our friend and big brother, DeLorean. A classic moment was when Desmond Howard won the Heisman Trophy in 1991. It was like we were speaking a language of our own as we celebrated Desmond's success, right along with his family.

Without a doubt, Raquel and I hit it off and were virtually inseparable for the rest of our freshman year. As we prepared to start our winter semester in January 1992, we stayed up to the wee hours of the morning talking until we both fell asleep. When we finally woke up, we realized that we had already missed our first classes of the day. At that moment, we decided we would be roommates the following fall semester.

Summer Break

Ring, ring, ring!

Ring, ring, ring!

"Hello?"

"Hi! This is Lisa. Remember me?"

"Yes, Lisa."

"Can I come work for you yet?"

"No, Lisa. You still need to get Accounting 271 and 272 under your belt."

"Okay!"

Click.

I had gotten into the habit of calling the recruiting manager at Arthur Andersen every summer since our initial meeting to inquire about working for them. I was relentless in my pursuit. I wanted to remain top of mind and demonstrate my commitment to begin my career with them after graduation.

In the meantime, I returned to the bank with one year of college under my belt. At the same time, my department hired two additional interns—an Indian woman named Rajal from Michigan State University and a white male named Justin from Bowling Green University. Whereas I had served more time at the bank, including my years as a high school co-op, Rajal and Justin were both older than me and had more years of professional work experience. As such, they were given assignments that allowed them to interface with management regularly. On the other hand, I had been confined to the storage closet where I sifted through boxes of files in search of an elusive list of documents requested by the external auditors. My reward for doing this thankless and 'think less' job was a thousand and one paper cuts!

"OUCH! Dammit!"

Out of frustration, I went to my auntie Betty, who worked in the same department, to voice my complaint. Ms. Betty and I were not related by blood, but we had developed a special bond. Therefore, I was comfortable confiding in her.

"Auntie Betty!" I said in a distressed tone.

"What's wrong, chile?"

"They keep giving Rajal and Justin all the good assignments, while I'm stuck in the storage room shuffling through a bunch of boxes."

"Listen to me and listen good," Auntie Betty exclaimed. With a single sheet of white copy paper in her hand to help illustrate her point, she firmly said, "If they tell you to move this sheet of paper from here to there, you do it! You understand me?"

"Yes, ma'am!"

In essence, she was teaching me a valuable life lesson about following simple instructions, serving with excellence, and showing gratitude. Since then, I have viewed every assignment, no matter how big or small, as both an opportunity and a test. It is an opportunity whenever you learn something new, gain experience, or develop a new skill. As a test, your supervisor observes your attitude and how well you understand and execute the assignment. In my case, Auntie Betty never heard me complain again. In hindsight, the task that I thought was menial had become part and parcel of the work associated with being an auditor in public accounting, my future career aspiration. It just goes to show you how little I knew at the time.

While I was working at the bank, Raquel was in Chicago continuing her internship with a pharmaceutical company. In our spare time, we spent countless hours talking on the phone, running up our parents' phone bills. We also took turns visiting each other's hometowns. For instance, I spent 4th of July weekend with her in the "Windy City," where she took me to all the popular tourist sites, like Sears Tower, Navy Pier, and the Michigan Mile. My all-time food favorites included Garrett's Popcorn and Harold's Fried Chicken. Yum, yum!

The following month, Raquel came to visit me. I will admit, a night on the town in Detroit in the early 90s paled in comparison to the exciting time I had during my visit to Chicago. Outside of showing her the Renaissance Center and having dinner in Greektown, Detroit's dark and desolate downtown sadly did not have much to offer. As I tried to keep a positive attitude about my city, I proudly pointed in the direction of the Ambassador Bridge, saying, "Look, Raquel! There's the bridge to Canada. Isn't it pretty?" In turn, she looked at me with a blank stare and asked, "Lisa, what are your plans after graduation? Will you relocate to another city or do you plan to stay in Detroit?"

Regardless of her preference for me to leave, I told her, "I plan to stay in Detroit."

Puzzled by my response, she asked, "Why?"

With great confidence, I said, "Detroit is going to come back one day, and I'm going to be part of it. You just wait and see!"

Sophomore Year—What's Different?

It was official: Raquel and I had become roommates! In planning ahead, we secured the same room in South Quad that she had during freshman year. We decked out our space with all the furnishings of a home, including small kitchen appliances, a sitting area, and an entertainment center. I supplied the 51-disc CD player while Raquel provided an extensive collection of music by hip-hop

CHAPTER 4—GO BLUE: LESSONS BEYOND THE CLASSROOM

artists Naughty By Nature, AMG, Arrested Development, Dr. Dre (*The Chronic*), and her reggae favorite, Shaba Ranks, just to name a few. It was not uncommon for us to receive a knock at the door from the residence hall advisor, asking her to lower the volume on the stereo. As you might expect, Michigan memorabilia was everywhere. On the wall just above our sitting area, we hung a navy-blue Michigan flag with a maize, big block "M" in the center.

So far, sounds normal, right? Wait for it…

On the left-hand side wall near the entrance to our room were three prominently hung posters that featured three historic figures: Abraham Lincoln, Ronald Reagan, and George Herbert Walker Bush; all former Presidents of the United States—and all Republican.

What the SH*T-and-a-half!

That's right! You read it correctly. My roommate was not only bold, brilliant, and busty; she was unapologetically Republican. A Black female Republican. Her political views have since changed, but in college, she was a staunch, card-carrying Republican. Whenever our mostly liberal classmates visited our room, they were shocked and intrigued by the posters. They saw them as an invitation to debate, which was risky considering Raquel was a political animal. Me, not so much. I just marveled at how these brave souls often left our room badgered and bruised after getting into a verbal wrestling match with Raquel.

Whereas I did not engage in the political debates, I would not miss the opportunity to vote for the first time that year in the presidential election between Arkansas Governor William Jefferson Clinton and incumbent President George H.W. Bush. I was raised by a mother who participated faithfully in the electoral process. Not only did she vote every cycle, but she also worked for the Detroit Election Commission, where she diligently counted absentee votes. Therefore, I had an obligation, duty, and responsibility to VOTE. Although Raquel and I may have voted for different candidates, we never let politics get in the way of our relationship or decision to remain roommates.

While Raquel was focused on politics and becoming a lawyer, I concentrated on getting into the B-School. Economics 201 and 202 and Accounting 271 and 272 were the four known "weeder" courses designed to separate the wheat from the chaff, the strong from the weak, and the women from the girls. Simply put, I needed to perform well in all four courses to get accepted into the Michigan Business School for the fall 1993 cohort.

Managerial or Cost Accounting (ACC 272) gave me the most difficulty. If you work in manufacturing, you likely can appreciate the foundational learning that was part and parcel of this course. Unfortunately, I did not find the lectures to be quite as appealing as my professor had hoped. To make matters worse, I often trudged through 10 inches of snow to get across campus to take this class, which was not unusual. Michigan was not in the habit of canceling classes due to bad weather. For us, there was no such thing as a snow day. In addition to the snow, the temperature outside could have been 10 degrees with a wind chill of negative 25, but that did not stop us from going to class. Hell, polar bears could have been slipping and sliding on the DIAG with icicles hanging from their butts, and at U of M, classes would have been in session. Unlike today, entire school districts and universities shut down when there's just 4 inches of snow. Wusses!

But I digress.

Truthfully speaking, I could have done better in cost accounting if I had been a little less distracted. Unlike some of my peers, my attention had not been consumed with pledging a sorority, partying excessively, or falling in love with the star football player. Whereas I did a fair amount of partying, I did not follow through on joining a sorority like I originally planned. As for love interests, my "would-be boo" on the football team broke my heart when I saw him hugged up in a blanket with another girl after one of the 2 a.m. fire drills at South Quad. During those drills—which would drive the drowsiest of students out their rooms and down the back stairwell—it was a sure-fire way to see who was creeping with whom.

Since none of those things were responsible for causing me to have a temporary lapse in focus, what was it?

Money!

That's what.

And, in the words of Tasha Mack from the TV show, *The Game*, "I was about that life!"

It all began in the dorm room of one of my dear friends from Cass Tech, Mr. Jamal Halifax. We called him Jam, for short. In high school, he was my dance partner. It was well-known that at a party whenever we heard, "Drop the Bass" by DJ Magic Mike, we'd find each other on the dance floor, and you guessed it–DROPPPPP! From time to time, I'd ask Jam to take me on candy runs when I needed to restock my supply, and he'd happily oblige.

Therefore, when he invited me and others to his room to hear about a business idea, I trusted him implicitly. Before the presentation started, he introduced me to his best friend Gerard, an engineering student from GM Tech, who was accompanied by a young, sharp, attractive, White married couple named Alexander and Allison Smith. They were both engineers who complemented each other quite well.

As Alexander, or Alex for short, set up his portable dry erase board and easel, I could not help but notice the duct tape that was holding this contraption together. You could tell his whole ensemble had traveled some miles. I could have easily prejudged the presentation by the size of the crack in the board, but I decided to keep an open mind instead.

After introducing himself, Alex asked this question, "How many of you know why you're here?" No one said anything. We all just stared at him with puzzled looks on our faces. He then commenced to answer the question for us. He said, "You are here because someone thought enough of you to invite you to see and hear some information that could possibly change your life."

Wow! That's good sh*t, I thought.

"You need to turn to that person and say, 'thank you'!" he continued.

We all looked at Jamal and said, "Thank you."

"With confidence, I can tell you that this information will change your life because it certainly changed ours," referring to himself and Allison. "Prior to someone showing this to me two years ago, I had no idea how I would get out of the rat race."

Rat race? I wondered. "What do you mean by that?" I asked.

CHAPTER 4—GO BLUE: LESSONS BEYOND THE CLASSROOM

"Great question," Alex replied. "What's your name?"

I replied, "Howze. Lisa Howze." Sort of like, Pope. Olivia Pope.

"To be in the rat race means that you earn just enough money to pay your bills, keep a roof over your head, put food on the table, and maybe drive a decent car. With all your hard work, you never really seem to get ahead. Instead of taking regular vacations, you live for the weekends." He paused to take a sip of water, and then continued with this thought: "You know you are in the rate race when on Sunday night, you get that nauseating feeling in the pit of your stomach as you think about the sound of your alarm clock going off at 6 a.m. on Monday morning to let you know it's time to get up and do it all over again."

"To make matters worse," he continued, "I was destined to keep up this routine for at least forty years unless I did something different."

Whoa! Alex was really painting a bleak picture of what life would look like once I entered the workforce full time.

As he continued his presentation, he reminded us of how we were all taught to go to school, get good grades, graduate, and get a good …"JOB!" we all said in unison, finishing his sentence.

As an engineer, Alex made over $80,000 per year but traded his most limited resource, time, to get it. It made sense, therefore, when he wrote this formula on the whiteboard: **TIME = $**. Most people follow this formula of exchanging time for money. For example, if you are an hourly employee, the only way to earn more money on your job is by working more hours. However, if you have a fixed annual salary like Alex, you earn the same amount of pay whether you work 40 hours or 60 hours in one week. In fact, your rate of pay per hour decreases as you exceed a 40-hour work week.

Alex described this scenario as **Plan A**, where "you work 40 hours a week for 40 years, only to retire with 40% of the pay that you cried wasn't enough in the first place."

"How many of you like the sound of that plan?" he asked. No one's hands went up.

"What if I told you there is a better way? Would you be interested in learning about it?" All hands went up.

On the whiteboard, he wrote: **PLAN B**.

"Plan B, ladies and gentlemen, is about you having your own business. It's about controlling your own destiny and living life on your own terms. In other words, PLAN B is about **FREEDOM!**"

"How many of you want to be free?"

Again, all hands went up, including both of mine.

Feeding off our energy, Alex was like an artist who examined his subject before returning his attention once more to the canvas. With the black dry erase marker in hand, he drew a circle in the center of the board. Pausing momentarily to look around the room at all the faces that were fully engaged, he then wrote the letters "Y-O-U" in the center of the circle. Then he said, "This is you!"

(Pause right there.)

Depending on your experience, you could probably guess what type of business my friend Jam had invited me to see. If you said, Amway, you would be correct! However, this presentation was more than an introduction to multi-level or network marketing, also referred to as direct sales. I had been exposed to a new way of thinking; unlike anything I was being taught in my college coursework. At that time, there was no Center for Entrepreneurship at the University of Michigan, like there is today.

After the presentation, I went back to my room, but I could not sleep that night. My mind was racing with all sorts of ideas about my future and everything that a life of freedom could bring. Within a couple of weeks of seeing the initial presentation, I told Jam that I was ready to get started. After getting my Amway kit, I immediately plugged into the system and did everything that Gerard, Alex, and Allison told me to do. I subscribed to the principle of "books, tapes, seminars, and major events". I attended the weekly presentations that were held at a hotel in the city of Troy, which was nearly a one-hour drive away from campus in Ann Arbor. I recruited fellow students and other guests to attend these presentations as well. I used the products and made customer sales too. I was open and teachable, and more than that, I was hungry!

However, my academic focus was starting to wane big time! Between the weekly presentations in Troy, the follow-up team meetings at the local Big Boy restaurant, and my daydreaming about riding around campus in a convertible Chrysler LeBaron, I regularly did not make it to the undergraduate library to crack open a book and study until well after midnight. It was clear that

I had gone off the rail when I received a less than stellar grade on my mid-term exam in cost accounting. If that wasn't enough, my work-study job was in jeopardy as well.

I worked as an accounting clerk for a non-profit center in downtown Ann Arbor, where I was responsible for updating the accounting ledger with donations received to support the organization's environmental education efforts in the surrounding community. One day, in my exuberance, I naively showed "The Plan" to my boss Karen, hoping she would join me in my new business venture. Instead of gaining a new business partner, I inadvertently placed a red neon sign on my back that flashed: WATCH CLOSELY!

It all came to a head one afternoon after I had sat through a long day of lectures and hung out late the previous night with my Amway buddies. Everything was business as usual at the job, or so I believed. I greeted Karen on my way to the back where she had a stack of receipts waiting for me to enter into the ledger. Approximately fifteen minutes after sitting down, my lack of rest hit me hard! It felt like a ton of bricks had fallen on my head and knocked me unconscious, except I was still sitting upright. I tried to shake it off, but it wasn't working.

When Karen came around to check my progress, she caught me as my head slowly tilted forward and my neck violently snapped back, seemingly in one continuous motion. I'm sure this was not the first time that she saw me nodding off on the job, but she intended to make it her last. Therefore, she invited me to follow her outside to the front steps of the Center to have a little talk. I guess she figured the outdoor air would be good to help revitalize my sleep-deprived soul. With all sincerity, she said, "Look, Lisa. I know what you've been doing, and I am elated that you have chosen to take on an entrepreneurial endeavor. However, if you're going to work here, I need you to be 100% present. So, either you curb your outside activities or find yourself without a job. The choice is yours."

Let's just say I did not work for the Center much longer.

In addition to not sleeping, I really did not take time to eat either, and it was beginning to show. While other students were packing on "the freshman fifteen," I was just the opposite, shedding pounds left and right. It took one of the football players that I recognized from South Quad to stop me on the street one day and ask, "Are you alright?" I replied, "Of course, why wouldn't I be?" Before I could reach my dorm room, word had already gotten back to Raquel, who informed me that someone saw me on campus and accused me of looking like "Pookie." When I say this was not a compliment, please believe me. In the 1990s movie "New Jack City," which featured actor Wesley Snipes, comedian Chris Rock played the role of a crackhead named Pookie, who at his lowest moment probably only weighed about a buck thirty-five. Translation: I really needed to get it together!

Although I had gone through this temporary phase with delusions of grandeur, I did not lose total sight of my original goal, which was to get admitted to the business school. On schedule, I submitted my application and waited for a response. Then, just before spring break, I received a letter from the "Michigan Business School" according to the return address on the envelope. Nervously, I opened it, and what it said on the inside was worthy of celebration. I GOT ACCEPTED! This meant I had accomplished my first of three goals.

"Yippee!"

| GOAL #1: Get accepted into the Michigan B-School. ☑ |

Besides my mom and dad, the first person I wanted to share the good news with was Dr. G., my business management teacher from high school. Before I could make it back home to Detroit, I learned that Dr. De Lois Gibson had passed away from a massive heart attack. I was heartbroken! Although she was firm and did not allow me to get away with anything, I truly appreciated her for believing in me. I am grateful for the impact she had in and on my life. Thinking about her makes me sad along with knowing that she did not live to see me make this great accomplishment. However, the message she inscribed in my high school memory book brings me joy. It reads as follows:

"Lisa,

Your interest in people will be a source for achievement. Your beautiful smile will make life pleasant for you. Do your very best and never give up on your ideals.

Best wishes,

Dr. De Lois Gibson
Bus. Mngt. & Bus. Law"

Junior and Senior Year—Time to Get Focused

As a junior in my first year of the BBA program at the Michigan Business School, it was time to buckle down, eliminate distractions, and get laser focused. As such, I had to let go of my Amway distributorship. I had no other choice, especially after consistently hearing "No" from my peers whose biggest objection to joining me in the business was time. I figured if *they* didn't have time, hell, I didn't either! We were all in the same boat–all striving to get this thing called "a college education" done. Undoubtedly, the business school proved to consume all my time and attention.

As I reflect on my overall experience in Amway, I am not ashamed to admit I did not make a billion, gazillion dollars. However, the value I gained after one year of personal development was immeasurable. I literally had undergone a mindset shift that changed my life forever and wired me for success. For example, I learned what it meant to have posture when engaging someone professionally. My mentors taught me to focus on my customer's needs and not my own. The same principle applied to working with prospective and actual business partners. In fact, it was Zig Ziglar who said, "You can have everything in life you want, if you will just help other people get what they want."

Another guiding principle I adopted from Amway prescribes that, "You are who you are based on the books you read and the people with whom you associate." At the tender age of 19, Amway gave me the notion to write a book. The idea of creating something one time and producing a profit from it repeatedly intrigued me. I also learned that associations matter. Through the power of association, the grades you earn in school, the size of your bank account, and the quality of your conversations are largely dependent on who is in your inner circle of influence. I'll tell you right now, if you don't like the results you're getting, then you need to either change your friends or *change your friends*.

Last but not least, during the summer leading up to my junior year, I will never forget how a 26-year-old guy named Cody Vanderbilt, flew over our heads and landed a helicopter in the middle of a field at Domino's Farms in Plymouth, Michigan. We were all there eating pizza and celebrating Cody's early retirement from his J-O-B. Thanks to Amway, at age 26, he no longer had a 9 to 5, and he no longer was in the rat race. Instead, he was financially free. From that moment, I knew I wanted to follow in his footsteps and retire by age 26. The bar had been set, and the image had been etched into my memory. Like my friend and mentor Shawn Blanchard always says, "It is impossible to un-see success." Finally, my all-time favorite lesson from Amway is this: "Life will either give you excuses to fail or reasons to succeed."

What was one of my early successes at the Michigan Business School? I learned from the error of my ways in cost accounting and took a different approach when I applied myself to the coursework in Intermediate Accounting (ACC 312). To prove to myself, *"I'm no dummy!"* I studied regularly, was attentive in class, and met with my professor during his office hours as needed. As a result of my hard work and dedication, I earned an A- in the class.

"YES! Way to bounce back, Lisa!"

Feeling vindicated, I was ready for the next challenge.

Once I accepted that the next two years of my life belonged to the BBA program at Michigan and leisure walks outdoors in the middle of the afternoon were a thing of the past, I resigned myself to four locations within the Business School footprint: the 2nd-floor student lounge, the library, the private study rooms in the basement of the Paton Accounting Center, and the computer lab.

When the latter closed, my backup option was the lab at Angell Hall, a centrally located building on campus that stayed open 24/7 and had considerably more computer stations and printers. I spent many painstaking hours at Angell Hall, writing term papers and completing group projects. A recurring nightmare happened there each time the computers crashed, and I had not saved my work. I'd be so angry, but I had no one to blame but myself. Instead of sulking over the loss, I salvaged what I could from earlier versions and continued from there.

The saving grace of those experiences is that I did not go through them alone. I had a study partner and friend, who we will call Carlotta Wilkins, or Carlie, for short. Prior to starting the BBA program, Carlie and I did not know each other. I was from the inner city of Detroit, and she grew up tending to cows and pigs in a small country town outside of Ann Arbor. The one thing we had in common was a fierce commitment to succeed. Our additional bond came through us each owning a 1984 Chevy Chevette–hers in forest green and mine in fire engine red. Although not flashy, those little cars got us where we needed to go, including the midnight runs to Taco Bell and White Castle when it was time for a study break.

Carlie and I tag-teamed as leaders within the student chapter of the National Association of Black Accountants, Inc. (NABA). After attending our first meeting, we quickly became immersed in the organization. She served as secretary then treasurer, and I served as treasurer then president during our junior and senior years, respectively. In those roles, we recruited other accounting and finance students, organized events, and had direct contact with the recruiting managers and partners from the Big 6 accounting firms.

Of course, I had my eyes set on Arthur Andersen. Whenever they were on campus for a career fair, I'd make a beeline for their booth. There was one recruiter I recognized from my visit to Andersen's offices when I was a graduating senior in high school. With perfect eye contact and my right arm extended to shake hands, I said, "Remember me? I'm Lisa Howze." At this point, they could no longer tell me I had to wait until I had completed Accounting 271 and 272 to come work for them. I had crossed both of those bridges, and I was ready for an internship!

Carlie and I interviewed for internships with all six of the firms to ensure we covered our bases. Then, the fun began, as we waited with bated breath to hear back from each of them. When we received our first responses, the letters had identical messages that started with, "We regret to inform you that..." We were both thinking, "Okay. That's just one. Maybe it wasn't meant to be. Let's see what the next one says." Our second letters were a mirror reflection of the first. The third one was no different, saying also, "We regret to inform you that…" At this point, we were becoming a bit discouraged, but instead of lingering in doubt and regret, we decided to turn our disappointment into a game and celebrate each rejection letter that followed. Depending on who called whom first, our conversations went as follows:

"Hey, Carlie!" or "Hey, Li Li!"

"What's up?"

"I got another ding letter!"

"Me too!"

Then in unison, we'd go, "Ding, ding, ding, ding, ding!" and burst out in laughter.

Included among the ding letters was one from my beloved Arthur Andersen. All was not lost, however; Carlie ultimately received an internship with Saturn, a division of General Motor's Pontiac brand in Memphis, Tennessee, and I returned to my existing internship at Comerica Bank.

Do you remember when I told you how I didn't apply for any scholarships prior to enrolling in classes at Michigan? Fortunately, during my senior year, one of my accounting professors recommended me for a $3,000 scholarship from Amoco Oil, which I received. "Thank you, Professor Griffin! Thank you, Amoco!"

The news of the scholarship boosted my confidence going into the recruitment season for full-time employment, although I only agreed to meet with four out of the six major public accounting firms. Arthur Andersen was included with one other firm that I decided to put on ice. Admittedly, I was still in my feelings about being turned down for an internship the previous year, not considering how competitive those opportunities were.

After snubbing them on their first visit to campus, thankfully, Andersen decided to visit Michigan a second time. What made them return? I don't know, but I'm glad they did. I signed up to be included in their interview schedule, and things went extremely well. Within a couple of weeks, I received an offer letter with a starting salary of $30,000 per year plus overtime. I had received a similar offer from each of the other firms I interviewed with as well. While one of my peers announced that she had accepted an offer with Coopers & Lybrand, she was curious about which firm I'd be joining. As I kept my cards close to my chest, she concluded that I was probably going to make the "bougie" choice and go with Arthur Andersen. She was correct about one thing: I planned to choose Andersen but for different reasons.

Yes. Andersen represented the crème de la crème of all the firms for me. However, my friend did not realize my decision to start with them was already predetermined. From the day Dr. G. connected me to Roger Short, who then connected me to his former colleagues at Arthur Andersen, the ball had already been set in motion. Then, in the same high school memory book that included the message that I shared with you earlier from Dr. G., I affirmed it in my response to the question that asked, "Where will you be in five years after (high school) graduation?" I filled in the blank with, "Working as an entry-level accountant for Arthur Andersen."

In my case, there was no denying destiny. As you consider yourself and your goals, what is for you will be for you. It may not always come when you want it, but it will be there when you need it. Always remember that delay does not equal denial.

Before accepting Andersen's offer of $30,000, I submitted a counteroffer for $31,500, plus the cost of taking a CPA exam review course. Without batting an eye, they approved my request. Here's the lesson: You never get in life what you deserve; you only get what you are willing to negotiate. If you don't ask, the answer will always be "NO!" Finally, there I was—a little Black girl from the westside of Detroit, who was within a few months of becoming the first in her immediate family to graduate from college and start a professional career. This was HUGE! My ancestors would have been proud.

> **GOAL #2: Land a job in public accounting.** ☑

Next, it was time for the grand finale!

Graduation Day

♫ "THIS IS HOW WE DO IT!" ♫

Instead of Pomp and Circumstance, imagine bobbing your head to the rhythmic sounds of "This Is How We Do It" by R&B singer Montell Jordan, while in your graduation processional line. This hit song will always and forever be associated with my graduation day– April 28, 1995. Whenever I hear it played on the radio or at a social event, my mind immediately gets flooded with fond memories of my mom's presence and the joy I shared with my fellow classmates. As such, there are three iconic photos that helped to capture the significance of this day. The first photo was taken of my mom and me in my dorm room, after ensuring I had gathered all my belongings. From there, I took her on a tour of the B-School, so she could see where I had spent many sleepless nights studying. Since the day was just as much hers as it was mine, I wanted to make the most of it. Along with meeting some MBA friends of mine, I introduced her to my tax accounting professor who said to her, "You have a very special daughter here. I enjoyed having her in my class." Beaming with pride, my mom kindly nodded her head and smiled in agreement, as if to say, *"I know. I raised her."* As I mentioned previously, my mother had always affirmed me as her 'little star' for as long as I could remember. So, she had every right to be proud.

After leaving the B-School, we headed over to the Crisler Arena, where the graduation ceremony was within an hour of starting.

As my mom got reconnected with my brother, I had a chance to catch up with a few classmates, just in time to take the second iconic photo. Adorned in our caps and gowns, five young, gifted, and talented Black women, with majors in accounting, finance, and information systems, gathered at the bottom of the concrete steps that led to the entrance of the Arena to smile for the camera: "Cheese!" We each had our own stories. We each had our own hills to climb. Through it all, we made it, and our families were proud. The extra beautiful thing about this photo and its timelessness is that you can see my mother standing in the background at the top of the stairs, wearing a long black trench coat with her black handbag clutched underneath her arm. As she looked off into the distance, she appears as a guardian angel, carefully watching over me.

As we lined up to proceed inside, somewhere nearby, someone was playing, "This Is How We Do It." My classmates and I nearly lost our minds as we moved and grooved to the bassline, stepping forward a few paces at a time. It was the best feeling ever! Once inside, someone captured a profile image of my mom sitting in the stands of the arena, patiently waiting for the ceremony to begin. Unlike the version of my mother who dropped me off at South Quad four years earlier, this version was fully engaged and present. As I was approaching the stage to hand the reader my name card with the phonetic pronunciation of my last name, I can only imagine the expression on her face when she heard: Lisa LaShawn "Nubian Princess" Howze! I am sure she was ecstatic like everyone else who cheered me on in the crowd, including my dad and Mama Fatty who sat in a different part of the arena.

"I DID IT, Y'ALL! I DID IT! I GRADUATED FROM MICHIGAN!"

How did I do it, you ask? I set a goal; I crushed that goal. I set another goal; I crushed it too! I didn't stop until the job was done. I was determined to not be a statistic. I was determined to succeed and not fail. I was determined to make my community proud. And the proudest one of all was my mom who got a chance to see her 'little star' rise!

> **GOAL #3: Graduate in four years.** ☑

A Life Lesson Learned Post-Graduation

After graduation, I ended my internship with Comerica Bank to enjoy the summer before starting my new career with Arthur Andersen in the fall. Meanwhile, I took a part-time job at my church as a clerical assistant. In this role, I earned $80 per week to process offering envelopes. This was a significant pay cut when compared to how much I was making at the bank. I didn't mind it because the lessons I learned that summer about generosity and financial stewardship were priceless.

For instance, as I entered the information from each envelope into the accounting software, I noticed the names of certain members who consistently made generous contributions to the church. The box that they checked on their envelope read, "Tithes." Curious about this concept of tithing, I wanted to know how I could do it too. After receiving guidance from my pastor, I calculated my tithe at $8 or 10% of my weekly earnings. When my income increased upon starting at Arthur Andersen, my tithes grew from $8 per week to over $130 every two weeks.

That was a big jump, right? Do you think I would have been able to "give away" $260 per month if I had not already started to follow the principle of tithing when I was only making $80 per week? The answer is no. However, since I demonstrated that I could be trusted with smaller amounts of money, I was blessed with so much more. Because of those early lessons that I acquired beyond the classroom more than 25 years ago, I have continued to enjoy financial success; and for that, I am thankful.

CHAPTER 5

THE CPA ADVANTAGE: BUT NOT WITHOUT ADVERSITY

In October 2020, the Michigan Association of Certified Public Accountants (MICPA) posted a statement on LinkedIn that said, "Women play a pivotal role in the CPA profession, and the MICPA is proud to recognize and celebrate this year's (2020) *Women to Watch Experienced Leader Award* recipients." As an MICPA board member, leader in higher education, and African American woman, I was proud to be recognized by the profession along with three other deserving honorees. When they asked me, "Lisa, what does this award symbolize for you?" I immediately expressed my appreciation for my parents and teachers like Dr. Gibson. They each had great expectations for me to achieve my goals and live life above and beyond their wildest imaginations.

In addition, I feel obligated to give back. Through my example, I want the next generation of young leaders who have even a slight interest in accounting to see the profession as a viable career option. Then, when that young person is asked, "What do you want to be when you grow up?" I want them to think of me and know that they can be whatever they want to be. The possibilities are truly unlimited.

When I set my sights on becoming a CPA as a graduating high school senior, I never imagined how being a part of this profession would give me access to rooms, people, and opportunities that are not often afforded to little girls that look like me. In fact, Black CPAs[1] have always been the most underrepresented group within the CPA profession, representing for many years less than 1% of now over 665,000[2] CPAs in the United States. Therefore, in a field that has been dominated for over a century by middle-aged white men in blue suits, white shirts, and neckties, my presence is rare. However, to meet the ever-growing needs of a diverse marketplace, leaders recognize the need to change the face of business. This challenge is even greater, given how the pipeline of accounting students has declined over the years, along with interest by young professionals to seek the CPA credential.

As a participant in these conversations, I use my voice to advocate for black and brown students for whom it has been said, "They cannot be what they cannot see." This statement speaks to the importance of representation in the profession. For this reason, organizations like the National Association of Black Accountants, Inc. (NABA), the National Society of Black CPAs (NSBCPA), and the Association of Latino Professionals For America (ALPFA) exist. In working with NABA's Accounting Career Awareness Program (ACAP) and the MICPA's High School Leaders program, I can testify of young African American men and women who have successfully entered the profession after being exposed as high school students to the rewards of this profession. Therefore, as an ambassador, I will continue to do my part to stand in the representation gap.

CHAPTER 5—THE CPA ADVANTAGE: BUT NOT WITHOUT ADVERSITY

Here's the question we get asked in the profession all the time: "Is it worth it?" It's a fair question. Students have the right to know what the advantages are to becoming a CPA, especially when they are required to commit more time and money to their education to even be eligible to sit for the CPA exam. This is where my story comes in. Whether you are an accounting student, professional engineer, or software developer, for that matter, the purpose of this chapter is not to convince you to become a CPA, but to illustrate how my experiences early in my career helped to shape me into the professional that I am today. Some of these experiences will sound familiar to those who have been working in your own career field of choice. For those of you who are yet to get started, stick around for a sneak preview of what may be on the horizon for you.

Before I dive in deeply, let me quickly say that being a CPA comes with instant credibility. Without ever saying a word, those three letters that follow my name speak volumes about my character, work ethic, and ability to solve problems. It was Tesla founder Elon Musk who said, "You get paid in direct proportion to the difficulty of problems you solve." Therefore, if you choose this profession and decide to stay in public accounting long enough to make partner or move on to take a new position in industry, as a CPA, you can literally write your own ticket. If you are anything like me, you can chart your own path, which included running for public office. Not to get ahead of myself, but later you will learn how I leveraged being a CPA to give myself a competitive advantage in the political races that I was part of in my hometown of Detroit.

Where we left off in Chapter 4, you learned that my journey to becoming a CPA began when I accepted an offer to join Arthur Andersen right out of college. However, due to my *stinking thinking*, I nearly let the CPA Advantage slip through my fingers. If I had not quickly regained my senses, I could have torpedoed my career well before it had a chance to get started. In that case, there would have been no need for the profession to celebrate me as a woman to watch. Let's dive in and see what happened.

25 Years Earlier

Labor Day weekend in Detroit had come and gone, taking with it the world's largest free jazz festival. The Montreaux-Detroit Jazz Festival had a reputation for drawing hundreds of thousands of jazz enthusiasts to Hart Plaza for an unmatched cultural and family experience. With the Detroit River and Renaissance Center as its backdrop, there was something magical about the festival that combined the melodious sounds of jazz musicians and vocalists with the savory, sweet smell of barbecue filling the air. That whole vibe is the meaning of summer in Detroit. However, with every note played and lyric sung, summer was slowly coming to a close. When they turned off the stage lights after Herbie Hancock's performance, it was my cue to gather my lawn chair and water cooler and start heading back to the car. With every step, reality sunk in that my summer break had come to an end, as a promising new chapter was set to begin.

When the alarm clock sounded at 5 a.m., I sprung out of bed. It was Tuesday, September 5, 1995, and my long-awaited dream to start my career as a staff auditor with Arthur Andersen had finally come true. In adhering to the strict professional dress code, I reached into the closet for a crispy white shell and the navy blue, single button suit with the pleated skirt that hung just below my knee. While it would have been more comfortable to go bare-legged, I managed to dance my way into a pair of coffee brown pantyhose without snagging them and getting a run. My unwrapped hair hung long and straight with a slight bend to the ends that helped to frame my fresh face. To finish the look, I stepped into a pair of black leather pumps that had a conservative two-and-a-half-inch heel. From head to toe, my appearance made it clear that "I understood the assignment!"

Bright-eyed and bushy-tailed, I arrived at the One Detroit Center building in downtown Detroit at 7:45 a.m. when I took the elevator to Andersen's office located on the 27th floor. Upon checking in with the front desk receptionist, I was given a New Hire Orientation package and directed to the conference room. As I moved through the office, I quickly scanned the place for faces that looked like mine. While it was comforting to see that many of the support services personnel, including the receptionist, were African American women, I secretly wondered where the Black professionals were who helped to wine and dine me during the recruitment process. Were they real or had I imagined them? It was important that I find my tribe because by the looks of things at orientation, I was the only African American in my starting class of 10.

To block out the noise in my head, I tried to focus instead on the information being shared. The presentation on investing in the Firm's 401 (k) plan piqued my interest the most. They made it clear that I did not have to follow their advice. If I wanted to squander my money by partying on the weekends or buying the latest shiny new object, I was free to do so. However, one thing I understood as an accountant is that numbers do not lie. When they used a chart to show me an example of a person who delayed making contributions to their 401 (k) by as few as five years compared to the person who started immediately, I noticed a drastic difference in the future retirement savings. Therefore, my biggest takeaway from that session was "invest early and often." Besides, I did not want to "mess around, not take care of business while I was young, and get to be 40, 50, or even 60 years old and not have a da*n thang to show for it!" as one of my uncles so eloquently put it. As a result, I quickly completed the paperwork with instructions to contribute at the maximum level, and I'm so glad I did.

If you are someone who has yet to participate in your company's retirement plan, please know that you do not need to be Warren Buffet to win in the stock market or take advantage of the U.S. tax code. By making regular 401 (k) contributions, not only will you be able to build a nest egg for your future, but you will also save on taxes you pay to "Uncle Sam" at the end of each year.

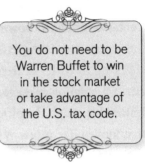

You do not need to be Warren Buffet to win in the stock market or take advantage of the U.S. tax code.

My first week in the office was followed by two weeks of intensive training at Arthur Andersen's state-of-the-art, resort-like facility in St. Charles, Illinois. There, I met a diverse group of associates from other Andersen offices across the country. While we all may have taken a Principles of Auditing course at different universities, the instructors in "New Hire School" were committed to teaching us how to apply the Arthur Andersen way to auditing a set of financial statements. During breaks, we had access to an abundant supply of fruit, snacks, drinks, and candy. You name it, they had it. To stay alert, I mixed coffee with hot cocoa, thinking that I would lessen the effects of the caffeine since I was not a "real" coffee drinker. The heart palpitations that I experienced proved it. Aside from my poor judgement in beverage choices, I appreciated how the Firm spared no expense in making sure I used good judgement

CHAPTER 5—THE CPA ADVANTAGE: BUT NOT WITHOUT ADVERSITY

when working with their clients. Andersen believed in grooming the best accounting professionals the industry had to offer, and I was grateful to be one of them.

When I returned to the office, I received my first assignment to work on the audit of the City of Detroit's federal grant programs. The engagement team's job was to ensure that the city was using the federal properly. If we found them to be out of compliance with the grant requirements, the city could risk losing the funds that supported programs relied upon by city residents. At the time, I did not fully understand the significance of the work we were doing. However, while working in a different capacity decades later, it all made sense. You will see what I mean a few chapters later.

In the meantime, while on the city's account, my senior (supervisor) made the mental connection that I graduated from the same high school as another staff member on the team. Eager to see who this person was, I followed my supervisor into the next room. As we approached, I saw someone who looked like me–another "sistah!" Turning to me first, my supervisor said, "Lisa Howze, meet Danielle Avis. Danielle Avis, meet Lisa Howze." Judging by the big grins on both our faces, Danielle and I were equally excited to discover each other. Like hidden jewels, when you find someone who shares your interests, experiences, and values, you hold onto them and never let them go. Who would have known that a brief introduction in the drabby gray conference room at the City of Detroit would lead to a more than 25-year friendship? During our days and years at "Ole' Uncle Arthur," we certainly needed to lean on one another as we tried to find our way in an environment where most of the people that we encountered did not look like us, except at the city.

Then, there was Kory and Michelle—two African American senior auditors who schooled us on what it meant to be "Black while in public accounting". They made it their personal business to "get to" the newbies early in our journeys because they knew how easy it was to become disillusioned by the red-carpet treatment that we all experienced at St. Charles. Therefore, their job was to open our eyes to the sobering realities of what could be expected during the first two years at the firm. Since Danielle had already had "the talk", it was my turn.

As I sat across the table from them, the look in their eyes told me that class was officially in session. First, they stressed the importance of passing the CPA exam and getting promoted to senior like them. The latter was largely dependent on my ability to navigate the inter-office politics of the 26th and 27th floors, client assignments, relationships with firm partners and managers, and performance evaluations. Although I had a fairly good experience on my first audit engagement, Kory and Michelle warned me that typically the bar was set higher for African Americans to receive an "Exceeds Expectations" on an evaluation compared to our non-African American counterparts.

As they took turns swapping stories about their personal experiences, I felt like my head was on a swivel, trying desperately to keep up. At one point, my mouth gaped open in disbelief, which only justified the need for the "Drop Squad"-like conversation in the first place. In the end, the one comment that kept playing on a loop in my head was that "many of us don't stick around to make partner." Damn! As discouraging as those words may have sounded, the numbers spoke for themselves. Except for one senior manager who seemingly had been in a holding pattern to make partner for years, there were no African Americans who ranked higher than a second-year senior, which meant no one even stayed long enough to make Manager. Instead, the average length of time was two to four years, with most leaving after two years.

This shocking information made me wonder why the firm was having such a hard time retaining us. Whatever the case was, over time, I got it in my head that, *"This job is only temporary. There are no guarantees for long-term success. However, while you are here, your real job is to learn as much as you possibly can. Then, use your knowledge and expertise to help your community, while paving the way for the next generation."* And finally, *"Don't leave until you have gotten what you came for!"*

My top priority in starting at the firm was to pass the CPA exam. Honestly, I expected to have passed it already between the spring and summer after graduating from Michigan. Although I had taken a CPA review course during my senior year, my first attempt at the exam resulted in me only passing one part, Business Law, while failing the other three parts. Keep in mind, this was under the old rules when we were tested over a two-day period and needed to initially pass two out of the four parts to make any of it count. Since I clearly missed the mark, my little talk with Kory and Michelle was perfectly timed to help me focus on taking the exam again in November 1995. Three months later, the results were in, and the outcome was different but not by much. Would you believe I passed the Auditing section but failed everything else–including the part I had previously earned a passing score? *Go F*cking Figure, Lisa!*

In frustration, I balled up the results, threw them to the floor, and vowed to never take the exam again. Unfortunately, the only person I would be hurting was me. During the next exam cycle, I sat on the sidelines and carried on with my pity party while others, like my colleague Maria, maintained their focus. Maria was an experienced staff auditor who had been at the firm one year longer than me. After several attempts of her own, she finally passed three parts of the exam at once. "Maria, how did you do it?" I asked in amazement. She said, "I studied in the morning before work, during my lunch break, after work each evening, and at least nine hours a day on the weekend."

Although I did not utter these words aloud, I walked away thinking, *Humph! I'm not doing all that! That's wayyyy too much! Wait. Pump the brakes, Lisa! You literally just asked this woman what she did to pass three parts! She gave you the blueprint, and you have the audacity to fix your feeble mind to think you're not going to do it! Seriously? GTFOH!*

After my inner voice finally knocked some sense into my head, I used an Excel worksheet to map out a plan over several weeks leading up to the next scheduled exam. Each day, I accounted for the number of hours studied and review questions answered. In the end, the strategy worked! Like Maria, I passed three parts. On the next go-round, I passed the fourth and final part as well.

> What happens when you miss a goal? Do you try again?
> What if you fail a second or third time?
> Do you give up, or do you stand up and try again?

Today, the bronze-framed CPA certificate that hangs on my wall at home reminds me how important it is to get out of your own way and not give up on your goals no matter how difficult it seems. The certificate reads:

State of Michigan

Department of Consumer and Industry Services,

Board of Accountancy

"Be it known that

Lisa LaShawn Howze

has qualified under the law regulating the practice of public accountancy and may use the title of

Certified Public Accountant

In the State of Michigan under this Certificate No. 024993

Upon display of a current Michigan registration. The right to practice in Michigan is dependent on current licensure.

It was signed and dated by the chairperson and secretary-treasurer of the State Board of Accountancy, on October 9, 1997.

At that point, I had been with the Firm for a little over two years. My original goal was to stay at least five years to make manager.

However, in June 1997, when the Firm announced promotions to Senior Auditor, my name was not on the list. To say I was highly disappointed is an understatement. It felt like I had been run over by a Mack truck, as my hopes and dreams lay flat in the streets. As a result, I had fallen into a momentary state of depression. While there, I secretly resented my friends and peers for moving ahead without me. I was in a bad place, but I knew I could not stay there for too long. Who could I go to for consolation and direction? Kory and Michelle were not an option because they had since left the firm. So, what did I do? I had no choice but to talk to myself, saying:

> *"Look, girl! I know you're upset about not getting promoted but look on the bright side: You still have a job. You're in the perfect industry to build a career. Besides, they're still willing to pay you while you learn. Take the extra time. Get some additional experience under your belt. Then, position yourself to step into your promotion as a new senior this time next year."*

Afterwards, I was like, "Alright, bet. Let's go!"

I followed my own advice, and as promised, one year later, in June 1998, I was ecstatic to see my name and photo appear in the "People making the news" section of the Detroit Free Press. This time, Arthur Andersen had included me among their list of staff members promoted to senior. It was my first newspaper appearance with many more to follow. More on that later.

With summer underway, it was the calm before the storm. By fall, I knew that I would need to start planning for "busy season" when I'd be the supervisor in charge. In the meantime, the firm sponsored me to attend my first NABA national convention in San Francisco. Who knew the Bay Area could be freezing cold

CHAPTER 5—THE CPA ADVANTAGE: BUT NOT WITHOUT ADVERSITY

in the middle of July, unlike other parts of California? Even so, I was warmed by the richness of my networking experiences with countless Black accounting professionals from across the nation. Besides the technical sessions, keynote speeches, and late-night card parties with my newfound friends, there were two highlights from the convention that I will never forget:

First, one of Arthur Andersen's national leaders reserved an entire restaurant for what seemed like 50 to 100 associates from offices across the country, including six that traveled with me from our Detroit office. While at the restaurant, I took pleasure in sampling a variety of white wines from Chardonnay to Pinot Grigio to Riesling to Zinfandel. Why not? We were in wine country! Second, we enjoyed a live musical performance by R&B singer Jeffrey Osborne who sang his ever popular "You Should Be Mine (The Woo Woo Song)." He had us all singing along, "Can you woo, woo, woo?" OMG! The entire experience was spectacular, or shall I say, *it was all that and a bag of chips*!

When I returned to the home office, I was so excited and filled with gratitude that I did not hesitate when asked to participate in the upcoming NABA Central Region Student Conference to be hosted in Detroit that October. There was an African American senior manager in our office, who we will call Rodney Lake who served as one of the conference co-chairs. As such, he recruited every Black professional at the firm to assist in conference planning. We all knew how much was at stake and wanted to ensure we made both Rodney and the Firm look good. For example, Danielle and I took the lead on scheduling students for interviews, while our colleagues worked on fundraising, conference speakers, and various other aspects of a well-executed conference. When it was all said and done, the conference was a huge success. Together, the NABA Detroit Chapter and our team at Andersen, led by Rodney, truly embodied NABA's motto of "Lifting as We Climb!" It was a proud moment for us all.

> Can I just take a moment and be totally transparent with you?

No amount of success comes without adversity. Unfortunately, the world only sees and cares about the end results, not the sacrifice. For instance, they want the cake but blatantly disregard the ingredients that went into baking it. Thus far, I believe I have done an effective job sharing my early career struggles, but there are some stories that remain untold. Stories with truths that frankly may ruffle a few feathers or uncover some hidden wounds. Whatever the case, if I chose not to share them, I would be doing you and me a disservice. So, you ready? Let's dive in deeper.

When Kory and Michelle suggested that I look out for inter-office politics, they were describing a notable difference between the products division engagement teams that operated from the 26th floor and services division engagement teams that operated from the 27th floor. In today's corporate vernacular, you hear statements about companies creating an inclusive work environment. Well, the air of exclusivity on the 26th floor was so thick; you could cut it with a knife. In contrast, the 27th floor had a vibe that was more welcoming and inviting. Even so, my compadres and I could not afford to let our guard down.

No amount of success comes without adversity.

CHAPTER 5—THE CPA ADVANTAGE: BUT NOT WITHOUT ADVERSITY

While we had no real control over client engagements assigned, the clients usually were not the problem. No matter the industry, all clients hated to see the auditors coming. It was just a given. However, if you treated clients with dignity and respect, they would bend over backwards to get you the information you needed. Whenever the partner came into the field, staff easily became nervous and intimidated. Partners, however, were more interested in managing client relationships, risks, and the bottom line–not staff. In addition to picking up the tab for lunch or dinner, some partners were good for instigating a teachable moment that I found to be more meaningful than how to cross-reference a footnote in the financial statements.

Quick story! I was assigned to a banking client where the engagement partner was superbly intelligent but a royal pain in my backside! Whenever he was present, I had to be on my Ps and Qs because he was bound to test me. For example, one day he asked, "What is 100 basis points (or 1 percent) of $1 million?" With a bit of hesitation in my voice, I said, "Ten thousand dollars!" He replied, "Are you sure?" as he dragged out each word. Even though I was correct, I totally second-guessed myself. Later, I determined that he was less concerned about the accuracy of my answer and more interested in the level of confidence I displayed while giving it. In essence, he was helping me sharpen my saw. I thought that was pretty dope!

Here's where the rubber met the road. During my first two years at the firm, I worked with different audit seniors on client engagements in a variety of industries, including banking, retail, manufacturing, technology, government, and non-profit. When I received my evaluations, I consistently scored above-average ratings for professionalism, work paper documentation, and auditing skills. However, I could not catch a break in the technical skills category. I was not alone; my African American colleagues were getting similar results on their jobs too. Did I think this was a coincidence? Absolutely not!

The rule of thumb was, if you did not receive an "Exceeds Expectations" in technical skills, you could not receive an overall "Exceeds Expectations" on your evaluation. Kory and Michelle warned me about this. Therefore, when I received an overall rating of "Meets Expectations," like my Black colleagues, I was told, "You're right in line with where you're supposed to be. Most staff with your level of experience receive 5s and 6s." I thought, *so you want me to feel good about being "average" when I know "good and well," there are some folks in my starting class who have the same "level of experience" as me but are receiving 8s and 9s, which meant "Exceed Expectations" overall?* Not to sound redundant, but "Go F*cking Figure!"

Black folks were livid about this blatantly disparate treatment in the evaluation process. Why? Because it impacted our advancement and our pay. As a result, we formed the firm's first Employee Resource Group (ERG) to support one another and provide a safe space to voice concerns and air grievances that we later brought to the attention of the Firm's division partners. Meanwhile, we affectionately called ourselves "BPs," and our gatherings were called "BP meetings," in which BP stood for *Black people* or *Black professionals*. We had nicknames for each other like Water, VeeGee, E. Money, J. Black, R. Kelly (not to be confused with the R&B singer), Cheesy, CL Smooth, Shuckey Duckey, Sloppy, Budd, and I was Detail. I can't begin to explain the origin of those names, but when we used them, it was with a high degree of respect and warmth toward our fellow brother or sister who was part of the same journey. When we gathered privately to break bread, we were

CHAPTER 5—THE CPA ADVANTAGE: BUT NOT WITHOUT ADVERSITY

like a family that had been drawn closer together by our shared experiences. Ironically, we attribute the friendships that we hold today to Ole' Uncle Arthur.

> Now may be a good time to put the book down to go to the kitchen to pop a fresh batch of popcorn! The plot only thickens from here. Don't worry! I'll hold your place.

In the mid-1990s, keep in mind, there was no training on emotional intelligence, unconscious bias, or micro- and macro-aggressions, as it related to diverse cultures in the workplace. Therefore, it was unfortunate that although the BPs were close, we could not always display our closeness in plain sight. What do I mean by that? At firm-wide business assemblies, we consciously chose not to sit together. To avoid negative attention and the constant nagging question from our white colleagues, "Why are you always sitting with so and so?" we separated into different areas of the auditorium. Sometimes we sat alone. Other times we sat with members of our engagement teams. As you absorb this information, I hope you recognize that this behavior was not normal! Instead, it was learned behavior, subconsciously taught to us by individuals who would never be questioned about where or with whom they sat. Unfortunately, African Americans have historically needed to make such calculated decisions to survive in the workplace, adding both mental and emotional stress.

> Are you ready for one more?

Imagine me standing in the office, engaging in normal conversation with two other Black women when a partner comes along and says, "Hey, break that up! What are you all doing, conspiring?" That was an interesting choice of words he used; don't you think? Was there ill intent on his part? Hmm! I don't know; you tell me. Would his reaction have been the same if a different group of people were congregating in a similar manner? I doubt it. What looked like "conspiring" with one group could easily be described as "collaboration" with another. Again, go figure! Then, when you think about these examples and others that I did not mention that carried a similar vibe, is it any wonder why Black professionals rarely stayed to make partner, let alone manager or senior manager?

Here's the reality: it does not matter if you are black or white; not everyone who starts their career in public accounting is going to stay, let alone make partner. To believe any differently is not realistic. While some attrition is expected, it becomes too costly to repeatedly lose talent because people are made to feel uncomfortable, different, or other than. Disparate treatment over time can diminish a young assoicate's aspirations to stay longer and climb higher, while robbing the organization of their potential contributions. Therefore, if firms are going to make the investment to attract diverse talent, then it only makes sense to make the necessary investment to retain them.

After being 20-plus years removed from my experiences in public accounting, I have since learned to appreciate all that was good about that part of my career journey while not harboring any ill feelings about what I may have considered to be bad. Case in point, on the subject of employee evaluations, I believe there is too much focus on the rating. In my opinion, the lessons that you learn from your shortcomings are a better indicator of your long-term success. For example, in situations where I have been on both the giving and receiving end of an evaluation, neither I nor the persons that I had the pleasure to evaluate would have gained the necessary insights to become a better leader or improve processes to generate a greater result, if the overall rating had been "Exceed Expectations" right out the gate. I know this borderline plays into the idea that as a Black woman, "I have to work twice as hard to get half as much!" However, there is nothing wrong with working hard if you learn something new in the process. What you decide to do with that knowledge is solely up to you.

Whereas the BPs and I experienced moments of frustration at the firm, they were just that–moments. No one was forced to leave, but as our individual goals changed, we left when we felt it was time to leave. In addition to the firm compensating us while we were on "Job Search," the beautiful thing was that there was no shortage of opportunities. We all had marketable skills that other employers wanted. If you had the CPA credential to go along with those skills, those employers were willing to pay a premium to get you. For instance, when I left public accounting in October 1999, I accepted a corporate accounting position in the energy industry and received a $20,000 bump in my annual salary. My colleagues enjoyed similar success, with some eventually starting their own CPA firms and consulting practices, and million-dollar joint ventures. None of this would have been possible without the training and professional experiences that were afforded to us in public accounting.

Therefore, being a CPA is part of my DNA. It is the lens through which I process and solve problems. All my unique experiences in public accounting have since allowed me to bring tremendous value to the organizations and clients I serve. In my personal life, I am rarely at a disadvantage when making financial decisions, like refinancing my home, leasing or buying a vehicle, or other related matters. Because of my accounting and finance background, I am also an asset to my family, friends, and community at large. While I have had the honor of being recognized by the profession as a "Woman to Watch," my greatest satisfaction comes from seeing a new generation of young professionals passing the CPA exam and even becoming partners at their respective firms. I am sure they would all agree that the journey may seem hard at first, but if you stay the course, obtaining the CPA advantage is more than worth it.

P.I.M.P.-O-LO-GY

*C*an I let you in on a little secret? Life is too short to continue in a career that does not make you happy. It would be a shame to have worked hard your whole life but never reach your full potential. As such, it is not unreasonable to question whether you have made the right career choice or wonder if you are on the right path. Trust me: I had to process those same questions for myself. When I decided to not overthink it, trust the process, and stay open to possibility, that is when a series of PIMPs began to show up in my life.

Wait. Did she just say, PIMP?!

Yes, I did, however; not in the sense that most people may be familiar with the term. Therefore, allow me to introduce you to two new perspectives for what I mean when I use "PIMP" as an acronym. A PIMP is someone who has been carefully and strategically **placed in my path**. A PIMP is also a **person** who **inspires** you to be **more productive** in your life and career. In other words, these individuals inspire and motivate you to level up.

Before I get into the next phase of my career that depicts life after public accounting, it is important for you to understand the characteristics of a PIMP as defined in the context of this chapter and the rest of this book. I want to make sure you can recognize a PIMP when you see one.

There are four types of PIMPs: pushers, influencers, mentors, and promoters.

First —The Pusher

A pusher could be a good friend or close confidante. This person sees something great in you that you may not see in yourself. When you doubt yourself or express fear, their job is to constantly remind you of who you are and your capabilities. They know what it looks and feels like to be pregnant with possibility. When it is time to deliver and the pain becomes unbearable, they won't let you give up. Instead, they encourage you to bear down and "Push!"

Second —The Influencer

Influencers usually are leaders in positions of power. They are credible individuals with a high degree of integrity. They tend to have large networks and a following of people who hold them in high regard. Because of their ability to sway popular opinion, influencers are careful about what they lend their name to. When you have the proper relationship with an influencer, your *street cred* goes up by association.

Third —The Mentor

Unlike the pusher, mentors do not push. Their job is to model and, therefore, set an example for you to follow. They may even share information about their own career path, as well as provide guidance, motivation, and emotional support. In addition, a mentor may help with exploring careers, setting goals, developing contacts, and identifying resources. A mentor's time is valuable, and your job as a mentee is to not waste it.

Finally —The Promoter

The promoter's philosophy is, "I love it, and I think you will too!" Promoters are always sharing good information and feedback about their experiences. Unlike most others, this promoter does not get paid to promote. Instead, their greatest payoff is seeing you win.

A mentor's time is valuable, and your job as a mentee is to not waste it.

Now that you have been properly introduced, understand that each PIMP has a purpose. I'll say that again, every person you encounter has a purpose. If they are in your path, then trust that they are a part of the plan. You won't recognize it at first. I certainly did not. However, as I reflect, countless people come to mind that I am positive were strategically placed in my life for a reason. Their presence was not by accident nor coincidence. If anything, I attracted them to me based on where my heart and mind were focused at that time in my career.

Every person you encounter has a purpose.

THE LAW OF ATTRACTION AND PUBLIC SPEAKING

While most people shy away from public speaking, I always knew that I wanted to be a motivational speaker. I know—it's hard to believe coming from an accountant. As much as I cared about getting the numbers right, I cared about people even more. It was Teddy Roosevelt who said, "People don't care how much you know until they know how much you care." I was always fascinated by other speakers who had the unique ability to capture an audience's attention and then transport them to an imagined place where their hopes, dreams, and aspirations lived, while their feet remained on the floor. If—but for a moment—that person in the audience believed it was possible to be, do and have in life whatever their heart desired.

I was often that person, and I knew in my heart I wanted create similar experiences. Whether I was speaking to an audience of one or one thousand, I didn't just want them to hear me: I wanted them to feel me too. According to late poet and Nobel Prize winner Maya Angelou, "People will forget what you said and did, but they will never forget how you made them feel."

NABA National Convention
Washington, D.C.—July 2000

I had been working at my new employer for under a year. They paid for my registration and accommodations to attend the NABA national convention in our nation's capital that summer. NABA always did an excellent job putting on a robust, well-executed conference every year. I always looked forward to hearing the keynote speakers featured at the scholarship luncheon and awards gala.

In addition, there was no shortage of technical sessions from which to choose. One session that caught my attention was in the Entrepreneurial Track. The presenter was a woman named Traci Lynn, who was also a motivational speaker trained by Les Brown. When I arrived at her session, it was standing room only. People really wanted to hear what she had to say. As I listened to her speak, she started to awaken my entrepreneurial spirit. It was a feeling that never let me rest. It was like an unfulfilled hunger that started in the pit of my stomach, moved to the center of my chest, and then created a yearning in my throat. I had it bad!

While listening, my mind went back to the summer of 1993 when I was in Amway and Cody Vanderbilt helicoptered into Domino's Farms after having retired from his corporate job at age 26. The image of that chopper making its descent onto the field stayed in my head all this time. As a 20-year-old, I decided that I wanted to emulate him and retire at age 26, too. Back from my trip down memory lane, I raised my hand. Without hesitation, Traci acknowledged me, and I began to tell her how I had dreams of retiring at age 26, but it had not happened yet. I was soon to be 27. She replied, "Not achieving your goal by a specified time does not make it an unworthy goal. Just change the date." I felt relieved by her answer. Then, I asked her, "Should I be concerned about burning bridges?" She said, "People are too busy worrying about burning bridges. I say, sometimes you just need to BLOW IT UP!" BOOM! A thunderous sound that erupted inside the room, as the other attendees who like me were astonished by this speaker's no nonsense approach. She was unapologetically real, and I appreciated it, as she gave me something to consider. After the session wrapped up, I met her at the back of the room to purchase her audio products.

Nearly Two Years Later
Roostertail, Detroit, MI—April 2002

In April 2002, NABA Detroit was preparing for the 29th Annual Scholarship dinner at the beautiful Roostertail, a private event space overlooking the Detroit River. This immaculate venue is known for

STRENGTH

hosting extravagant events for celebrities, politicians, and newly wedded couples. NABA scholars, sponsors, members, and guests were anticipating an exquisite experience, and as a first-term chapter president, I wanted to ensure it was a night to be remembered.

Therefore, my goal was to create positive energy and set the tone upfront. During the reception, I circulated throughout the ballroom, greeting guests and leaving them with this promise: "You're going to have fun tonight!" When I asked if they were ready, I received a resounding, "Yes!" It was like music to my ears. After completing my rounds of shaking hands and kissing babies, I took my seat at the dais next to the keynote speaker, Mr. N.Z. Bryant, an incredible speaker who happened to work in the financial services industry.

In the audience were three people who meant the absolute world to me. To my left, my mom sat at a table sponsored by Deloitte. To my right, my dad and Mama Fatty sat at a table sponsored by Plante Moran. I could only imagine the chatter that was coming from each of those tables. Mom likely said something like, "That's my baby! I always knew she would grow up to be special. My little shining star!" At the other table, I'm sure Mama Fatty was the vocal one who said, "That's our daughter! She makes us so proud." Parental support was in full bloom that night.

To begin the program, the emcee centered everyone's attention. After making brief remarks, he introduced and invited me to the microphone. Although it was not time to give my official presidential update, I used the time to warm up the crowd. Let's look back on what I said:

> "Good evening! I am Lisa Howze. I had the pleasure
> to personally meet and greet some of you earlier. My

CHAPTER 6—P.I.M.P.-O-LO-GY

official remarks will come later in the program. In the meantime, I would like to ask you to do me a favor. Is that okay?" In unison, they replied, "Yes!"

"Okay. I would like you to participate in an exercise before we get started." While gesturing to my right, I said, "When I point to this side of the room, I want you to say, 'Lisa, no!'" Then, gesturing to my left, I said, "When I point to this side of the room, I want you to simply say, 'Noooo!' Can you do that for me?"

Again, they agreed, and I began by pointing to my right. Sounding like a discordant group of amateur singers, they were all over the place with, "Lisa, no. No, Lisa. Nooo!" I interrupted. "Wait, wait, wait! No, you guys didn't get that right. Let's try that again." The second time was a charm, as I had both sides of the room harmoniously saying their respective parts. "Alright, you got it this time! This was just a test run. When I come back, we're going to do it for real. Okay?"

I took my seat, and the emcee proceeded with the program. After dinner had been served and N.Z. had given a soul-stirring speech, the hour had come for me to activate what I had envisioned that morning as I prepared for this moment.

Me: "Somebody said it couldn't be done."

Right side: "Lisa, No!"

Me: "Somebody said it couldn't be done."

Left side: "Noooo!"

Me: "Yeah, they said that!"

I then began to recite the poem, "It Couldn't Be Done" by Edgar Guest.

> Somebody said that it couldn't be done,
> But she with a chuckle replied
> That "maybe it couldn't," but she would be one
> Who wouldn't say so till she'd tried.
> So she buckled right in with the bit of a grin
> On her face. If she worried, she hid it.
> She started to sing as she tackled the thing
> That could not be done, and she did it.
>
> Somebody scoffed: "Oh, you'll never do that;
> At least no one has ever done it";
> But he took off his coat and he took off his hat,
> And the first thing we knew he'd begun it.
> With a lift of his chin and a bit of a grin,
> Without any doubting or quiddit,
> He started to sing as he tackled the thing
> That could not be done, and he did it.
>
> There are thousands to tell you it cannot be done,
> There are thousands to prophesy failure;
> There are thousands to point out to you one by one,
> The dangers that wait to assail you.
> But just buckle in with a bit of a grin,
> Just take off your coat and go to it;
> Just start to sing as you tackle the thing
> That "cannot be done," and you'll do it.

From there I named a list of accomplishments that we achieved that year, including awarding over $20,000 in scholarships; launching *NABA Detroit Spotlight*, the chapter's new newsletter; and, partnering with Salvation Army and their Adopt-a-Family Christmas program. I remember being told by a seasoned member within our chapter to only focus on one or two initiatives during my first year as president. My "Candy Girl Mentality" kicked in, and I told mysef, "That's just not good enough. If we can do more, we'll do more." So, more is what we did!

When the event was over, a lady who reminded me of Estelle Getty approached me, shook my hand, and said, "You're a dynamo!" Between her comment and the smiles on the faces of my parents, I was one proud young lady!

She Ready!

"When the student is ready, the teacher will appear."

—Buddhist proverb

Earlier, I shared the concept of people placed in my path. Well, there is one particular person who played a very special role in my life. I credit her for igniting a fire in me that once lit, it was near impossible to put out. Just like you are holding my book in your hand right now, what if I told you she gave me a little book that literally changed my life? It is true, and as you continue reading, you will understand how.

STRENGTH

Crazily, in spring 2003, I was taking three classes in grad school, serving my second term as president of NABA Detroit, and working full-time. To say I was busy is an understatement. However, my reward for being focused and diligent came in the form of an invitation to a private luncheon at one of Detroit's finest restaurants located in an area known as Greektown.

Sweet Georgia Brown offered exquisite dining. When you entered the restaurant, you immediately felt special. The ambiance was classy and intimated a space for powerbrokers and sophisticated movers and shakers to convene and consummate business deals. The dining room designated for the Sisterhood Collaborative was situated to the left of the host stand. For a party of 17, the seating arrangement was carefully orchestrated, as if the organizer knew exactly what she was doing by pairing certain women together.

For example, seated to my right was the owner of a private tour and transportation company that I later did business with on behalf of NABA. On my left was a young woman who had founded a non-profit agency that provides job seekers with professional attire and career training skills. She later went on to become an author, a guest on the Oprah Winfrey Show, and two-time ringer of the bell on the NASDAQ trading floor. Every woman there was either a business owner, leader of an organization, or pillar in the community. I felt extremely fortunate to be in such great company.

On the table in front of each guest was a decorative bag filled with an assortment of gifts, including a lovely, little, burgundy softbound book entitled *The Prayer of Jabez*. My eyes were instantly attracted to the metallic gold letters printed on the cover and the gold-trimmed pages. Fast-forward a couple weeks after the

Sisterhood Collaborative luncheon when I stepped away from the office during the lunch hour to simply sit in my car and refresh my mind. While there, I decided to open this small treasure of a book to see what nuggets of information and inspiration I could find.

To my delight, I learned about a Biblical character named Jabez, who was said to be more honorable than his brothers. In the four parts to his simple, yet bold prayer, he asked to be blessed, to have his territory enlarged, to have help when life got too hard, and to be protected from harmful situations that might lead him to cause pain. In the end, Jabez's request was granted.

As I read the story, I felt as if the author, Bruce Wilkerson, was challenging me to pray this simple prayer and then get ready to see my ordinary life transform into something that was well beyond my imagination. The ideal of that was both exciting and incredible. Can you imagine if someone made you a promise so big that it seemed too good to be true? I thought to myself, *"If what he is saying is true, I want to know how this could be possible."*

For the very first time in my life, I was being told that it was not selfish to ask for favorable treatment. Can you imagine how different my life would have been growing up if I could have gone to my mom or dad and asked for whatever I wanted without the fear of them telling me "NO!"? What if, instead, they were just standing by waiting to hear from me to then give me access to all the gifts they already had in store for me? Wouldn't that have been awesome? Well, our friend Jabez had no problem asking.

Second, this idea of an enlarged territory was equivalent to me asking for more influence and favor with people, which would be necessary considering my dream to become a motivational speaker. I have since learned that with more influence comes more responsibility.

Next, the third part of the prayer suggested that I would reach a point in my life where I'd need to depend on someone other than myself. Granted, I had been independent and strong-willed all my young life, and I found it difficult at times to ask or wait for someone to assist me. However, in the next chapter and in the "Courage" section of this book, I had to activate the "call-a-friend" option more often than I ever imagined.

Admittedly, I did not understand the last part of the prayer when I first read the story. However, based on where I sit today, I get it now. Like the 'old folks' used to always say, "Just keep living!"

In addition, as a result of reading this book, I adopted the concept of divine appointments, which are perfectly orchestrated meetings or encounters that create an opportunity for you and I to help or be helped by someone else. It is a concept that only affirms my belief that there are no accidents in life. Everything happens for a reason, remember. Given the series of events leading up to the Sisterhood Collaborative luncheon, I knew without a shadow of a doubt that the woman who had given me this small book was the PIMP of all pimps and had been placed in my life for a reason.

Three Years Earlier
First Meeting of The Blonde

Fresh out of public accounting, I wanted to apply what I learned at Arthur Andersen to help small businesses. I purchased a laptop and started a home-based business called Howze Business Consulting.

CHAPTER 6—P.I.M.P.-O-LO-GY

By day, I worked in corporate accounting and built my business at night. I supported small business owners by helping them establish policies and procedures for effective business operations, along with bookkeeping and tax preparation services. To grow my clientele, I figured I needed to go where they were likely to be.

A local college hosted regular small business workshops at a hotel in downtown Detroit, and I was sure to attend. During one of the panel discussions, there was one panelist who stood out from the rest—not only in appearance but in the way she spoke. She was a light complexioned African American woman with blonde hair who spoke with great confidence and authority. In her description of an encounter with a would-be thief that tried to make off with some merchandise from her downtown store, I remember thinking to myself, "This lady ain't no joke!"

When the session ended, I do not recall having a conversation with her. I only remember getting one of her signature metallic gold business cards that was folded in half with print on both sides, thus representing each of her four businesses, including an upscale and resale clothing shop.

The Second Meeting
November 2002

A co-worker invited me to go with her to a networking event hosted by the Detroit Renaissance Chapter of The Links, Inc. at the Charles H. Wright Museum of African American History. The event was well attended by everybody who was anybody in Detroit. As we made our way through the crowd, there was a circle of people who seemed to surround this one energetic, "blonde-haired" woman. Honestly, I never caught a glimpse of her face.

I just remember my co-worker saying, "Lisa, get her card!" as the masterful networker spun from left to right, handing out her business cards. When I held the card in my hand, it was like déjà vu. I had seen this card before. It was metallic gold, folded in half with print on both sides that represented four different businesses.

Coincidence? I don't think so!

Four Months Later
Planning NABA Detroit's Entrepreneurship Event and Panel Discussion—March 2003

"If you treat it like chicken, they'll treat it like chicken. But, if you treat it like steak, they'll treat it like steak."

I'd never had anyone to speak to me in this manner. The words sounded strange, but I understood them explicitly. In that moment, I thought to myself, "This woman is mentoring me already." The woman that I am referring to is the mystery blonde with whom I previously only had two brief encounters. None of that mattered when weeks in advance, I suggested to the NABA planning committee that I "knew" a couple of businesswomen who would be ideal panelists for our upcoming entrepreneurship symposium.

To make good on my word, I needed to find that darned metallic gold business card! When unsuccessful, my inner genius kicked in when I decided to search the Internet. There was only one problem: I could not remember how to spell her name. I began to type what I thought it was: "Desiree Coleman?" Nope, that wasn't it. How about, "Desmarie Coleman?" Nope, that wasn't it either. I then activated my Cagney & Lacey detective skills and typed into the search: "Resale clothing in downtown Detroit." The results came back with: "Fashion Sense" and listed Desma Reid-Coleman as the proprietor. BINGO! That was it!

I called the phone number included in the listing and reached "Mama Jones", the store manager who was also the 68-year-old mother of the proprietor. Barely able to pronounce her name correctly, I asked for "Desma Reid-Coleman." Mama Jones replied, "She's not in today. May I ask who's calling?" I stated my name and that I was calling from NABA. Well, Mama Jones thought I was saying "NAWBO" which stands for National Association of Women Business Owners, an organization for which her daughter had recently served as president of the Greater Detroit Chapter. You can see how the two could easily get confused, right? Nevertheless, it worked in my favor when I received a nearly immediate return phone call. This was a miracle in and of itself since *Ms. Desma* was always traveling and just happened to be in town long enough to respond. The conversation went a little something like this:

"Lisa Howze? This is Desma Reid-Coleman. I heard you were looking for me at the store."

"Yes. Thank you for returning my call. As I shared with your mom, I am president of the National Association of Black Accountants - Detroit Chapter, and we're planning a symposium to feature female entrepreneurs. I heard you speak once at an event for small business owners a couple of years ago, and I thought you would be perfect to serve on our panel."

She then asked me, "Do you have a program?" I replied, "I can get one." Translation: "I had not planned to, but since you brought it up, sounds like a good idea." Who was I fooling? It was apparent that I had not created a program, and that's why she hit me with the "chicken versus steak" comment. In essence, she was teaching me the concept of perceived value. If I did not think it was important enough to create a program, how could I expect others? It only takes a little **extra** effort to go from ordinary to extraordinary.

In the end, she agreed to participate but not before letting me know that normally she would require an honorarium, as she rarely did anything for free. However, she figured I was special since I was able to get through her gatekeeper. Mama Jones rarely let anyone get easy access to her daughter.

After this conversation, I went back to my team with good news that not only had I secured Ms. Reid-Coleman for the event but another woman who was the successful owner of a public relations firm in Detroit. Together, they formed a dynamic duo.

On the day of the event, I sat awestruck in the back of the room, as they each shared pearls of wisdom with me and the young audience of accounting professionals and students. As I listened, I could feel the butterflies forming in my stomach again. These ladies were awakening my entrepreneurial spirit once again.

When it was over, I had to quickly intercept Ms. Reid-Coleman in the hallway before she got on the elevator. I told her how much her participation meant to me and our members. I mentioned how I could relate to her story of being an entrepreneur in her youth, as it reminded me of my lemonade stand and candy sales in high school. In that moment, it was as if she were seeing a younger version of herself, and I was seeing who I could become in the future. She then said, "Say, listen. I'm hosting a luncheon in a few weeks with an exclusive group of women. I'd like to invite you. Just be clear, not everyone gets an invitation. So, consider yourself special. And, by the way, from now on, call me Des."

CHAPTER 6—P.I.M.P.-O-LO-GY

After the luncheon at Sweet Georgia Brown's, I became her shadow. Everywhere she went, I followed. If you saw her, you saw me, as she was constantly inviting me places, including her speaking engagements, where I was sure to grab a front row seat. In addition, she exposed me to her accomplished and influential circles of friends. Therefore, after reading *The Prayer of Jabez*, I was persuaded that our paths intersecting multiple times over the years was not by chance; it was by design.

Out of that one relationship came many others. The next connecting point to my aspiration to become a motivational speaker was through a woman named Helen, whom I had met at a Christmas party Des invited me to. While in the middle of a conversation with a group of other ladies, Helen sat next to me and happened to mentioned Toastmasters. My ears perked up immediately because I remembered Dr. Traci Lynn, the speaker from D.C., mention Toastmasters in her audio tape that I listened to three years earlier. I said to Helen, "Toastmasters? I think I've heard of that organization. Tell me more." She explained that it is an organization that helps individuals build their communication and leadership skills, and thus, get better at public speaking. Sensing my excitement, she asked me if I want to attend her Club's holiday party. I told her, "Just let me know when and where, and I will be there!"

At this point, I realized that the Law of Attraction is real!

Invitation to Join Toastmasters

When I arrived at the restaurant where the Toastmasters group was gathered, I was welcomed with a warm round of applause. I felt so special. Before taking a seat, I signed my name on the guest list. Not more than five minutes later, someone else arrived. When everyone began to applaud that person as well, I thought, "Oh, they must do that for everybody!" I guess everyone deserved to feel welcomed and supported. I certainly did. This was my kind of environment. Good vibes only, for sure!

The president of the Club, a young woman named Allia Carson, called for everyone's attention and then announced that we were getting ready to play a game. As she explained the rules, excitement built among the guests, including me. What she described was like a relay race, except we weren't running; we were speaking. Allia kicked things off by saying: "I woke up this morning, looked in the mirror, and noticed I had a coarse grey hair, springing forth from the top center of my head like Alfafa in the TV show, The Little Rascals. How could this be? I am only…" Mid-sentence, Allia stopped speaking and the next person picked up the story with, "…23. This is not supposed to happen to me!" As we continued around the table, the story became more layered and funnier by the minute. As it was nearing my turn, I recognized that I would be the last person in the relay to speak. I liked the idea of being the anchor. Your girl nailed it, too! As the game ended, we filled the atmosphere with tons of laughs, hand claps, and high-fives. It was so much fun!

Next, the vice president of membership grabbed a handful of applications and extended an invitation for guests to become members of the club. Waving my right hand from side to side, like I was in church on Sunday morning, I shouted, "Yes, yes, yes! Sign me up!"

Crossover Service 2004

Speaking of church, I received an invitation to attend the Crossover Service at Union Grace Missionary Baptist Church. It had been years since I had gone to a party on New Year's Eve, so being in a worship service suited me just fine. At one point in the service, the organist began to play the melody to gospel artist Donald Lawrence's song entitled, "Bless Me (Prayer of Jabez)." Ring a bell? It was not a coincidence and more like confirmation that I was in the right place at the right time.

With tears rolling down my cheeks, the song began:

> "Bless me, bless me
> Oh Lord, bless me indeed
> Enlarge my territory.
> Oh Lord, bless me indeed
> (I pray for increase)
> Bless me indeed
> (I pray for increase)"

As you continue to read, you will see, like Jabez, the Creator granted my request.

CHAPTER 7

PAIN HAS A PURPOSE

*A*lthough I was an experienced public speaker, Toastmasters helped to put a framework and structure to what came naturally for me. Ironically, when asked to give my introductory "Icebreaker" speech, I was a bit nervous. The idea of baring my soul to a bunch of strangers made the butterflies in my stomach do a different type of dance. However, as the saying goes, 'in for a penny, in for a pound'; I could not afford to play it safe. To be authentic, I convinced myself that in addition to sharing my successes, I needed to get comfortable talking about subjects that frankly made me uncomfortable. Hence, I reflected on my early upbringing with four older brothers whose job it was to help guide and protect me but at times were the source of my growing pains. In other words, whenever they brought heartache to our mother, they in turn were hurting me.

Memories of how the second eviction made me feel anxious and alone rushed back to my mind like a raging river. In a flash, I got chills thinking about how numbingly cold those winters were when the lights and gas in our house had been shut off. I also remember the embarrassment I felt each time I had to tell my friends that my phone number had changed, after getting disconnected for the umpteenth time. Through it all, however, I made it! Therefore, it felt only appropriate to title my speech, "Against All Odds."

Standing behind the rostrum, I appeared to be well-composed, strong, and confident. No one could see that my left leg was shaking out of control like a leaf, but I felt every tremor. Rather than give in to my nervousness, before I knew it, a thunderous sound erupted from my diaphragm when I open my presentation with, "Three, five, seven, nine, and eleven: What do you do when all odds are against you?"

The power in my voice commanded the people on the front row to sit up straight and pay attention. Encouraged by their positive body language, I grew in confidence as I continued to speak. Then, in an exaggerated pause, I took a deep breath, looked around the room, and locked eyes with a young man seated near the back row. I asked him, "When you look at me today, what do you see?" Although I was not expecting a response, he exclaimed, "I see a beautiful Black woman!" Flattered by his candor, a warm smile crept across my face as everyone else broke into a chorus of chuckles.

In turn, I asserted, "You see a proud, gifted AND 'beautiful' Black woman who has been educated among the leaders and best, worked for one of the largest accounting firms in the world, and is now on the verge of earning a second degree in finance." Intrigued by my accomplishments, they leant in closer. "However," I resumed, "you would be surprised to know that I was not always this outgoing." As an example, I shared how in first grade at lunchtime, I was terrified to go to the cafeteria with all the other kids. With tears in my eyes and a sullen face, my only resort was to stay behind in the classroom to eat lunch with my teacher. This inexplicable phobia I had as a child when coupled with the stress of not knowing what I would have for dinner once I returned home from school make it difficult to understand how I even made it. I could have easily become a statistic. My life could have easily gone astray, but somehow I managed to turn life's lemons into lemonade which ultimately made me profits. When answering the question, "What do you do when all odds are against you?" my response is: you rise.

After completing my first ten speeches in Toastmasters, my profile was beginning to rise. I achieved the first milestone of becoming a competent toastmaster (CTM) and then went on to become an advanced toastmaster (ATM). By that time, I was winning speech competitions within my club and competing at Regionals against members of other Toastmasters clubs in the area. I distinctly remember this one competition that was held at Fellowship Chapel, a church on Detroit's northwest side led by the esteemed pastor, civil rights activist, and president of Detroit Branch NAACP, Rev. Dr. Wendell Anthony. During my passionate delivery, I caught the attention of an experienced toastmaster from a different club, who said to me after the competition, "Great job! You sound like a politician. Have you ever thought about running for office?" I graciously thanked him but quickly dismissed the idea of politics, as not being for me. Little did I know!

And Still I Rise

While I never imagined going into politics, I was no stranger to running for office in NABA. In July 2003, during my third term as chapter president, I became the first chapter president from the central region to be named "Chapter President of the Year." The award added an extra boost to my self-esteem as I led the chapter into the new calendar year when there were two major events on the horizon that would determine our success as a chapter and my legacy as chapter president. As the host city for the 2005 national convention, the Detroit Chapter had the honor and privilege to give our NABA family across the country a taste of Detroit as we planned to deliver a spectacular experience one year earlier at the 2004 national convention in Orlando, Florida. While it was customary for the host chapter to plan a "promotional party" to showcase what visitors to their city could expect the following year, we were adamant to let everyone know that "We're Detroit, and we don't plan parties. WE PLAN EVENTS!"

Before leaving for Orlando, our chapter had created a promotional video that highlighted the Detroit Pistons' 2004 NBA National Championship win. It also featured several iconic images of sites around the city including Comerica Park, the Fox Theatre, Joe Louis' fist, and the fountain at Hart Plaza, just to name a few. When we played the video at the membership luncheon, the audience was immediately captivated by the Motown sounds of Aretha Franklin's "R-E-S-P-E-C-T" playing in the background. It was the perfect segue into my passionate verbal appeal encouraging members to come to Detroit the following year. After hearing my speech, a member approached me stating, "I'm coming to Detroit next year! I was not planning to come, but now after hearing you speak, I'm definitely coming to Detroit!" Those words were like music to my ears.

We sealed the deal on Friday night when we showed Orlando and the rest of our NABA family why "It's A Great Time in Detroit!" Our promotional event was replete with an auto show, a fashion show, and a remarkable performance by a Motown Revue singing group. To top the night off, we hired a dope a** DJ from one of the nationally syndicated morning talk shows, to keep things rocking well beyond the normal cutoff time. It was certainly a night to remember.

Amid all our planning that year, the Chapter had received a local push when Maureen McDonald, a freelance writer for the Detroit News, whom I had met through Ms. Desma, wrote an article entitled, "Accounting group plans to host national convention in Detroit next year!" It appeared above the fold on the front page of the Business section. When the newspapers hit the stands, I drove around the city and suburbs to every CVS Pharmacy I could find to buy as many copies of the newspaper I could get my hands on. The first copy I took to my mom and exclaimed, "Look, Mama! I did it! I made the papers (again)! Your little star made the papers!"

Rise and Decline

Within weeks of graduating from Walsh College with a 3.6 GPA in the Master of Science in Finance Program, my star was yet again on the rise, but my mom's health was headed in the opposite direction. She had slowly been vanishing before our very eyes. It became apparent to me that something was wrong when she declined the invitation to attend my graduation ceremony. My heart sank to the floor at the thought of her not being present to support me at one of the most important times of my life. Although other family members and friends were there to help me celebrate, no one could fill the void that was left by my mom's absence, thus making it a bittersweet moment.

Finishing grad school was a relief. I had regained my life and was not interested in anything new filling the vacant space in my calendar. I thought I was home free until six weeks later I received an invitation from New Center Toastmasters Club President Allia Carson to attend her "graduation" of sorts. Because she had been supportive of my journey to become a professional speaker, attending her graduation was the least I could do. When I reached

STRENGTH

the venue, I proceeded to the ballroom where I sat among what looked like 500 people. The place was so crowded, I don't remember ever seeing Allia before being directed by one of the leaders to grab my belongings and follow him into a different room. In that moment, I realized this was not a traditional graduation. I was thinking, *it's been a long day. I am tired, and I am not in the mood for this tomfoolery! WTH!*

Once gathered, the facilitator instructed all guests to identify an area of our lives that we wanted to work on. I reluctantly wrote at the top of the notepad they had given me, "Relationship with biological mother." We were then told to find a partner and personally share the area we chose and why. At this point, I was starting to get irritated because I really didn't want to "work" on this and certainly not with a total stranger! After 10 minutes passed, the facilitator asked for volunteers to openly share what they decided to work on. I don't know how this happened, but my arm developed a mind of its own and decided to extend my hand above my head to be recognized. I thought to myself, *WTF are you doing? We agreed that we were getting out of here, but now you have singled me out!* The betrayal was real. Of course, I ended up sharing some of what I discussed with my partner. It wasn't a whole lot of detail, but it was enough to get me unwittingly noticed. Consequently, when the session was over and I had one foot pointed toward the exit, a young Caucasian woman stepped into my personal space and said, "So, Lisa. What are you up to?"

Dammit! Just when I thought I was going to get in and out, I was suddenly being confronted by some random person that I didn't know from Eve! On the surface, her question seemed simple. However, my intuition suggested there was something more to it. Indeed, she wanted to know what I was up to in life, and if there was a big idea that I was willing to dedicate myself to that could possibly change the trajectory of my life forever. Who knew that one little question could pack so much meaning?

Hesitantly, I shared that I wanted to quit my job to pursue my dream as a motivational speaker and trainer. "That is a pretty big deal!" she replied. "But I also heard you say that you wanted to work on your relationship with your mother. Is that still true?" I was thinking, *first of all, Lady! Why are you getting all up in my business?!* Since it's not always wise to say everything that you're thinking out loud, I replied, "That's a pain point for me, and I'd rather not talk about it." She then hit me with this reverse psychology. "What would it be like if you could work through that pain and live a life that is not bound by the events of the past and instead gain access to the type of relationship you've always wanted to have with your mother?" I said, "I would love that!" She then replied, "If you take on this work, not only will you create the possibility of a better relationship with your mom, but you will experience more freedom in pursuit of your other goals as well. How does that sound?"

"That sounds good!" I answered.

She then directed me to the table at the back of the room to register for the next session of The Landmark Forum, set to start within two weeks.

Wait a minute: Pump the brakes!

I know you're probably thinking, *Lisa, WTF! Your, MOTHER? Really? You had a PROBLEM with your mother? Based on everything you've told us thus far, how could this even be a point for concern? This woman was your biggest cheerleader! She attended mostly all your school events and ceremonies! For goodness's sake, she caught the bus in the middle of the day to bring a duffle bag full of Faygo pop to your school so you could continue your sales for the day! Not to mention, she stood tall and proud in support of you at your college graduation from Michigan. Granted, she was not able to see you walk across the stage to get your grad degree but DAMN! C'mon, this woman was a saint! How could you take issue with her?*

Okay, okay! I hear you! Loud and clear. In my defense, let me put some things into perspective for you. At the time, I was a soon-to-be-31-year-old woman who was carrying around the hurt of a 15-year-old girl. For 16 years, I viewed my mom through an altered lens initiated by a traumatic experience involving one of my brothers. This horrifying event ripped through my mother's soul like a jagged edge knife, causing emotional, mental, and financial distress, which in turn had a negative impact on me. His life, her life—our lives were forever changed.

Flashback to Sophomore Year in High School

It all occurred one pivotal Saturday morning in the fall of my sophomore year. That was the same day that I visited the neighborhood candy store. Imagine watching a split screen television, where on one side, you see a pleasant exchange between me and the proprietor of Leddy's Wholesale Candy. Mind you, I'm not just making an investment in my first case of M&M candies, but I am also cementing the cornerstone of my financial future. Conversely, on the opposite side of the screen, all hell was breaking loose at my house, less than a mile away! There, my mother was pinned against the dining room wall with a 9mm handgun pressed

CHAPTER 7—PAIN HAS A PURPOSE

to her head by a police detective who was yelling, "Where is he?!" This detective along with three other cops had forcefully entered our house, hell bent on arresting one of my brothers. After intense interrogation, lots of hollering and screaming, the police found, handcuffed, and took my brother into custody. As my mom watched these officers forcibly remove her son from the home, her limp body suggested that they had taken her vitality along with them.

Fortunately, I was not there to witness any of this, which I honestly believe was the Creator's way of protecting me. Unfortunately, my absence prevented me from fully understanding the depth of my mother's pain and heartache. Counseling is probably something that we all needed but did not have the wherewithal to seek. Instead, we resorted to coping mechanisms. For me, I poured myself into my budding candy business, school, and work. My mom was not so lucky. She had no other outlets. Her children were her everything. As she lost a son to the penal system, I felt like I had lost a mother. So much of her time, energy, and attention had become consumed by the aftermath of that horrid event including the trial, conviction, and life sentence that followed. Over time, an invisible wall formed that made my mother appear emotionally unavailable to me. It was a bitter pill that I had a hell of a hard time swallowing.

The sequence of events played in her mind repeatedly. If she was not talking about it, she was recounting what happened in notebooks and on random pieces of paper. She lived in a constant state of paranoia, thinking that our phone line had been wire tapped by the police. It was unbearable to watch her suffer with intense anguish day in and day out. The more absorbed she became in my brother's plight, the wider the wedge seemed to get between her and me. The emotional abandonment I felt was only exacerbated by her physical absence when she would leave home before daylight to travel two or more hours to visit my brother at various prisons around the state and return home after dark.

When she wasn't visiting him, she was making her presence known at police headquarters, where she would frequently go in search of answers. There truly was no limit to her fight. In fact, one of her visits to police headquarters took place on the same day as parent–teacher conference at Cass. When I went to school the next day, Ms. Rankin, my 11th grade AP English teacher, asked me to stay after class to talk. She inquired, "Is everything okay at home?" I shrugged the question off, like, "Yeah. What makes you ask?" Out of concern, Ms. Rankin informed me that while meeting with my mom during parent-teacher conference, my mom broke down in tears in front of her. Hearing this shattered my heart into a million and one tiny pieces.

Thirty-one years later, as I pen this portion of the story, I now realize that even in her moment of ultimate weakness, my mom demonstrated tremendous strength and love for both of her children. In my brother's case, she was willing to go through hell and back to fight for her son's release. At the same time, she continued to be a faithful steward over her baby girl's education.

Damn!

I didn't see it that way back then. However, the Landmark education experience that I was getting ready to embark upon some 15 years later would be the start of me gaining a new perspective and dealing with those areas hidden from my view called blind spots.

Taking on the Landmark Forum

Transformational is the word that best describes the Landmark Forum. As a participant, I learned to see life through a different lens, noting three distinct layers: 1) there's what happened; 2) how I felt about what happened; and 3) the story I have been telling myself to support my belief about what happened. In my first 31 years of living, you can imagine I told myself a lot of stories and gave meaning to more sh*t than a little bit. However, in a span of three days, the Forum set out to blow up all those bull*h*tt*n' a** non-supportive beliefs that were likely generated by those same made-up stories that had been holding me back.

If I can be totally transparent with you, at the time, I did not know there was anything holding me back. I was a homeowner, had two college degrees, drove a brand-new car, wore nice clothes, and had money in the bank. By the world's standards, I had it going on. Who would I be to disagree? However, what if I told you that I was merely playing to my strong suit? High achievement had always been my strength, but Landmark was teaching me that sometimes we can use our strengths in one area of life to overcompensate for a weakness in a different area of life. For me, I had an advantage with strong money management skills, but I was emotionally bankrupt. Case in point, my strong sense of independence is a result of being limited to doing lots of things on my own as a child, not by choice but necessity. When all I wanted was a sense of belonging and acceptance from my brothers and their visiting friends, I remember one of them yelling, "Go in the house! There are no girls out here for you!" Instead of seeing it as protection, those words registered with me as a form of rejection that stung to my core. From that bitter moment forward, I told myself that if I wanted to get something done, I had to do it myself. *I'll show them.*

The Forum leader walked my cohort and me through several impactful exercises in which we learned to identify aspects of our lives that were no longer true, relevant, or helpful. By isolating the behaviors and emotions that hold us back, we can unlearn them and then relearn new ways of being that help us move forward. The only purpose for revisiting the past is to complete the past, and that takes work. When you do not complete the past, you will surely repeat the past. In other words, unresolved issues as a kid become recurring problems that get triggered as adults. In turn, false narratives end up driving our lives.

In the case of my incarcerated brother, for nearly three decades, I blamed him for taking my mother away from me during the critical years when I was an undergraduate at Michigan. Never once did she visit me between the day that I was dropped off in front of South Quad and the day I graduated. As I have matured, I can appreciate the great burden she must have felt as a mother bear who had lost one of her cubs to the penal system. Whereas I desired it, I did not require as much attention. Thankfully, she had poured positive energy into me when I was younger. I, therefore, had to find the strength within me to carry forward and succeed against all odds. It only took me 30 years to finally get it. Therefore, completing the past allows you to look at old situations with a new set of eyes. With this renewed understanding, you have permission to create a new story that is more supportive and empowering. With a fresh perspective, you can break free of the negative emotions, unfulfilled expectations, and fear of moving forward without this false sense of security that your original story provided you.

Are you ready?

CHAPTER 7—PAIN HAS A PURPOSE

Where Are You Taking Her Now?

Built into each Landmark Forum schedule is a one-day break, which I chose to use as an opportunity to visit my mom. When I reached her house, I was in for a surprise. While she was seated at the dining room table, three of my aunts, whose presence was unusual, were standing over her with raging concern. As I tried to assess what was happening, they insisted that my mom needed to go to the hospital to have her heart check given the size of her swollen legs. When the ambulance arrived, my mom didn't seem to put up much resistance. She calmly stepped inside the wagon on her own accord and off she went. Prior to then, the only time my mom had been hospitalized was when I was six years old, and she had broken her ankle after slipping and falling on ice. Therefore, I thought her visit to the hospital would be short and sweet after the doctors would have run a series of routine tests.

When I called my mom's hospital room the next day, I said, "Hey, Ma! How are you feeling? What did the doctors say? When are you coming home?" She was evasive in her response. I couldn't understand why, so I asked again. "Do you know when you are coming home?" She still didn't answer the question. Suddenly, I found myself on the phone by myself—she had hung up. Thinking, *well, that was strange,* I got dressed to make a personal visit to her at the hospital. Before I could get out the door, my phone started ringing. On the line was a social worker who wanted to confirm my identity before telling me their plans to transfer my mom to another facility.

"Wait a minute! WHAT? You're sending my mother where? WHY?"

Instead of giving me direct answers, the social worker asked a series of strange questions that made absolutely no sense to me. I could not understand how in the hot hell my mother could go into the hospital for one thing—swollen legs—only to later have her sanity called into question. WHAT! Can somebody please tell me how that happens? I mean, honestly, did my aunts truly understand what they were doing when they called 9-1-1 that night? Apparently not, because the ripple effect of that one decision had devastating consequences that followed. Stay with me to see what I mean.

When I finally got a chance to lay eyes on my mother, she had been heavily sedated with medication. For the entirety of my visit, she remained taciturn. When I spoke to her, she said nothing in return. After visiting her consistently for several weeks, the doctors lessened the dosage of her medication, making her a bit more lucid. When I asked, "Mom, are you ready to come home?" Surprisingly, she said, "No!" That was not the answer I was anticipating. In a twisted way, she had grown comfortable being in this place. It was no Club Med for me, but for her, it seemed she was able to get a much-needed break from the stresses of life.

After approximately 10 weeks in this place, the doctors finally agreed to release her to my care. After which, we soon discovered that my mother required more assistance than either of us anticipated. For example, when it was time to take the single step into my house from the side door entrance, she was too weak to raise her right leg high enough, and I was not strong enough to lift her. Therefore, I ran to get help from my next-door neighbor who gladly assisted us. Once I finally got my mom situated in the living room, the weight of this new responsibility hit me like a ton of bricks. I was so overwhelmed I wanted to cry.

CHAPTER 7—PAIN HAS A PURPOSE

This was new for both of us. For years, my mom had been everyone else's caregiver, and now she was in need of deliberate, intentional, and loving care. In my case, I had never been responsible for anyone other than myself. "Ms. Independent" needed to make some major adjustments to make this work.

Being in denial did not help. So, I did my best to embrace it.

In the beginning, I felt ill-equipped and emotionally impaired and questioned whether I was up to the task. Simply put, I was not ready to accept that my mother was no longer the strong woman I had always known her to be but being in denial did not help. So, I did my best to embrace it.

Since I had a side-hustle network marketing business in the self-care and wellness industry, one evening, I decided to treat my mom to a spa-like foot massage. I filled the foot tub with warm water and two heaping scoops of rejuvenating foot soak crystals. After dipping her feet, I told her to sit back, relax, and enjoy the good treatment. After 20 minutes of soaking, I initiated a three-step process that included a brown sugar scrub to exfoliate, special attention cream made of menthol and eucalyptus oil to moisturize, and a lemon-scented body butter to seal in all the goodness. By the time I finished, my mom's feet were happy, and she felt like a brand-new woman. Suddenly, I thought about how, in Landmark, I set the intention to work on my relationship with my mother. While I never would have chosen this path, I could appreciate how God orchestrated this moment to allow me to treat my mom to a wonderful pampering experience. In her words, "Well, I'll be!"

While I was growing as a caregiver, I never lost sight of my goal to become a motivational speaker. As I continued to work on my craft, my voice echoed throughout the house, and all my mother could hear me repeatedly say was, "I choose. I-I-I choose. I choose. I-I choose. I choose to be an uncommon woman." To her, instead of choosing, it sounded like I was losing my mind. At least that's what I overheard her tell one of my brothers. In reality, I was preparing for my first paid speaking engagement. To help me practice my oratorical skills, I enjoyed reciting a poem entitled "Uncommon Woman", which is the female representation of a famous quote that states, "I do not choose to be a common man." The following are a few lines from the poem that resonate with me even today:

> "I choose to be an uncommon woman. It's my right to be uncommon if I can. I seek opportunity, not security. I do not wish to be a kept citizen, humbled and dulled by having the state look after me. I want to take the calculated risk; to dream and to build, to fail and to succeed..."

These powerful words remind me that in failure and success, you always have a choice.

> In failure and success, you always have a choice.

Landmark Education Advanced Course
January 2005

Fast-forward to January 2005 when I was taking Landmark's Advanced Course, the second installment in their Curriculum for Living program. The more I became immersed in self-awareness, the more l grew personally and professionally. As I deepened my connection to my word, I grew in integrity. As I strengthened my connection to others, I grew in commitment. And, as I was given plenty opportunity to nurture my dream as a speaker, I grew in confidence that it was time to "bust a move" like the late '80s rapper Young MC and leave my job. Therefore, on the day of the one-day break prior to the closing session, I had plans to go to work and tell my boss, "Deuces!" However, before leaving home, I had sense enough to run the idea by my mom first. Without hesitation, I asked, "Momma, can I quit my job?" In no uncertain terms, she replied, "Sure, you've been working long enough!" Just like that, it was confirmed: MY MOMMA SAID I CAN QUIT MY JOB!

I had never been so excited to go to work on a Monday than I was this day! With an extra pep in my step and a song in my heart, I rejoiced in how no one in my department knew what was about to happen that day other than me. Or so I thought. Before I could meet with my manager that afternoon, I received an urgent phone call around 2 p.m. from my brother Tony who exclaimed, "Mom's had a stroke! Get over to St. John's Hospital right away!"

When I arrived in the ER, I found my mother disoriented, incoherent, and confused. I was heartbroken to see her in this state, considering our talk that morning when she had given me the green light to quit my job and follow my dreams. Obviously, I had to put those plans on hold, which made me wonder if this interruption was a sign from God. If so, what was He trying to say? Only time would tell.

After a couple of days in the hospital, my mom's condition improved, and she was able to recognize me, Tony, and other family members who came to visit. This time when she was released to come back home with me, I knew it would not and could not be business as usual. I requested to take a family medical leave of absence from work to be in a better position to manage her care. She was assigned a home care specialist, physical therapist, and an occupational therapist to aid in her recovery. After a few sessions, she was able to bathe, dress, and feed herself with some assistance, and use a walker to get around the house. Unfortunately, whenever it seemed like she was making progress, she would experience a setback in the form of mini strokes. The technical term for these episodic events is transient ischemic attacks or TIAs, which are represented by a temporary period of stroke-like symptoms. Each time this happened, it resulted in a call to 9-1-1 and an ambulance ride back and forth to the hospital. Feeling the weight of this responsibility all over again, it was time for me and God to have another talk.

"Lord, why me?"

Before He could respond, I thought to myself, *"Wait. Why not me?"*

After shifting my thinking, I was like, "Okay, then," and then asked two follow-up questions for clarity:

"What is my purpose?"

And "What would You have me do?"

Since everything happens for a reason, all I could do was trust the process and be open for instructions. When I stopped "ripping and running" the streets, as my mother called it, I could finally be still, look within, and listen for the still small voice that was telling me to create. "Create what?" you may ask. The good news is I did not need to look far for the answers. Everything I needed had already been provided in the form of my gifts, talents, knowledge, skills, and abilities.

For example, as a numbers person with a passion for helping people succeed at entrepreneurship and in their personal finances,

CHAPTER 7—PAIN HAS A PURPOSE

I laid the foundation for a new business called Fundamental Accounting Solutions. To tap into my desire to motivate people to live more fulfilling and productive lives, I also created a brand called Driving Motivation. The logo's design featured a luxury steering wheel with a microphone as its hub, and underneath it was the tagline, "Empowered Steering for Life." When people wore a Driving Motivation t-shirt or carried one of my signature tote bags, I wanted them to feel confident, self-assured, and committed to achieving their goals. I even created an introductory set of Driving Motivation Cards that each included a unique message of empowerment.

Finally, I developed a product called The Mileage Tracker System that targeted entrepreneurs, specifically sales professionals and owners of home-based businesses. The tool was designed to help them "keep track" of miles driven for business purposes and maximize their tax deduction. Sexy? Of course not. However, I have found that things that are both boring and necessary tend to make some people rich. If only I had the tech savvy to create a digital mileage app like the ones that exist today, I'd be a gazillionaire! Honestly, it was therapeutic for me to engage my mind in those creative activities, as the stress of caring for my mom who had been diagnosed with dementia only intensified.

As my 12 weeks of family leave time wound down, I was anxious about returning to work and getting adequate care for my mom. Although not ideal, the best available option we had as a family was to place her in a nursing home. Her first few weeks there were tough. Over time, she started to experience spikes in her blood pressure that caused her to be sent to the hospital. Once stabilized, they would send her back to the nursing home. This ping-pong action occurred frequently, with each time causing extreme physical strain on her and emotional stress for me. In fact, during one of her hospital-stays while the NABA national convention was underway in Detroit, I received a call from a nurse at 2 o'clock in the morning requesting me to come see about my mom. Since I was a child, I have always dreaded the 2 a.m. phone call because my mom was usually on the receiving end of some bad news associated with one of my brothers. When I got to the hospital, I was greeted by her care team of doctors and nurses that wanted to get my consent on the extent of aggressive treatment they should apply to my mom in case of a life-threatening medical event. Uggh! I did not like making those tough decisions; it was too overwhelming to deal with at only 31 years of age.

At times, I felt like I had ice water running through my veins based on my ability to be responsive to my mother's healthcare needs while continuing to lead in other areas of my life. Case in point, serving as chapter president during the NABA national convention was no small feat. However, with the support of an amazing team of leaders, including the co-chairs, members, and volunteers, we were able to execute our plans with precision. In fact, the Detroit convention was reported to have been one of the most successful conventions in NABA history at that time. In addition to hitting the numbers, we showed impeccable hospitality to our guests who enjoyed themselves while in our city. They were greeted by Mayor Kwame Kilpatrick who delivered the keynote message to NABA scholars, while Rhonda Walker, a local TV news anchor and founder of the fledgling Rhonda Walker Foundation, served as mistress of ceremonies. During the membership luncheon, I had a proud moment when I completed my $3,000 personal commitment to become a lifetime member of the Association. In the end, I fulfilled my responsibility and concluded the four years of my presidency on top!

CHAPTER 7—PAIN HAS A PURPOSE

However, after everyone else packed up to go home, I was left with the reality that my mother's health was becoming more and more debilitated. The one anchor that helped me cope was my faith. Although I had a church home, I had become a regular visitor at Union Grace Missionary Baptist Church, which I reference earlier toward the end of Chapter 6. Given my frequent visits, the first lady of the church took notice of me. One Sunday after service, she and the leader of the Seniors' Ministry asked if I would be returning for the evening program. I explained that I would not be returning given my obligation to my mother. As this duo regularly visited the sick and shut-in, they asked for my mother's name and the location of her nursing home. To my pleasant surprise, on one of my next visits, I found a handwritten letter sitting on the nightstand next to my mother's bed that read:

"Dear Ms. Howze,

Your daughter, Lisa, came to visit us today at Union Grace. She told us that you were here and that you were not feeling well. Although you may not be able to read this, our hope is that Lisa will read it to you on her next visit. We will be praying for you and your daughter.

Sincerely,

First Lady Tracy and Sister Kim Mack"

Reading those words filled my heart with so much gratitude. I have never forgotten the love and kindness they showed toward my mom and me!

Summer had turned into fall, and Mom had made no measurable improvements. During another one of her hospital stays, I stood

STRENGTH

outside her room talking on the phone with my older sister Sabrina. As I updated her on our mother's status, she suggested that perhaps Mom was tired and wanted us to let her go. Maybe she was right, I thought, as I reentered by mom's hospital room. While reaching for her hand, I whispered, "Mom, I just want to let you know that it's okay if you want to let go. You've done your job. You no longer need to hang on for us. We'll be okay." Unable to speak, my mom took her right thumb and stroked it over the top of my hand—a small gesture that spoke volumes. By doing so, she assured me that she loved me and heard what I said. It was an amazing moment of awareness on her part that offered tremendous comfort to me. It is a precious memory that I will cherish forever.

Shortly thereafter, I reached out to Hospice Care of Michigan to officially enroll my mom into the hospice care unit at her existing nursing home facility. No more medicine. No more nasty food. No more ping pong visits to the hospital. At that point, it was all about keeping her comfortable. One night after work, I decided to go sit with my mom for a little while, hoping my presence would add to her comfort. I'm glad I did because not more than 24 hours later, I received an urgent message on my answering machine from one of the nurses at her facility to come there immediately. I was certain of what I'd encounter upon my arrival. To not face it alone, I called and asked my brother Tony and good friend Danielle to meet me there. When we walked into my mother's room, I saw her lifeless body lying there. It was confirmed. My mom made her transition on Tuesday, November 22, 2005, just two days before Thanksgiving. What a way to start the holiday season!

Well, at least, she was finally at peace.

CHAPTER 7—PAIN HAS A PURPOSE

In the days immediately following her passing, I really did not have a chance to grieve. I was too busy planning her memorial service and writing her obituary. My college friend Carli helped me pull together a collage of photos that reflected my mom as a daughter, sister, aunt, mother, and grandmother. Each image held a lot of history and told an amazing story, especially the ones of her and me together. During the eulogy, my then pastor commented, "Whenever you saw Lisa, you saw her mother." It was noticeable to others how much she cared for and watched over me. To this very day, I am convinced that she still watches over me.

Following her memorial service, I wanted to get away from everything and everybody as quickly as possible to spend some quiet time alone. During Christmas break, I planned a trip to Chicago via AMTRAK. The four-hour train ride gave me a chance to relax and clear my head. During this journey, I started thinking about life differently. I felt the urge to simplify my lifestyle, give up material possessions, and most of all, stop chasing money. I resolved that less was more. Fancy cars and expensive clothes no longer held the same value for me. Rather than running after riches, I chose to pursue purpose instead. The scary reality is that I may have never reached this level of understanding had I not endured the bitter moments of this profound valley experience.

Pain has a purpose, and your purpose will always be greater than your dream.

You may recall that in January 2005, I thought I had it all figured out. I was persuaded to press forward, quit my job, and pursue my dream as a motivational speaker. Fortunately for me, God stepped in and said, "No, not now, but your time is coming!" I did not know why I was being forced to wait. I had no idea what was on the horizon for me, but God knew, and time would surely tell. What was clear to me was that while I was chasing a dream, the pain of losing my mom placed me on a path to discover my purpose. In trusting the process, I learned that my dream was about me, but my purpose was about serving others. Therefore, if you take nothing else away from this chapter, please remember that pain has a purpose, and your purpose will always be greater than your dream.

SECTION II
COURAGE

The audacity to do it anyway

CHAPTER 8

THAT WAS A GOOD JOB

*"If you have nothing left to lose—
you have everything left to gain."
(Anonymous)*

After losing my mom just before the Thanksgiving holiday in 2005, little did I know that 2006 was going to be a year of accelerated change. It was as if her passing gave me permission to hit the reset button. For example, I quickly cut ties with a non-supportive relationship, in which I had been constantly overextending myself but getting very little in return. You know the kind, right? Amid that "break-up," I switched churches. Although I had been there a total of 15 years, I stopped growing spiritually at least three years before my departure. Therefore, it was just time. In either situation, I could no longer continue to go along just to get along without sacrificing my mental, emotional, and spiritual well-being. As I moved into a new season of my life as a motherless child, I decided to refocus my attention on the projects that I had begun the previous year.

At center stage was the Driving Motivation brand along with a new financial wellness program I developed under the Fundamental

Accounting Solutions umbrella. In combining the two concepts, I called it the "Behind the Wheel Financial Empowerment Series (BTWFES)." While creating the course, some friends of mine in the financial services industry, who were also my trusted financial advisors, tried to recruit me to become a financial planner as well. Could you blame them? I had the right pedigree—CPA, finance professional, trustworthy, skilled at sales, charismatic, outgoing, goal-oriented, and attentive to detail. However, I always resisted their offers, which seemed ironic, considering how strongly I felt about educating people about money and helping them manage their personal finances.

Although I did not commit to join their practice, I decided to at least get my own financial house in order. This meant creating a budget, reviewing old receipts, and seeing where I could eliminate unnecessary spending. In the process, I came across a paper napkin that was folded tightly in the bottom of my purse. When I read the handwritten message on the napkin, my mind instantly went back to October 2004. I had been invited to speak at a health and wellness conference hosted by a church on Detroit's westside. It was my first paid speaking engagement that came with a $250.00 honorarium. After I finished my presentation, there was a general assembly of all speakers and guests in the church's auditorium. The speaker for the hour was none other than First Lady Crisette Ellis of Greater Grace Temple, an apostolic church on Detroit's northwest side. She was poised, polished, and purposeful in her delivery, as she left the audience with this message: "Write the vision and make it plain." Those words struck a chord with me and lingered in my heart well-beyond the event's end.

In fact, I found myself one week later sitting in the company cafeteria, thinking about my future, and asking myself, "Why am I here?" The next question was, "How does what I do help people?" Have you ever asked yourself these questions? If so, what was your response? For me, the questions were not rhetorical. I was seriously looking for answers. Then, I remembered First Lady Ellis's instructions to "write the vision and make it plain." Therefore, I grabbed a nearby paper napkin and wrote on the back of it: **"JUNE 30, 2006, IS MY LAST DAY AT DTE ENERGY! I WILL HAVE $25,000 IN CASH! ..."**

In essence, I made a written "Declaration of Financial Freedom," which included two very important elements: a date and a dollar amount. Somehow, however, I lost track of it as my attention became more consumed by the debilitating changes in my mother's health. It was as if something had said, "Now, it's time to remind her of what of she said nearly 18 months ago." As such, in March 2006, the paper napkin resurfaced from the depths of my purse. Coincidence? Nah. Prophetic? Absolutely! When I read the words, I thought: W*ow, I wrote that! Hmm? I'm almost there, too. (Referring to the amount I had in savings.) Let's make a run of it!*

For the next several months, **"Operation Get the Money/Keep the Money"** was underway to amass as much money as possible from every imaginable source. The great thing about pursuing my financial goal was that I had already initiated the simplification process months earlier. For example, the first expensive habit that I eliminated from my budget were the St. John knits that I had grown accustomed to wearing. I saved a fist full of cash from that one action alone. The lease on my 2003 Honda Accord was scheduled to expire within a couple weeks, so I was already counting the savings there, with plans to keep the replacement vehicle monthly note under $200.00. One car salesman found that to be a laughable ambition, but I guess he really didn't know me. I also cut out the after-work dinner and drink affairs with co-workers and friends. Cutting back on the things you enjoy doing can be hard, but these were all temporary sacrifices intended to serve a higher purpose. In addition to making the cuts, I generated more cash from filing my tax returns which tended to yield a four-figure refund because of my home-based business. With every dollar accumulated and saved, I got more and more excited about reaching my goal!

Unabashedly Free

As I stared at myself in the mirror on a Monday morning in March 2006, I realized that after eight hours of toiling with the coils of curls on top of my head, I still did not have a hairstyle. In this 995th entry in my natural hair chronicles, I faced a dilemma, in which I thought: *I could either stay home and try to tame my mane, or the good folks down at the electric and gas company are going to have to deal with me like this!* By "this" I meant my unshaped afro that I patted a thousand times and used a hot straightening comb along the front edges before I felt comfortable that *this is it* to head into the office. The question that begs an answer is, "Why was *this* an issue in the first place?" The different reactions I received from my colleagues and coworkers told it all.

First, there was "Curious Cassie" (a.k.a "Becky") who was fascinated by my hair's shape and texture. Without even thinking, I instinctively pulled away as she reached to touch it. Time out! Dear White People: I say this with the deepest sincerity and love for mankind. Please, please, please…STOP trying to touch a Black woman's hair! C'mon, y'all. In case no one has ever told you, it is simply not cool, and it creates an uncomfortable situation for the recipient of your advance, especially in the workplace. Not to mention, it would be considered totally out of bounds if done in reverse. Therefore, if it is not okay to touch "Becky's" hair, then it certainly is not okay to touch "Keisha's" hair either. I advise that you admire with your eyes and not your hands. 😊

The second person I encountered was a middle-aged Black man, who served in management and had been with the company for nearly 30 years. Do you know he had the audacity to say to me, "Black women with afros don't get promoted!"? WHAT?! Obviously, he didn't know me, nor did he know what I knew. Rather than allow his uninformed remarks to take up space in my head, I just smiled and walked away. The whole time I was thinking, *F*** what he heard, I'll promote my damn self!*

The third and final noteworthy encounter I had that day was with another African American sistah who was a few years older than me. When I decided to visit her desk, I thought she would be able to appreciate my freedom of expression, but I was wrong. When I rounded the corner to enter her cubicle, I was immediately met by, "Aww, hell naw!" Translation: *"Gurrrl! What is you doin'? You know you cain't com' up in here with yo' hair lookin' like dat! You gonna make these White folks lose their damn minds!"* All I could do was laugh and shake my head at the same time.

Three different people responded in three unique ways to my one act of courage in showing up as my authentic self. Emboldened with self-confidence, I repeated the afro hairstyle at work on at least two other occasions. In fact, one of those times was in the presence of upper management when I was invited to the executive suites to discuss my role in a new system implementation. No one said a word about the big a** elephant in the room. Therefore, I could only conclude that they either accepted it, tolerated it, or did not care to make it an issue. Whatever the case, it did not matter to me because I had a date and a dollar amount, and any insecurities

I may have had concerning my hair had since faded away. Who knew that I was ahead of my time? Since then, Black hair in the workplace has continued to evolve and take on many shapes and forms. It has even found itself at the center of present-day political debate spurred by the CROWN Act legislation that helps to fight against hair discrimination in the workplace. I appreciate the advocates and allies who support Black Americans in showing up as our beautiful, excellent, and authentic selves.

I Can See It

Between the months of April and June 2006, things started to move at an accelerated pace. My previous declarations started to take form in real life. For example, after once again seeing Les Brown speak in Detroit at the Charles H. Wright Museum of African American History, I said to myself, "Someday, I am going to speak on that stage as well." Guess what happened? I did, thanks to Dr. Ken L. Harris, Jr., who at that time was the founder and leader of the International Detroit Black Expo. The theme of my speech was, "Do the Unthinkable and Live the Impossible!" It was unthinkable to believe that I could replace my Honda Accord with a car that had a note for less than $200 per month. However, when I enthusiastically shared with the audience that my new note was only $191.43, I showed them that it was possible. Two weeks later, I hosted my very first Behind the Wheel Financial Empowerment Series workshop at a local hotel. In keeping ticket prices low to get as many people in the room as possible, it was unthinkable to believe that I could generate sponsorship revenues that were equivalent to over 100 ticket sales. However, when three financial services professionals in my network agreed to sponsor a table, I once again showed myself and others what was possible.

CHAPTER 8—THAT WAS A GOOD JOB

By June 2006, I was attending the NABA national convention in Hollywood, Florida. While at a networking reception, I bumped into one of my mentees. Marquetta Clements, who had first-hand experience with my impassioned speeches as chapter president, informed me that the employee resource group at her firm was looking for a speaker for their upcoming conference. In her role as president of the Black Employee Network (BEN) at Deloitte, she asked, "Would you be interested?" I replied, "Of course! I would love to." When she asked, "How much do you charge?" I was trained to respond, "What's in your budget?" Rather than negotiating a fee over the loud music with Lil Jon's "Snap Yo Fingers" playing in the background, she suggested we continue the conversation when we both returned to Detroit. I agreed, but before leaving Florida, I had already started working on the proposal, which undeniably set two parallel paths in motion.

Meanwhile, when I got home from the convention, I was dog-tired by the end of the week! While attempting to catch up on some ZZZs, my phone rang. If anybody was going to shake me out of my sleep, it better had been for good reason. When I looked at my caller-ID, it was my good friend Danielle Avis on the other end of the phone. Danielle had a knack for getting me to do things I never intended to do. In this case, it was the 12-hour "Women's Lock-in Service" at our church that Friday evening. No matter how hard I tried to convince her that I was physically and mentally beaten down, she was not buying any of my excuses and insisted that I go. In the end, all it took was a "C'mon, Li Li!" to get me up, dressed, and out the door.

The theme for the women's lock-in service was P.U.S.H., which stood for "pray until something happens." From sun down to sun up, we heard from different speakers, shared personal testimonies, and encouraged each other in our faith. Every woman in that sanctuary came in search of a breakthrough, while being surrounded by sisters whose job it was to help her P.U.S.H. In my opinion, the most impactful exercise of all occurred in two phases just before dawn. First, we were instructed to share one personal goal with the sister next to us. The sister that I was partnered with confided in me that she wanted to work on her marriage. In turn, I told her that I wanted to quit my job. Apparently, I had shared my desire with her in the past. Therefore, her quick response was, "Oh, girl! You still talking about that?" Translation: *"I've been hearing you say that forever! So, why don't you make like Nike and 'Just Do It!'"* She had a point, which made the second part of the exercise that much more important.

We were asked to take out a piece of paper and write one word that explained why we had not acted on our goal. The overachiever in me did not write just one word but two. Afterwards, like everyone else, I folded my paper and dropped it into the collection basket as it passed. One by one, the facilitator, whose name was Jennifer, sifted through the odd-sized pieces of paper and detected a common theme. In most cases, if not all, the women named FEAR as the reason for their inaction. No one seemed surprised, but they did feel relieved that they were not alone. As the session ended in prayer, it was not the end for me. Instead of immediately joining the other women for breakfast in the fellowship hall, I lingered in the sanctuary to talk with Jennifer about how I was the one who wrote 'SECRET FEAR' on my paper.

Why secret fear?

It was safe to say that outwardly, "I was big, bad, and bold Lisa Howze," but on the inside, I was that frightened little girl who was afraid to pull the band-aid of my "boo-boo." I explained how in

CHAPTER 8—THAT WAS A GOOD JOB

October 2004, I had written on a paper napkin that "June 30, 2006 is my last day at DTE Energy!" She looked at her watch and then back at me before saying, "You got one week, Boo! What ya gonna do?" I said, "HUH?! Do you think I should tell the other ladies?" She said, "Yeah, c'mon! Let's go tell them."

When we reached the fellowship hall, I nervously cleared my throat to get the ladies' attention. Then, I repeated to them what I had just shared with Jennifer. Upon hearing my declaration, one young lady enthusiastically asserted, "I'll help you write the letter!" To that, I replied, "Huh?!" This thing was getting more real by the minute. I truly did not expect to receive so much support, considering I had only been an official member of the church for a little over five months. To put icing on the cake, one of the church mothers chimed in with some sage advice. In a low, raspy voice that made me listen closely, she said, "This is what I want you to do: Go home, cleanse your body, dress in all white, and anoint your head with this oil." She gave me a small vial of oil that had been blessed by a minister. Her final instruction was to lay prostrate on the floor and wait to hear what the Lord had to say about my plans.

I went home and followed her instructions to the tee. As I lay in the middle of the floor, I quietly waited to hear from the Lord. Several minutes had gone by, but God had not said anything to me yet. So, you wanna know what I did? I started talking to Him. I said, "Look, Lord! You usually speak to me when I am in a restful state. I know it's only been about five minutes, but it feels like an eternity. Hurry up and start talking because I gotta pee!" Then, as clear as day, I heard Him say, "I've already told you, and I've already shown you. You know what to do. Now, get up!"

Although June 30 was only a few days away, I knew I could not leave abruptly. I needed at least another week to get my ducks in a row and give proper notice. Once I became clear about how my health care coverage would be impacted, all my others moves were strategically planned and carefully calculated. However, there was one wild card that added a bit of uncertainty. I did not know the status of the speaking engagement proposal that I had submitted to Marquetta. When my initial email and several follow-up phone calls to her went unanswered, I began to worry because my resignation was imminent. As a result, I reached out to my good friend Arica who also worked at Deloitte with Marquetta to see if she could give me some insight. Excited to hear her pick up the phone, I rattled off the following:

> "Hey, Arica. Have you talked to Marquetta? I submitted the proposal like she asked, but I have not heard from her. She hasn't returned any of my phone calls either."

> Arica sighed and said, "Yeah, about that… She received your proposal, and to be honest, Lisa, your speaker fee came in quite high. So, she was considering another lady from out of town whose fee was not nearly as high as yours."

> Anxiously I replied, "I figured that might be the case. Listen, I don't care about the money! I just want the opportunity! What's your budget? Just tell me! Whatever it is, I'll meet it!"

Arica told me they budgeted the speaker's fee at $1,000. "Good lookin' out, Arica! I will revise the proposal and get it over to Marquetta first thing in the morning." To show my sincerity, I

CHAPTER 8—THAT WAS A GOOD JOB

lowered my fee to $999. I figured there was no way they could deny me for coming in under budget.

After hitting send on the email to Marquetta, my heart skipped a beat when I received an auto-responder message indicating that she was out of the office for the week and not checking messages. WHAT!? Next, my mind started doing all kinds of mental gymnastics: *This can't be happening! I mean, today is the same day that I plan to give my manager two weeks' notice. What should I do? I can move forward in faith, remembering what God had spoken to me, or I can give into fear and live the rest of my life wondering what-if.* I chose to move forward with God's promise and continued to get dressed for work. Before leaving home, I checked my email one last time. In a twist of fate, there was a message in my inbox from Marquetta that read: "Congratulations! It gives me great pleasure to inform you that we have selected you to be our speaker for the Deloitte BEN Conference on August 11, 2006."

When I tell you I was excited, you don't understand! I shouted for joy all over the house. Do you hear me? When I think back on that day, I can't help but see the test that led to my testimony which affirms that "Delay does not mean denial!" Furthermore, I must say that the Lord has a strange sense of humor. He plays way too much! Ha!

Right when he had his second cup of fresh-brewed, perking hot coffee, I peeked my head into my supervisor's office: "Ethan, can we meet this afternoon for about half an hour? I'd like to give you an update on the status of my projects." He agreed to 2 p.m. From there, it was just a matter of time before I dropped the hammer on him. BAM! With each passing hour, I could feel myself getting closer to freedom. My belly filled with great anticipation as I carefully put the finishing touches on my letter of resignation. I grabbed two manila folders, placing the summary report of my current work assignments in one and my letter in the other.

When the clock struck two, he led the way into the small conference room, as I closed the door behind us. As we sat across the table from each other, I thanked him for taking the time to meet and then led into a discussion about my open projects and what I expected to complete within the next two weeks. (Wink, wink.) While he was looking over the summary document, I calmly slid the letter in front of him and stated, "This is what I really wanted to share with you." In a state of shock, he looked at the letter, then looked at me, and back at the letter again. "Was there something that I did?" he asked. In my head, I was thinking, *no, numb nut! I'd never give you the satisfaction.* However, what I so eloquently said instead was, "No. This is a decision that I arrived at on my own. I've always wanted to live my dream as a motivational speaker, and this is what I intend to do."

Taking the focus off me, I intentionally switched places with him by assuming the leader-coach role. "Ethan, can I ask you a question?" After nodding his head in the affirmative, I asked, "If you were not doing this job (as Accounting Manager), what would you be doing?" He responded, "I'd be a veterinarian." Wow! Caring for animals was a far stretch from the debits and credits and number crunching that had shaped both our careers. While I was moved by his vulnerability, I felt sorry for him because he was not doing the thing that possibly could have brought him more joy and fulfillment. Since I didn't ask him in follow-up, I'll ask you:

Why do you think he was not doing what inspired him most, like being a veterinarian? In what ways are you like or unlike Ethan?

As for me, I was determined to not allow whatever was holding Ethan back to stop me from pursuing my dreams. Fast-forward two days later, while attending Sunday service at Union Grace, my pastor preached a sermon that referenced the act of faith demonstrated by the Apostle Peter who was called to "step out of the boat." He further exclaimed that "when you step out, others will follow." This message confirmed everything that I had just done.

Two weeks later, on July 21, 2006, my *Reigning Day* had finally come! When I walked into the office that day, I was dressed to the nines in a two-piece carefully-tailored red knit suit that had gold piping that wrapped around the collar and ran down both sides of the extended lapel. The matching skirt fit perfectly like a slender hand inside an Isotoner glove. My satin gold shoes served as the ultimate complement to complete the look. I proudly wore my hair in a protective natural style that was a combination of cornrows and two-strand twists. If you were to compare my image on Day 1 on the job in public accounting to my last day at DTE Energy, you would see a stark contrast. For instance, when I started my career, I was willing to conform to the conservative norms that were established by the profession. However, on my Reigning Day, I rewrote the rules and established a new order for women like me who dared to radiate greatness as her true self.

Now, tell me. Who do you know quits their job and throws themselves a private party in the office on their last day? Me, that's who! I reserved the large conference room and invited co-workers and friends that helped to shape my experiences at the company. Some members of management even popped in to offer their support and well-wishes. As I reflected on memorable moments and explained my motivations for leaving, I appreciated looking around the room and seeing the reassuring faces of sisters who were part of a group of women that I met with regularly. In parting, I gave a shameless plug for the expected release of my financial empowerment CD entitled, "Reigning Day: How to Master Money and Buy Back Your Freedom." I circulated sample copies of the introductory track on the CD as an additional sign of my confidence and commitment to step into my new destiny.

During my final elevator ride down to the first floor, I bumped into the director of the department. In that exchange, I handed him a business card that included my photo and contact information on the front and the logos for Driving Motivation and Fundamental Accounting Solutions on the back. The puzzled expression on his face was priceless, as he looked back and forth at the card and me. In total amazement, he said, "You planned this?" as if it were hard for him to believe that I could contrive a well-calculated and deliberate departure. Perhaps it would have been easier for him to accept a scenario in which I let my emotions push me into calling it quits without thinking through what happens next. Fortunately, my push came from the paper napkin that was buried in the bottom of my purse that contained two things: a date and dollar amount. Can I let you in on a little secret? None of this would have made a bit of difference if my plans had not been aligned with my Creator's purpose and plan for my life.

Today, I am not surprised by people's reactions when I tell them I quit my job only 11 years into my professional career. When they hear the name of the company I left, they instinctively say, "Ooh, that was a good job!" They are not wrong. It was a good job for a great company that overall treated me well. Therefore, I was totally aware of what I'd be giving up, but I was unwilling to trade my hopes, dreams, and future aspirations for a false sense of security. By choosing my passion over my paycheck, I made a conscious decision to live life without regret and open myself to receive all the blessings coming my way.

CHAPTER 9

I DIDN'T SEE THAT COMING!

*I*n the two-and-a-half-year period (2006-2008) that followed my exit from that "Good Job", all hell had broken loose. For instance, the housing market crash caused the U.S. economy to go off the rails and thrust the country into the Great Recession. Millions of people lost their jobs, stopped paying their mortgages, and ultimately lost their homes due to bank foreclosure. My neighborhood in northeast Detroit was hit the hardest. Homes that had previously been occupied by teachers, police officers, and firefighters were reduced to empty shells that reflected a new norm of vacancies that stretched to many other neighborhoods across the city. Also, on the home front, automotive giants General Motors and Chrysler Corporation were on the verge of collapse when their executives went before Congress to request financial relief through a government bailout. Not even Whodini could escape the effects of this distressed economy!

To add insult to injury, inflation was wreaking havoc on people's pocketbooks. I personally suffered from sticker shock at the pump, as the price for regular unleaded gas soared to over $3.25 per gallon. What used to cost $45 to fill my car's tank increased by one-third to nearly $60. Depending on where you lived in the country, the total cost could vary, but you get my point. In addition, the skyrocketing cost of a box of cereal and gallon of milk seriously had me rethinking my grocery list. When I walked out of DTE Energy in July 2006, I had no idea that I'd be walking into the eye of the storm. As an entrepreneur, I was OUTCHERE in the deep, and there was no turning back!

On the personal front, Murphy's Law was in full effect. If anything *were* to go wrong, *it did*. There was no way that I could have predicted every negative situation or event that cropped up. However, I learned to take the bad with the good. For example, one week prior to my speaking engagement with Deloitte and the Black Employee Network (BEN), I traveled to L.A. for a three-day, speakers training event hosted by Norma Thompson Hollis, a native Detroiter who founded a Black-owned and operated speakers bureau and training company based in Los Angeles, California. Norma was another one of those people placed in my path (PIMP) in 2005 when we met at a sales conference in Atlanta, Georgia, where I was a vendor. I had shipped no fewer than four large boxes filled with The Mileage Tracker System and Driving Motivation branded t-shirts and tote bags. I was prepared to make a killing! Or so I thought.

Norma approached my table with a business card in hand and explained how she had been directed to come speak to me. During our brief encounter, she learned how passionate I was about public speaking, which made her tell me about the one-day training event that she had coming up soon in Detroit. I took her up on her offer to attend and was glad I did. It was through Norma that I learned to ask a client, "What is your budget?" whenever they asked, "How much do you charge?" If you recall, I applied what I learned with Marquetta when she first approached me about the speaking opportunity with Deloitte. With that being said, I was looking forward to going to Cali to soak up some more knowledge and sunshine, too.

Norma and her team did not disappoint. Their training went beyond speaking techniques and covered the business of speaking, including press kits, speaker one-sheets, client testimonials, and how to establish your speaker's fee depending on the type of event. After the three days were complete, I was inspired and eager to apply all the new things I learned once I got back home to Detroit… until there was a delay.

While en route to the airport with my sister Sabrina, we exited the 405 freeway at La Tijera and Century Blvd. In my rearview mirror, I could see a red convertible approaching quickly from behind with no intention to stop. Then, everything seemed to move in slow-motion, as I gritted all 30 of my teeth to brace myself for impact. BOOM! Instantly, I shouted in my best Erin Brockovich voice, "I can't believe this a**hole just ran into the back of our car!" With a pair of medical crutches in his front seat, this dude was noticeably intoxicated. What gave it away? Aside from him irresponsibly crashing into us, I saw a projectile of clear fluids violently emerge from the hollows of what I imagined to be an empty stomach, as he leaned his head outside of his car to vomit on the ground. From the looks of it, this guy was totally in bad shape.

Paralyzed from disbelief and shock, I remained glued to the driver's seat with my seatbelt fastened while my big sister, who stood 5'9" tall at 180 pounds with beautiful golden dreadlocks hanging down her back, got out of the car to confront this puny white dude with disheveled blonde hair and a serious drinking problem. Although we had already called the police, she was not going to sit by and let this drunken fool get away with what he had done. No, she didn't get violent with him. She simply demanded that he give her his driver's license, as she kept repeating, "You know you in trouble! You know you in trouble, right?" Apparently, her words started to sink in because within seconds, he put the pedal to the metal and fled the scene of the accident, burning rubber as he sped away. There was just one thing the idiot left behind…his driver's license!

When the police arrived, my sister handed them the guy's license, which they used to help track him down. They assured us that he could not have gotten too far outside the airport area and asked me if I wanted to ride along in their cruiser to look for him. From the moment I agreed to get into the back seat of that iconic black and white LA County police vehicle, I felt like I was in a Beverly Hills Cop movie—straight out of Hollywood! Nonetheless, it's a good thing I was not a real criminal because the flat hard plastic surface back there did not make for a comfortable joy ride. Sheesh!

After circling the airport a few times, the police spotted a red convertible Mazda Miata parked on the side of the street. The police vehicle that I was in parked at a distance, while the officers in a separate squad car approached the car of the presumed drunk driver, asking him to step out of his vehicle. While rolling down my window, they asked me to discreetly look to see if this guy was our perpetrator. Once I gave the head nod of assurance, the other officers clanked handcuffs on him and hauled his tipsy tail away to jail. He was going to pay dearly for the inconvenience he caused, and later you will see just how.

If you thought that was wild and exciting, wait until you read what happened later that fall.

CHAPTER 9—I DIDN'T SEE THAT COMING!

"He's been shot! He's been shot!" the man's anguished voice rang loudly through the phone. Who was the "he" in this scenario? My 17-year-old nephew. With no time to wait for an ambulance or a Detroit police squad car to come, the two men on the scene acted swiftly, lifting my nephew's seemingly lifeless body from the ground into the bed of a pick-up truck and rushing him to the nearest hospital. After a successful surgery, the doctors said two things that were extremely sobering about this near-fatal incident: 1) if the two men had not been there or hesitated to act as quickly as they did, my nephew could have bled to death; and 2) if the bullet that penetrated his neck had been any closer to his main artery instead of coming out through his jaw on the opposite side of his face, it would have ended his young life before it had a chance to get started. Within two days, he was released from the hospital and on a path to a speedy recovery. I was grateful for the miracle but emotionally wrecked, nonetheless.

Can you imagine overcoming one hurdle only to face another one shortly thereafter?

I'm sad to say that approximately two months after reaching his 18th birthday, this same young man found himself in a heap of trouble with the law. A portion of the money that I had saved to support myself and my entrepreneurial endeavors went toward his legal defense. During his trial, I could not help but think about my mom and imagine how overwhelmed and helpless she must have felt while listening to the proceedings in my brother's case, almost 20 years earlier. Finally, when the jury delivered its verdict, my heart sank to the pit of my stomach, as dreams of a promising future for my nephew went up in the air like smoke.

Damn!

How many stories similar to this do you know?

With this story, I hope to encourage young people to think twice about their associations, i.e., the people they call "friends." In addition, please understand that every rash decision made in the heat of the moment can lead to a lifetime of pain. Furthermore, every young person who gets into trouble after going left when they should have gone right is a part of somebody's family and hopefully connected to someone who loves them.

Given my experience as an auntie, I want to also speak directly to other women who have experienced the hardship of having a husband, son, brother, nephew, cousin, or significant other fall into the unforgiving hands of the criminal justice system. Unfortunately, when tragedy strikes, it does not care if you have a good-paying job or no job at all. Instead, it leaves behind the cartilage of broken hearts, ruptured futures, and disrupted plans. However, if you are who I know you can be, you have always been able to find the strength and courage to pick up the pieces and carry on–many times with no one else being the wiser. If that's you, I want you to know, "I see you, Sis! I see you, Mom!"

As you can see, life had dished me a healthy serving of unpleasant events that I did not see coming. The car accident, for example, set me back months, as I was unable to pursue any speaking engagements. Do you want to know what I was doing instead? Three to four days a week, I had a date with Dr. Pete, my chiropractor who made his living telling me what was *wrong* with me: "Your neck is crooked, your spine is out of whack, and one leg is shorter than the other." What!? If it were not for the fact that he was helping me manage my neck and back pain, my self-esteem would have been shot.

CHAPTER 9—I DIDN'T SEE THAT COMING!

Fortunately, in between doctor's appointments, I made time to record the official audio for my financial empowerment CD, "Reigning Day: How to Master Money and Buy Back Your Freedom." Through the lessons that I share with each track, I help set people free from their mental and emotional ties to money, while teaching them to apply four principles of personal money management. For those of you who desire to leave your place of employment and participate in the "Great Resignation," entrepreneurship is not for the faint at heart. "Everything you eat, you must kill," as the diehards say. Most times you will not know from where that next meal is coming. The only thing that is certain about life as an entrepreneur is uncertainty. While getting free is admirable, *staying* free is a whole other issue.

To ensure that I did not backslide into the "comforts" of a 9 to 5, I created a sign that I used for motivation. Encircled in the center of a sheet of paper were the words, "Corporate Accounting Job". I then drew a red diagonal line through it. Sounds extreme, but my fear was that if I did not wholeheartedly pursue my dream, I would live to regret it. As such, I doubled down and invested thousands of dollars in personal development. I became a student of thought leaders who had written books and/or hosted seminars on leadership, wealth, and business building strategies.

For example, I read T. Harv Eker's book, *Secrets of the Millionaire Mind* and participated in his signature experiential training event, the *Millionaire Mind Intensive* (MMI) twice. During MMI, I remember a situational exercise in which I partnered with another participant, and we took turns interviewing one another as if were guests on a television talk show. Later in Chapters 10 thru 13, you will see the skills that I developed in practice were on full display during real-life interviews that aired to hundreds of thousands and even millions of viewers in the metro Detroit market. In addition to MMI, I took a two-part seminar series, which helped me develop the skills and discipline needed to deliver highly interactive and thought-provoking learning experiences for individuals who would eventually become participants in my training events and programs.

By mid-year 2007, my activity started to pick up. For example, at the 2007 NABA National Convention in Philly, I received NABA's *Walking the Road Less Traveled Award* to acknowledge my ability to leverage my accounting background into a new area of interest. During the same time, I officially launched the *Reigning Day CD* and paired it with a financial empowerment training series that I designed to help members of the faith-based community become better stewards of their personal finances. Under the leadership of Reverend Dr. Steve Bland, Sr., Liberty Temple Baptist Church was the first religious organization to invest in my program.

Later that year, with the help of my mentor Desma, I was selected by NAWBO to speak at their national convention in Atlanta, Georgia. This one event led to two additional speaking opportunities with women-centered organizations. Moreover, Kathleen Alessandro, who was then president of the NAWBO Greater Detroit Chapter, asked me to take her place where she was scheduled to speak at a conference in Grand Rapids, Michigan, the following month. The host organization was the Institute for Continuing Legal Education, and the audience was mostly attorneys and members of the legal profession. The invitation to speak also included a complimentary dinner and a one-night stay at the Amway Grand Hotel.

When I pulled up to the hotel, I had no business being in the line for valet parking. Why? Because I had a problem opening the

CHAPTER 9—I DIDN'T SEE THAT COMING!

driver's door from the inside of my more than *gently used* luxury vehicle. This was not an immediate issue since the valet would be opening my door for me. However, as soon as he would have attempted to let himself out of the car, he was going to be in for a big surprise. To avoid the later embarrassment, I decided to come clean and give him the low down on what was up with my busted up door handle and how to let himself out of the car. This certainly was not the ideal scenario for a guest staying at this prestigious hotel, but what was a girl on a mission supposed to do? I guess I could have self-parked, but oh well.

As I lay awake in bed the following morning, it hit me! *OMG!* I thought. It happened. My mind flashed back to August 1993 when I was an Amway distributor in college. Les Brown, the international motivational speaker and author, was on stage speaking at the Georgia Dome in Atlanta. As I listened to him deliver an electrifying speech, I said to myself, "I think I'd like to do that someday!" By "that" I meant, use the power of my voice to stir souls and help people believe in themselves and their abilities. Les trumpeted one of his famous sayings, "If you can look up, then you can get up!" *Fourteen years later, here I am, staying at the Amway Grand Hotel, getting ready to speak at the Devos Place. Wow! Dreams do come true*, I concluded. I was truly grateful to be walking in my purpose.

The following winter, in February 2008, my purpose pointed me in the direction of Stillwater, Oklahoma. What was a city girl like me doing in those neck of the woods? I was visiting Oklahoma State University, where I was scheduled to speak at the Big 12 Student Conference. Although this was a non-paid speaking engagement, I found a way to generate income for myself. For instance, I researched and reached out to select financial services companies that were listed as conference sponsors. Two of them agreed to pay me $250 each to have their branding displayed during the two workshop sessions that I was leading. Without much effort, I generated $500 in revenue simply because I had the audacity to believe that I could. I shared this amazing feat with one of my brothers, in the same way that I had dropped the $700 in cash at his feet when I first started selling candy almost 20 years earlier. For me, it was both easy and fun to create money out of thin air.

After I shared principles of leadership and personal money management with the students, there was a general assembly that evening at a different building on campus. Rather than driving my rental car, I rode one of the commuter buses to the venue with a group of students who were also staying at my hotel. To my surprise, when we arrived, I learned that Stedman Graham (a.k.a. "Oprah's man") was the keynote speaker! I say that tongue-in-cheek because early in his remarks he said to the room mostly full of college students, "I know what some of you are thinking: 'That's Oprah's man!'" I said to myself, *"Yep!* You took the words right out of my mouth." As he continued with his message, he drew lessons from his book, *Who Are You?* in which he defined identity and self-awareness as the keys to living a successful life.

The event was over when his speech ended, but then, my search for a ride back to the hotel began. Unbeknownst to me, the commuter bus that brought me to the venue was not immediately returning to the hotel. Instead, all the buses were charged with taking students to an offsite party to turn up. As for me, I just wanted to turn in so I could head home the next day. I located the conference organizer and told him my dilemma. He said, "I'd be happy to give you a ride if you don't mind sharing the car with Mr. Graham who needs to get dropped off at his hotel first." Of course, he got zero objections from me! Who in their right mind would turn down a once-in-a-lifetime opportunity to ride with the man who had touched the hem of Oprah's garment? Who, really?

After waiting patiently, I asked, and Mr. Graham graciously agreed to snap a photo with me. As we walked toward the exit, he paused to grab a copy of OSU's student news publication. He told me, "Wherever I go, I always pick up a copy of the local paper. It helps me stay abreast of things happening in the area. You never know how it may come in handy." Those were priceless words of wisdom that I've never forgotten.

When we reached his hotel, he got out of the limo, and I said in parting, "Tell Oprah I said hello!" I honestly believed in my heart that meeting Stedman Graham was a sign that I was getting closer to meeting Oprah herself. I had always dreamed of being a guest on the Oprah Winfrey Show. I imagined sharing my story while sitting on her famous coach, where so many greats had sat before me. However, there was one show that made me reevaluate my ambition.

On the show, Oprah featured an ordinary woman who wanted to do something extraordinary for her community. This woman collected jars of pennies to raise money to buy food for the community food pantry. She even encouraged others to bring their pennies as well. Together, she believed their efforts could stamp out hunger for families in need. As a result of witnessing this woman's heart to serve, I had an "aha! moment". Whereas I wanted to go on Oprah and talk about my accomplishments and how "great" I thought I was, I quickly realized that it was not about me. While admirable, nothing I had done for myself mattered to others in the greater scheme of life.

As proven by this noble woman with the pennies, the stories that seemed to matter most were the ones about service to others. The late, great Reverend Dr. Martin Luther King, Jr. exclaimed this fact when he said, "Life's most persistent and urgent question is, '**What are you doing for others?**'" From this experience, I adopted my third fundamental belief that says, "It's not about me!" It's so much bigger.

As Stedman faded into the distance of his hotel lobby, I moved up to the front seat of the limo. I was in absolute awe with the whole experience. As the driver made his way back to my hotel, I kept repeating these words to myself: "He's taking me places. He's taking me places. He's taking me places." By "He", I meant the inner compass that had been guiding and directing my life. I was overwhelmed with gratitude; number one, for the ride and secondly, the opportunity to be in the presence of greatness. When I closed the door to my hotel room, I could not wait to further develop the words that my heart was telling me to write. After several revisions and a few tweaks once I returned home to Detroit, the following poem was born:

"Go for What You Know"
By Lisa L. Howze

He's taking me places.
Wouldn't you like to go?
Mysterious places, indeed.
Wouldn't you like to know?
He's taking me places.
My life is in His hands.
Carrying me when I need Him most,
Like footsteps in the sand.

CHAPTER 9—I DIDN'T SEE THAT COMING!

He's taking me places.
I cannot imagine, hence.
No place is too daunting,
For I am protected by the fence.
He's taking me places.
New doors, they open wide.
I see scores of friendly faces,
They invite me to come inside.
He's taking me places.
The stage is to set go.
Speak up loud; say it proud,
I am His, I'll have you know!

While I had been putting the finishing touches on the poem, I learned that first-term United States Senator Barack Obama had just won the Iowa caucus in his bid to become the Democratic nominee for President of the United States. This unexpected victory made me and the rest of the world take notice. It seemed like he was being guided by a similar source that was taking him someplace, too. Perhaps 1600 Pennsylvania Avenue? I will admit, prior to Barack Obama's run, I had no idea what a "caucus" was, and although I had previously been encouraged to run for precinct delegate or city council, I scoffed at the idea. Besides, a dark cloud seemed to hover over Detroit politics at the time, setting up the strangest dichotomy: On one hand, Barack Obama was set to make history as the first Black president if elected, and Detroit Mayor Kwame Kilpatrick, who easily could have been on a similar path, was facing indictment for perjury in a whistleblower case. Later that year, Mayor Kilpatrick was forced to resign from his post.

Fast-forward to June 2008 when I was preparing to give a presentation entitled, "Can You Spare Some Change?" at the NABA national convention in Atlanta, Georgia. In a way, my title was an ode to Obama who was running on a "CHANGE" platform. As more than 200 of my fellow NABA brothers and sisters gathered in a conference room to hear me speak, I was so honored. They represented chapters from every region of the nation and ranged from first-time attendees to long-time pillars of the association. As I stood at the front of the room while being introduced, my mind quickly flashed back to eight years earlier when I crowded into a standing-room-only conference room in D.C. to hear Dr. Traci Lynn speak. She was the first person to inform me that a goal is still a goal even if you must move the timeline. I carried that message with me the whole while, and now, my time had come to rock the mic!

Let's be honest! What was I going to tell a room full of accountants about money that they didn't already know? Rather than educate them about the principles of personal money management, I chose to edutain them instead by sharing a story about my candy selling days in high school. It all tied into the theme of my message about change. Here's the recap: When I first added potato chips to the line-up of goodies I sold from my locker and an oversized tote bag, I priced the chips at 45 cents per bag–a nickel less than the candy bars. I squatted low to the conference room floor to reenact a moment when I was at the bottom of a huddle of students, dishing candy and stashing cash. There was this one kid who had given me 50 cents for a bag of potato chips. As I continued to transact business with several other students, I noticed that one kid was still standing there. It seemed like an eternity had passed, and he just kept standing there! So, finally, I asked, "What are you waiting for?" He said, "My change, please." After angrily searching at the bottom of my purse for a nickel to give him, I stood up and exclaimed, "THAT'S IT! FROM NOW ON, EVERYTHING IS FIFTY CENTS! I DON'T HAVE TIME TO BE MAKING CHANGE! We only have 10 minutes in between classes, and I'm trying to make miracles happen!"

The room erupted with laughter! At that point, I knew I had them! They were highly engaged, asking great questions, and eating every chocolate morsel of sweet information out the palm of my hand. Pun intended! (Ha!) Seriously, though, the organic exchange that occurs between a speaker and her audience is near magical. Secretly, they had become co-creators in crafting the genius in the story I told. By far, it was a highlight performance in my speaking career. Despite having no sleep the night before the presentation, I never felt more alive.

I even had someone to capture video footage of me speaking along with shots of the audience's reactions. I planned to use an edited version of the presentation to load as content on my new website that was under development. Get this! The thumbnail image for the video was going to show me dressed in a business suit, standing in front of the U.S. Capitol, holding a torn cardboard sign that read, "Can you spare some change?" This satirical depiction was meant to capture people's attention, but the irony of the intended message ended up manifesting itself in real life over the two years that followed.

Ironically, in the fourth quarter of 2008, I had to take a long, hard look and reevaluate my own finances. As the state of the economy worsened, I found myself swimming in over $36,000 in credit card debt. My high-stakes game of "robbing Peter to pay Paul" had reached its peak, and it was not going to be long before my house of cards came tumbling down. When my niche market of accounting firms started showing signs of tightening their belts around training and development costs, I grew gravely concerned. If it had not been for the $15,000 payout that I received earlier that year for lost wages from the insurance company of the drunk driver who rear ended me in California in 2006, I would have been in dire straits much sooner. As the year ended, I was really messed up. I had no freaking idea how I was going to keep the dream alive and pay my bills. Something had to give. Despite how it looked, I knew that me giving up was not an option!

CHAPTER 10

POLITICS 101: THE CALL, THE RUN, THE RISE

Two Years Later

"*R*aise your right hand and repeat after me…"

"I, Lisa Howze, do solemnly affirm that I will support the Constitution of the United States and the constitution of this state, and that I will faithfully discharge the duties of the Office of State Representative according to the best of my ability."

I was sworn into the 96th Legislature of the Michigan House of Representatives on Wednesday, January 12, 2011, almost exactly six years from the date my mother first gave me permission to quit my job. Maybe this was the Creator's purpose and plan for me the whole time. I just wish my mom could have been there to witness this shining moment in her baby girl's life. In her absence, I had a host of other family members and friends who traveled the snow-covered roads and braved the blistering cold to witness me take the oath of office.

A question I often get asked is, "What made you run for office in the first place?" Are you wondering the same thing? I'll tell you just as I have told others: it all began with one simple phone call.

Allow me to provide some context. If you remember, at the end of the previous chapter, I was not 100% clear on what my next move would be, but I was hopeful since the country had just elected its first black president. When Barack Obama was sworn in as the 44th President of the United States of America, I was inspired to compose the following message that I sent to over 3,000 contacts in my database:

> Subject: Change is in the Air
>
> *I'm so excited about the inauguration of President Barack Obama! Change is certainly in the air, and I look forward to bringing about change in my own sphere of influence. As such, I'd like everyone to know how I intend to do it. So, please look forward to my BIG announcement on Monday!*

With my choice of words, I intended to create curiosity and build suspense. I could tell the strategy was working when one of my friends responded, "Girl, what is it? You know you can't be keeping secrets from Black folks! Tell me." Another one said, "I've already seen your website, so I know it can't be that! What is it?"

If only they could have heard the conversation that I had with myself immediately after sending the message. I said,

> *You know, that was a pretty tall order you just placed! How are you going to tell the people on Monday that you're **JUST** launching a website?*

Good question.

You know what? I'll worry about that when Monday comes.

That was on Thursday.

The Call

Midday on Friday, I received an email from my friend Donovan, a contractor who had just completed a renovation project at my home. Attached to his message was an invoice showing the balance I owed. Based on prior conversations about when I could pay, I was a bit perturbed, while thinking to myself, *"Man, I don't have the money yet. You'll get it when I get it!"*

Ten minutes later, my phone rang. Guess who it was? DONOVAN! I just knew he was calling me about that da*n invoice. Boy was I wrong! With absolute conviction in his voice, he said, "LISA, you gotta run for city council!"

"Huh? What! I'm not doing that! Are you crazy?"

In the two minutes that followed, I gave him every excuse I could think of to not run. With plans to launch a new website, develop and design training programs, and book speaking engagements, I asked him, "When would I have time to run for City Council?"

Not accepting "NO" for an answer, he insisted, "Look, man: you gotta do this! There is too much SHIT going on in the city right now! Council is out of control, and you gotta do something about it!" The whole time he was talking, I was thinking: *This is not happening. How could this be happening?* In that moment of denial and self-doubt, I felt an incredible weight on my shoulders. You know that feeling you get when your heart knows you have something to give, but your head questions whether you're ready and willing to give it? That's where I was, and Donovan was not letting up!

After I finally hung up from speaking with him, my plans were to call Danielle and tell her about Donovan's hair-brained idea. Before I could dial her number, my phone was already ringing, again! This time it was Donovan's wife, Monique. I asked her, "Did Donovan put you up to calling me?" She chuckled and then offered to assist while touting her experience as an Obama campaign volunteer. I couldn't believe they were tag-teaming me.

When I finally got a hold of Danielle, I tried to pass the buck by suggesting that perhaps she should run. To that, she responded, "Oh no, Li Li! This is you all day! You should definitely run; I'll support you!" Surprised by how enthusiastic she was, I still was not convinced and told her I'd be contacting another friend to get her opinion. Danielle cautioned me to pray before I called anyone else. Did I listen?

Nope.

Instead, I called to seek the advice of a sister-friend who was closer to Detroit politics and politicians. When I shared the idea with her, she said, "Oh, so you want to get dirty, huh?" suggesting that politics makes strange bedfellows, and I should be careful. In the end, however; she pledged her unwavering support.

My third call was to someone I looked to as a trusted advisor and confidante. Surprisingly, they were less than enthusiastic about the whole idea. Unfortunately, their jaded view of politics kept them from offering me any meaningful assistance in my decision-making process.

Perplexed and overwhelmed, I made my way to my dad and stepmom's house. As we sat in the living room, I told them I wanted to talk to them about something important.

Mama Fatty said, "Go ahead. We're listening."

"What do you think about me running for City Council?" I asked. They both agreed that I should do it, with Mama Fatty jokingly saying, "We'll vote for you. We'll vote for you *twice*!" Then, with all sincerity, she affirmed that, "Lisa, anything you put your mind to, you can do it. I know you can." Getting their support meant everything to me, although I still had my doubts. Isn't it funny how others will believe in you and see your potential before you believe and see it for yourself? The longer I sat with them, the heavier that burden on my shoulders seemed to get, as I sank deeper into their reclining chair. Shaking my head in disbelief, I said to myself, *this was not supposed to be the announcement!* And then I said, *NO, this was supposed to be the announcement; I just didn't know it.*

By the end of the night, it dawned on me that I had not prayed about it as Danielle suggested. Of course, there is nothing wrong with seeking the counsel of others, but I had gone the whole day without talking to the Source who created me. When I finally got some facetime with Him, shared what was on my heart, and listened for the response, I cried out to my Creator, saying, "If this is what You want me to do, I'll do it!" When Monday came, the headline of the announcement read: "Howze Declares Candidacy for Detroit City Council." Then, somewhere in the third paragraph, it said in essence, *"Oh, by the way, today, she also launches her new speaker's website."* Oddly enough, I dropped everything I was previously doing and never revisited any of it again, until now–nearly 13 years later.

The rest, as they say, is history!

The Run

While I had accepted the charge, there was only one problem: I had never run for political office. I truly was in unchartered territory. I had no experience, no money, and no so-called "name recognition". However, what I lacked in campaign fundamentals, I made up for it in faith and an uncanny ability to follow instructions. For example, when the people I trusted told me to start a Facebook page, I did. When there were places that they suggested I needed to be as a candidate, I went. Whenever a congressional district, block club, or police precinct held a meeting, I was there, introducing myself and collecting signatures for my nominating petition. Since there was also that year a special election to complete the unexpired term of fallen Mayor Kwame Kilpatrick, I used the related candidate forums and events as perfect opportunities to look, listen, and learn more about Detroit politics and meet new people.

While school was in session for me politically, life was still happening at a record pace, and sh*t was about to hit the fan, fast! I needed to figure something out quickly. Can you imagine what it was like to go without a regular paycheck for two and a half years? I'll tell you. Money was tight! I was up to my eyeballs in credit card debt and my property taxes were due. I didn't want to touch my retirement account, especially since it had already lost at least one-third of its value when the economy crashed in 2008. I just needed some breathing room to stop suffocating under the weight of one past-due notice after the next. I was so confused and filled with despair. One evening, I found myself on the couch in Danielle's accounting office, sobbing, and blubbering on about how I did not know what I was going to do.

Three days later my energy shifted, as I was reminded of some sage advice that said, "The best way to take your mind off your problems is to get busy helping somebody else." As such, I offered to volunteer at the upcoming media bootcamp for a friend of mine who happened to be an Emmy award-winning gossip researcher, media expert, and TV producer. I figured if I assisted with her event, I could focus on something positive and learn a thing or two about pitching stories and getting noticed by the media. After all, I was running for office.

Whoever coined the statement, "It only takes one good meeting to change your business," was correct. It is true in life and politics as well. In fact, I owe the jumpstart of my political career to one chance encounter with a woman I met while volunteering at the bootcamp. When given the opportunity to introduce myself in the larger setting, I said, "I am Lisa Howze, and I am a candidate for Detroit City Council." Shortly thereafter, I was visiting the ladies' restroom when a woman at the sink said to me, "I heard you say that you're running for city council in Detroit. You should meet my husband." Curious, I asked, "Who's your husband?" She handed me his business card and said, "Give him a call." I thanked her, and then we both returned to the bootcamp. This example proves that you never know who's in the room watching and listening. Therefore, no matter what is going on in your personal life, it is wise to always show up wholly and completely as your best self.

It turned out that the gentleman whose card she handed me was a Lansing lobbyist who was well-connected to the political landscape in Detroit. Through him, I met Mr. Sam Logan, then publisher of the Michigan Chronicle, a weekly African American newspaper that once garnered national attention in its early years for its "radical" approach to politics. Next, there was Doug Rothwell, a white gentleman who was the president and CEO of a business roundtable that focused on solving tough challenges within the region. Doug then connected me with the Detroit Regional Chamber and their candidate screening committee. With each of those introductions, I was off to a good start.

Meanwhile, my Facebook page was starting to gain some traction. Someone sent me a private message that said, "Congratulations on your decision to run for city council! It's been a while since we've worked together. If you decide to work with me for your campaign, I guarantee you that I will help you make it through the primary and place in the Top 5 for the general election." Isn't that just like some people who *slip into your DMs* and make lofty promises that sound too good to be true? Who was he anyway? Let's call him Erik Mateo. In my limited knowledge of Erik, I appreciated him for being the first radio personality to give me a live, on-air interview when I was president of NABA Detroit. Since that time, he had gone on to become a media-marketing guru who spent his career helping to develop high school interns at the radio station into award-winning journalists and radio personalities.

Even though he had the credentials to back up his claims, I admittedly was still a bit skeptical. When you couple politics with being a single woman, you will understand why I proceeded with caution before I finally agreed to work with him. It was one of the best decisions that I made, too! While many people know him as Erik, I affectionately

CHAPTER 10—POLITICS 101: THE CALL, THE RUN, THE RISE

call him "Squeaky," a dear friend and confidante. My journey to the Capitol steps in Lansing is just as much his story as it is mine, which you will later learn. For now, just consider him another one of those persons placed in my path (PIMP).

Meanwhile, one hundred and sixty-eight (168) candidates' names were set to appear on the August 2009 primary election ballot. You probably are wondering how I was able to separate myself from the rest of the pack. I had something that no other council candidate had; I had the CPA advantage. In a city that faced a structural budget deficit of $300 million, I positioned myself as "the ONLY certified public accountant running for Detroit city council." By virtue, that meant I was best suited to help fix the city's broken finances. The irony was I did not have a lot of money in my coffers to run a traditional campaign. However, Erik taught me one very important philosophy that says, "Power perceived is power achieved!" Therefore, we committed to taking the little money I had to get the biggest bang for our buck by running political radio ads that reached far and wide.

Why was this a power move?

First, our timing was impeccable. We hit the airwaves immediately after NBA hall of famer and former Detroit Pistons basketball player Dave Bing won the special election for mayor on May 5, 2009. In a self-recorded message, I touted my financial expertise by repeating the catchphrase, "I am the ONLY certified public accountant running for Detroit city council." Throughout the month of May, we consistently ran the ads during two popular local morning political talk shows.

For those paying attention, the perception was that my campaign had a lot of money. Instead, the secret weapon I had was Erik, who understood that political ad rates were relatively inexpensive. For example, a $100 investment could easily buy four to six, 30-second radio spots that aired at times when Detroit voters were guaranteed to be listening. By comparison, that same $100 could only buy about 20 individual yard signs, which would not be enough for anyone to notice.

How did we know if the ads were working?

When I attended the 13th Congressional District meeting after one week of running the ads, I was greeted by someone representing Congresswoman Carolyn Cheeks-Kilpatrick's office who said to me, "So, you're Lisa Howze! I was wonderin': *who the hell is THIS Lisa Howze?!*" I guess he had heard the ads, huh? Based on his reaction and how other candidates responded to me that day, I could safely say that the radio ads were working. Wow! Erik was right: power perceived is power achieved!

Before the month ended, I received an unexpected mention in the Detroit News when Nolan Finley, the newspaper's editorial page editor, named me along with a handful of other council candidates that he said the business community would be discussing over the weekend at the Mackinac Policy Conference.

Why was this a big deal?

For one, it was earned media that cost me nothing, which Erik described as the best kind of media. Second, this conference, which is an annual statewide event hosted by the Detroit Regional Chamber, was the place to be for any candidate running for public office that wanted to get an audience with the power players, movers, and shakers that could write checks and help advance their campaigns. I recognize this now, but back then, I was unaware and

CHAPTER 10—POLITICS 101: THE CALL, THE RUN, THE RISE

therefore unable to fully grasp the significance of the moment. In fact, if my team had given in to my resistance to make the last-minute 300-mile trek to Mackinac Island, I would have missed the moment altogether. All it took was a "you better get your a** up there!" nudge from Erik to get me moving in the right direction.

> Have you ever felt like you were late to the party? Your brain automatically assumes that you missed out on something that everyone who arrived before you had a chance to experience. Don't worry. Always remember that what is for you will be for you, and it is better to be there late versus not being there at all.

When I stepped off the ferry and walked across the connecting bridge to Mackinac Island, I noticed that people were leaving or had already left since the conference ended at noon on that Saturday. Instead of being discouraged and turning around to leave with them, I determined that if I had traveled that far, it had to be for a good reason. As it turned out, the one person that I was meant to connect with was sitting alone on a bench in a dimly-lit area inside the Grand Hotel.

Stephen Henderson was the editorial page editor for the Detroit Free Press—the more liberal newspaper in Detroit. I stepped forward with my hand extended to introduce myself. "Hi, Stephen. I'm Lisa Howze, candidate for Detroit city council. Your counterpart at the Detroit News wrote about me in Friday's newspaper." Stephen gave me a head nod to acknowledge the mention. When I asked him about the Free Press's endorsement process, he explained that all candidates for city council would receive a questionnaire in the mail. If the editorial board liked my responses, I would be invited to participate in a screening interview. I thanked him for the information and walked away thinking I hit the jackpot! That brief encounter made the early morning trip to Mackinac more than worth it. Mission accomplished!

When the Detroit Free Press Candidate Questionnaire came to my home, I filled it out and mailed it back immediately. As a result, the editorial board invited me in for an interview with Stephen and one of his colleagues. The topics discussed during the interview in many ways mirrored the questionnaire. For example, when asked, "How much is it going to take to win the election?" I responded, "$100,000." Then, they asked, "How much have you raised thus far?" I said, "$7,000." Their next logical question was, "Where are you going to get the other $93,000?" I said with complete confidence, "With your endorsement, I'll attract the rest!"

How could I speak with such authority and boldness?

It's simple. I never allowed my lack of resources to limit my imagination. Before I asked anyone for anything, I was always mindful to make good use of the resources I already had. Through disciplined behavior and a positive attitude, I believed that I could attract whatever I deserved, while also not being afraid to ask for what I wanted.

I never allowed my lack of resources to limit my imagination.

On the Sunday, two weeks prior to the August primary, I received an early morning phone call from Erik, which was nothing unusual. He always called me before the crack of dawn. When he started the conversation, the difference in his voice was that he sounded like a frog was caught in his throat. He said,

"Baby, you got it!"

"Got what?" I asked.

"The Free Press endorsement!" he replied.

At the sound of this incredible news, I immediately dropped to my knees and started thanking God. As tears streamed down my face, I thought about how far I had come. In the beginning, I didn't know anything about politics, let alone how to run a successful campaign. Before the radio ads, no one outside of the people closest to me even knew my name. In fact, I was told by a detractor, who was eager to get me out of the race, that no one would find my name on the ballot because I had no *name recognition*.

What if I had listened?

How about the time when I signed a bad contract and the other party threatened to make trouble for my campaign if I did not pay?

While in distress, what if I had become completely discouraged and decided to call it quits?

Trust me; there were plenty of times when I wanted to give up, but Erik was always there to encourage me to keep fighting by simply showing up. I'm glad I listened to him instead of the naysayers. Otherwise, I would not have been in the position to receive an endorsement from the Detroit Free Press. Four days later, I would not have also been endorsed by the Detroit News.

Finally, if I had given up and dropped out of the race before either of these endorsements, I would have never received the biggest endorsement of all when 12,511[3] Detroit voters filled in the oval next to my name, "Lisa L. Howze", on the August 2009 primary election ballot!

Yes, you read that correctly! More than 12,500 Detroiters agreed that the ONLY certified public accountant in the race for city council deserved a seat at the table. With their support in a citywide election, I came in 12th place out of 168 candidates. To top it off, I only spent a little over $12,500[4] at that point, which amounted to an average of $1 per vote.

To understand the significance of this, let me put it into perspective for you. During that same race, an incumbent council member defended his seat by spending $3.30[a] per vote and finished in 2nd place. On the other hand, another opposing candidate spent $6.26[a] per vote and finished in 14th place. Therefore, as a first-time candidate who had no prior campaign experience, I pulled off a major feat. In fact, my accomplishment astonished one labor union leader to the point that he kept asking, "How you do dat?! HOW YOU DO DAT?!" He could not believe that in a matter of six months, I went from being an unknown entity to one of the Top 18 vote getters.

---

[a] In the 2009 primary for Detroit City Council, incumbent council member Ken Cockrel, Jr. spent $164,117.32[5] and earned 49,743[3] votes, which amounts to $3.30 per vote, while Frederick Elliott Hall spent $69,452.32[6] and earned 11,088[3] votes, which amounts to $6.26 per vote.

The General Election

By proving myself in the primary, I was in a better position to attract the support I needed to be competitive in the general. To build what I called a four-legged table, I needed more of the following: key endorsements, campaign dollars, voter support, and ways to distinguish myself in a more concentrated field of candidates.

After receiving the endorsement of both major newspapers, other endorsements followed. For example, the Detroit Regional Chamber, which showed interest during the primary but was uncertain if I could pull it off, endorsed me fully for the general, while making a $5,000 contribution to my campaign. Then, there was a progressive political action committee comprised of prominent African American business leaders and political influencers that added me to their slate of candidates whose values and views aligned with their mission.

At a critical time during the campaign, however, the most significant endorsement I received came from a gentleman named Benny Napoleon. Why was this such a big deal? Because Benny Napoleon was that deal! As Detroit's native son, men and women alike loved to be in his presence. Before becoming Wayne County Sheriff, Benny served as chief of the Detroit Police Department, but he gained national and international acclaim when as a deputy chief he led the investigation that helped crack the case that resulted in the conviction of four perpetrators who plotted an attack on U.S. figure skater Nancy Kerrigan during the 1994 Olympic trials held in Detroit. Given his connection to clergy, as the son of a preacher man, his love for labor unions, and passion for people, many revered Benny as the Godfather of Detroit politics.

For this reason, anybody planning to run for office in the city of Detroit knew to go to Benny first to get his blessings.

Erik, who was like a little brother to Benny, knew this as well. After constantly being in his ear for several months about my campaign while out on the golf course, Erik said Benny finally called him one day and said, "Who's your girl? Lisa Howze? Tell her I'm going to get behind her." When Erik called me with this news, he added, "Get ready to go back into the studio! We're going to record a (radio) spot with Benny!" I was completely blown away! The fact that this political icon was willing to lend his name and credibility to me, a newbie in the world of politics, was beyond words. With Benny's support, I went from having zero labor union endorsements to instantly having dozens that I could list on my campaign literature. The phenomenon that was taking shape with support from the papers, business, and now labor, was remarkable.

Fundraising

After the primary, individual donations started to pour into the campaign. For example, I received an unsolicited donation of $1,000 from a complete stranger who attached a note that simply said, "Just win!" Then, there was my single most successful fundraising event that helped me move into a more spacious and visible campaign office. To appreciate its significance, I must share the backstory that unfolded two weeks prior to the primary election when I received a letter in the mail from the President of Walsh College. I thought: *This is strange; it's been five years since I graduated with my master's. Why would the president of Walsh be contacting me?* When I opened the envelope, the handwritten note read as follows:

CHAPTER 10—POLITICS 101: THE CALL, THE RUN, THE RISE

"Dear Lisa,

Congratulations on your run for Detroit City Council! If you are successful in the primary election, my husband says that he will help you.

Sincerely,

Stephanie Bergeron"

Surprised, I had to read the note again. The second time I focused on three keywords: "my", "husband", and "Bergeron." *OH, SH*T! JEFF BERGERON!* Jeff was a partner at Arthur Andersen when I started my career in public accounting. He later became the managing partner for EY's Detroit office when our professional paths crossed again. To have caught his attention during my campaign was huge! Once I advanced to the general election, as promised, he hosted a fundraiser for me in partnership with an attorney who was also influential in the metro Detroit business community. Together, they introduced me to several of their friends and associates who wrote generous checks to support my campaign. It was an amazing night!

Voter Support

Before the term "Influencer" became a normal part of our present-day vernacular, Detroit had passionate voters who regularly dialed into the radio station and used the political talk shows as a platform to share their perspectives and shape opinions on issues that mattered to them as Detroiters. While passing through the crowd at an event hosted by the radio station, someone shouted at me from behind, "Hey! Give me a couple of your yard signs." When I turned around, I was standing face to face with Ms. Edith Johnson, a middle-aged, Black woman whose raspy voice I recognized from the radio. I had become a fan of hers, and apparently, she had become a fan of mine. Ms. Edith was an influencer in Detroit politics, and to have her ask for my yard signs was major. Every opportunity she had to advocate for me on the radio, she did.

Candidate Forums and the Great Debate

Five incumbents and 13 challengers remained in the race, making it easier for voters to see us, hear our campaign messages, and decide which nine would prevail in the November election. Whereas I continued to distinguish myself as "the ONLY" certified public accountant running for Detroit city council, I noticed other candidates began to use "the ONLY" mantra as well. For example, someone said, "I'm the only police officer," or "I'm the only candidate who served as chief of staff" for a previous council president, or "I'm the only businessman who has two hot dog stands in downtown Detroit." Really, he said that! Never mind their vocation, like me, they understood that those two simple words were effective at drawing a distinction. I guess you can say I started something, huh?

When all 18 of us shared the stage at the "Great Debate" hosted by a church on Detroit's northwest side, I had been encouraged by Erik to do one thing: "Win the crowd!" The debate was moderated by three members of the media, representing radio, television, and print. They kicked things off with two softball questions—nothing earth-shattering that would sway voters one way or another. Then, came this question, "If you were going to give the current council a letter grade, what would it be?" Many of the challengers played it safe and said, either a "B" or "C". When one of the incumbent members responded, she said, "I'd give ourselves an A!" I turned my head quickly, like *WHAT! You got to be kidding me! Really?!*

Of course, the next candidate to respond was me. Without hesitation, I said, a "D minus"! I then broke it down: "D" for dysfunctional. A "D minus" for being a distraction. A "D minus" for being disruptive to the progress of the city of Detroit." Turning my attention from the moderators to the live audience, I ended my response with, "And, on November 3rd, you're going to have an opportunity to decide who you wish to discharge from their duties!" The crowd erupted out of their seats! Even the moderators had to pause before proceeding to the next question, while I calmly sat back in my seat, as if nothing had happened.

After the debate, a line formed with people waiting to shake my hand and share their reactions to my performance. One woman said, "Whoa! The accountant really came to life tonight. I didn't know you had it in you. Now, I know. Keep up the great work!" One news station aired a story about the debate during their 10 o'clock broadcast. While there were sound bites from various candidates' responses, they showed my entire response, which was later dubbed as my "D-statement". My camp was proud of me that night, and so was I.

As Election Day drew closer, I had been endorsed once again by the Detroit Free Press and Detroit News. In fact, the Free Press featured my photo, along with those of the eight other endorsed candidates, on the front page of the Local News section, where the headline read, "9 Who Can Make Detroit Work." Can you imagine how that made me feel? Proud. Motivated. Grateful. In essence, the press was telling their readers that I could be trusted to represent the city's 700,000 residents and make decisions in their best interest. To earn that level of confidence meant that I was running an effective campaign and successfully branding myself as a candidate who could add value to the quality of leadership in the city of Detroit.

At the same time, Facebook was giving off some positive vibes when someone posted, "I just saw Lisa Howze's campaign bus on Belle Isle." The 55-passenger chartered bus that cruised around the city's most treasured park had an 8-foot vinyl sign with my photo and campaign message strapped to each side.

The bus belonged to a transportation and private tours company owned and operated by a married couple at my church. I never thought about asking them to use it for my campaign until one evening after a strategy meeting with one of my campaign advisors. When I noticed him going apesh*t crazy about something, I asked, "What's got you so excited?" He pointed in the direction of the bus that was tucked away in a corner of the parking lot and said, "That's your secret weapon right there! All this time, you had 'North Korea' (which was his nickname for the massive machine on wheels) sitting right up under your nose! When we pull up on 'em in that sucker, they're not going to know what hit them!"

He was right. The reaction I received from fellow candidates when they saw my bus pull up at various polling locations on Election Day was priceless. Then, the adrenaline rush! There was nothing like stopping the bus and hurrying to get off so I could greet an excited group of Detroiters we saw that gathered around the city. I absolutely loved it!

However, beneath the surface of the handshakes, hugs, and smiles, I had an uneasy feeling on Election Day. The self-assurance I had going into the August primary was missing. For instance, on the

CHAPTER 10—POLITICS 101: THE CALL, THE RUN, THE RISE

eve of the primary, I felt a sense of calm and went to bed knowing that I had done everything I could do. The rest I left to a power much greater than me. By comparison, on the eve of the November general election, instead of feeling peaceful, I felt anxious.

Why?

I am embarrassed to say that there was division forming in the camp between certain members of the team. Unfortunately, I got caught in the crossfire. Instead of the high-spirited pep talk that you give to volunteers, supporters, and team members on the night before the election, my spirit was a bit weakened under the surface because I could sense the bad energy in the room. Most people would not have noticed, but I knew it.

When did it all begin?

The tension first reared its ugly head right around the time that I received the endorsement from Sheriff Benny Napoleon. As my campaign grew in popularity, some of my earlier supporters felt slighted as newer members moved into critical campaign roles that allowed those individuals to work more closely with me. My philosophy was that if you had access to donors who were willing to write checks, let's get the money. If you knew where the likely voters in the city were, then great, let's go reach them! However, if you wanted to engage in petty squabbles, jockey for position, or be a drag on my personal time, you could miss me with all that mess!

Why?

The grind of running for public office requires a special degree of stamina and focus. I, therefore, could not afford any unnecessary drains on my already depleted energy. As the election came down to the wire, I believe some individuals lost sight of the goal to help me get elected so that I could help put the city I loved on the road to financial recovery.

If that wasn't enough, do you remember the progressive political action committee that included me on their slate of endorsed candidates? Well, I lost their support. Even though no one said to me, "Lisa, you're off our slate!" it became apparent as I visited polls on election day and found that none of the slate's poll workers were handing out my literature. Why did it go down like that? Late in the campaign, I had taken a position on an issue that I was not aware would put me at odds with the PAC's policy agenda. When one of its trusted members approached me about the matter, I made it clear that I was not willing to change my position. Was I taking a risk? Absolutely! However, I'd rather choose principle over politics and personal gain any day. Can you say that about most politicians?

With my values intact, I continued to make my rounds to various polls, while giving Detroiters the best energy I had to offer. With a couple hours to spare before the polls closed at 8 p.m., my campaign bus completed its final route through a southwest Detroit neighborhood before returning me to my car. I had ample time to head downtown to the hotel to get ready for the Election Night Celebration that my team planned for me. When I checked into my suite, Erik was already there setting up the war room to watch the election results come in.

While getting dressed, I could hear the television playing in the background, as the announcer made early predictions about who the top three vote getters would likely be. As the reporting continued, it was not looking or sounding good for the home team. Erik suggested that I wait until the results were final before going downstairs to greet my guests. When it was all said and done, I finished in 10th place and received over 48,000[7] votes, which was two spots better than the primary with nearly four times as many votes. Keep in mind the race started with 168 candidates. Obviously, the team and I had done something right, but it just wasn't enough to claim the final seat on the nine-member council.

The victory speech that I had hoped to give would sound much different since it was confirmed that my run had ended in defeat. As I contemplated what I would say to my supporters, the elevator ride to the first floor seemed to take an eternity. When I finally reached the entrance of the restaurant and saw all the faces of family, friends, classmates, donors, and community supporters, I knew my message needed to be upbeat and positive. As I made my way through the crowd, there were people smiling, cheering, and reaching out to shake my hand. The love I felt from them was incredible. No longer did I feel like I was carrying the weight of the world on my shoulders. Instead, the crowd seemed to be carrying me on theirs, as I floated toward the platform to give my long-awaited speech.

As I adjusted the microphone, I spotted a little girl in the audience who was accompanied by her parents. At not more than eight years old, she had brown, saucer-shaped eyes that danced with excitement as she peered at me. Through her innocence, I saw a reflection of myself at that age and only hoped that my running gave her a glimpse of who she could become. Therefore, with her in mind, I told the folks who crowded into that restaurant to support me that although we came up short, there was no need to hang our heads in disappointment. "What we accomplished in a matter of nine months was nothing short of remarkable," and for that I was grateful.

When I stepped down from the platform, I made a beeline to the exit so I could extend congratulations to other candidates whose victory celebrations were at the same hotel. While in progress, I ran into the TV reporter who covered the "Great Debate" when I gave my illustrious "D-statement". As she shook my hand, she said, "Congratulations on a hard-fought run!" Her words meant a lot because they told me that people, including folks in the media, were paying attention.

When I returned to my room, I'm not going to lie; I was heartbroken. Everything that I had worked so hard for had come to a crashing end. I didn't know how I would move on, so I just curled into a ball on the couch and cried myself to sleep like a baby. It's a good thing no one was around to see my face that I am sure was not pretty. Honestly, I didn't care. I just wanted some relief from the pain that started in my head and then like a rope wrapped tightly around my heart. At some point later in the night, Danielle came back to the room to check on and keep me company. She offered thoughts about what she wished she had done differently. I told her it was no need for both of us to beat ourselves up because no amount of "Monday morning quarterbacking" was going to change the outcome. Her presence was enough to help me get through the night.

The following morning, I was still an emotional wreck. While steeped deeply in my feelings, I was all ready to hang up my campaign shoes and never run again. But then, the phone rang, and on the other end of the line was Sheriff Benny Napoleon. He was calling to suggest that I run for state representative. *Here we go*

CHAPTER 10—POLITICS 101: THE CALL, THE RUN, THE RISE

again! This was the "second call" in my elevation to a place I never imagined going. At first, I refused the offer, while confessing that my political career was over. Little did I know, it was just getting started.

Benny would not take "NO" for an answer and insisted that I run. Sound familiar? Finally, I stopped giving excuses and asked one simple, yet important question: "As a state representative, can I still serve the people of Detroit?" When he replied, "Yes," I said, "Okay, I'm in!" The following Monday, I was a guest on Angelo Henderson's show, where I announced my candidacy for District 2 State Representative. The ONLY certified public accountant was back for another run–this time in a district race!

Was it easier to run in a district race?

Short answer: Yes. Except, right after my announcement, I still was not convinced that politics was for me. First, I doubted myself, then I experienced impostor syndrome. I questioned whether I deserved to take the next step up. I rationalized how I had never been a precinct delegate, neighborhood city hall director, or block club president. Why did that matter to me? I had this ideal in my head that other candidates tended to have held one or more of those positions before even thinking about running for office either at the local or state level. I felt like I was cheating the system. That's when Craig, my new campaign manager, quickly shut me up by saying, "Look, Leese! Your path is not going to be the same as everybody else's. You might as well get used to it. Use this advantage to your advantage and keep it movin'!"

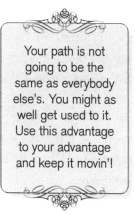
Your path is not going to be the same as everybody else's. You might as well get used to it. Use this advantage to your advantage and keep it movin'!

Craig was right. However, while I was seeking another political office, my creditors were seeking payment for the mountain of bills that had been piling up on my dining room table. The stress of not being able to pay my bills resurfaced once again. But guess what happened next? My phone rang, and on the other end was attorney Terence Thomas who had assisted me during my bid for city council. What started as a call to congratulate me on my decision to run for state representative turned into an invitation to work for his wife and my friend, CPA LaShanda Thomas, who had started a new accounting practice that "could use your help," he said.

During the first three months of 2010, I was able to catch up on my bills and get the strength back in my legs to run another race; thanks to LaShanda and Terence. During that same time, I received another unexpected blessing when someone contacted me about purchasing the web domain names that I reserved via GoDaddy.com in late 2008 for less than 50 bucks. If you recall, my finances were really fragile back then, and I was full of anxiety about what was next for me. Would you believe less than two years later I made more than 600 times my investment when I sold the following: CPABound.com, CPABound.net, and CPABound.org? Of all things, what made me reserve those site names? Well, let's just say that's another story for another time, but I think I said a few chapters earlier that "being a CPA has its advantages." Ha!

As a matter of fact, I continued to use the CPA brand in the nine-way primary race for state representative. Unlike my first campaign, I had name recognition, financial backing, and a comprehensive winning strategy to complement the radio ads that Erik strongly encouraged me to continue to run. As a result, I won the Democratic nomination with 36% of the vote, surpassing

CHAPTER 10—POLITICS 101: THE CALL, THE RUN, THE RISE

the combined votes of the 2nd and 3rd place candidates by two percentage points. My decisive victory set in motion my rise to the state Capitol!

While there were several election night celebrations taking place on the evening of August 3, 2010, the one person I wanted to share my victory with most was my dad. In the middle of the night, I got dressed and drove to the Samaritan Center, where my dad was under residential care. It had to have been 4 o'clock in the morning when I quietly tiptoed into his room. Leaning over his bed, I whispered in his ear to wake him, "Daddy. Daddy." Once he was aware of my presence, I said to him, "Guess what, Daddy? I won!" Immediately, my dad's face lit up like a Christmas tree. While grinning from ear to ear, he proudly said, "I always knew you could do it! Congratulations, doll!" I absolutely loved it when my dad called me "doll" or "darlin'". His affirmation meant EVERYTHING to me! Besides, I was happy to give him one more thing to brag about to his friends: His daughter was now "State Representative-elect Lisa Howze!"

The outcome of the general election in November was a foregone conclusion, as I garnered over 96% of the vote in a decisive win over my Republican opponent. However, what happened to Democrats across the state in 2010 was a whole other issue to be discussed in the next chapter.

Shall we proceed?

CHAPTER 11

LET'S GO HIGHER: MICHIGAN HOUSE OF REPRESENTATIVES

After all my efforts, would you believe I only served one term, or two years, in the Michigan Legislature? Do I have any regrets? Absolutely not. As one of 148 state lawmakers elected in 2010, I am fortunate to have used my time in office to build incredible relationships, work on meaningful legislation, and directly impact the lives of people I was elected to serve. Some highlights to help chronicle my experience include being assigned to the House Education and Insurance policy committees, being named vice chair of the House Democratic Campaign Committee, being recognized by Habitat for Humanity as Michigan's 2011 Public Official of the Year, and finally, having my consumer protection bill signed into law as Public Act 208 of 2012.

Whereas I would have loved to serve my constituents longer, I firmly believe every assignment has an intended expiration date. Clearly, my short time in the legislature was only meant to be a pit stop along the way to my next assignment. If I could offer you a word of caution, be wary of staying in certain places or situations longer than necessary. For some of you that might mean a job, and for others, it is a relationship. Whatever the case, please know that if you become attached to certain roles, positions, or titles, you may not be in position to answer the call that leads to your next opportunity. Because I understand my purpose, I focus my energy on completing my current assignment to then move forward with grace. If you follow my lead, I will teach you to do the same.

Every assignment has an intended expiration date.

First things first, I must admit that when I was elected to state office, I did not come into the Legislature as quietly as one might expect. With encouragement from my confidante Erik and a few other elected members from Detroit, I set my eyes on becoming chair of the Detroit Caucus. During the process, it is safe to say I ruffled a few feathers by challenging a second-term member who thought he was a shoo-in for the post until I upended his plans. Some judged my actions as an ill-conceived, premature power grab. In fact, I heard one of my opponent's supporters saying, "Who does she think she is? She doesn't even know where the bathroom is yet! How the hell is she going to lead the caucus?"

Right, wrong, or indifferent; who's to say? Truth be told, I didn't need everyone's support, let alone approval. To secure the leadership position, I only needed seven out of 12 votes. I reached out to my friend Sheriff Napoleon and asked him to weigh in with members of the caucus, but he declined to get involved. I respected his wishes and then concentrated on getting the votes on my own. I was confident that at least four of the five other newly elected members would be with me. Therefore, my work was cut out for me to persuade at least two incumbent members to join my side,

CHAPTER 11—LET'S GO HIGHER: MICHIGAN HOUSE OF REPRESENTATIVES

as I assured them that I had the other necessary votes. When they pledged to support me, victory was clearly within my grasp.

The official vote for Detroit Caucus Chair was scheduled on the same day as the swearing-in ceremony when everyone would be at the Capitol. Prior to then, we attempted to hold the vote at least two other times in district, but when my opponent saw momentum building in my favor, conveniently one or more of his supporters could not "make it" to the meeting to cast their vote. Without full participation, we could not proceed. However, on this day, it was do or die!

All 12 of us gathered in a conference room in the Capitol, where my opponent and I were expected to make one final appeal to our colleagues before calling the vote. When offered the opportunity to speak first, I declined because I understood the power of having the last word. After my opponent gave his remarks, I reminded my colleagues of how I had secured over 48,000 votes in my recent run for Detroit city council. I closed my case by saying, "If that many residents in the city of Detroit had confidence in me, surely you should as well."

Next, everyone wrote the name of the person they wanted to lead the caucus on a piece of paper and slid it to the center of the table. When the votes were tallied, the result was a 6-6 split decision. I don't know who was more surprised–me, my opponent, or our fellow caucus members. I was more than confident that I had secured the seven necessary votes. "Who flipped?" I wondered. Could it have been the person I invited into my home to discuss the merits of my candidacy and vision for Detroit and the caucus? Surely, it wasn't them. Maybe it was the person who called me on my cellphone as I was arriving at the Capitol the morning of the vote. When asked if I had the votes, I replied, "Yes. But wait! I still have your vote, right?" I needed to confirm because that person sounded like they were ready to switch sides. "I got you!" they assured me. But did they really?

The answer to that question will remain a mystery. However, that entire experience taught me a valuable lesson about integrity in politics. I know; it seems like an oxymoron, right? Well, it doesn't have to be. The principle is simple: once you give someone your word, you keep it. If for some reason you decide to change your mind, it's okay. Just be sure to let the other person know as soon as possible. No one likes surprises because they tend to breed feelings of distrust later. In the end, there was no outright winner for the caucus chair position. Therefore, as he was no longer my opponent, my colleague and I agreed to share the responsibility. In our roles as co-chair of the caucus, he handled internal (Lansing-related) affairs, while I handled external (Detroit-related) affairs. It was a reasonable compromise, but at times still difficult to navigate.

In the grand scheme of things, none of it mattered because one week later my father passed away. When I received the phone call, I was devastated. Although my dad had been sick and unable to care for himself for some years, I always saw him as being strong, invincible, and capable of living forever. It turned out that was not the case. Naturally, I questioned whether I could have done more to be present and make the most of the moments we had. However, as I got more and more absorbed into my new world of politics, time slipped away from me. Nearly four years later, I suffered another heartbreaking loss when Mama Fatty made a tragic transition that accelerated her timeline to join my dad in their final resting place.

CHAPTER 11—LET'S GO HIGHER: MICHIGAN HOUSE OF REPRESENTATIVES

By age 41, I was a parentless child. Losing my mom at age 32 was painful enough. Then, to lose my dad less than six years later was like losing another part of myself. He and I always talked about him someday walking me down the aisle at my wedding. I hated the idea that someday would never come. Not to mention how he would not get to see me accomplish so many other things in life as well. Nevertheless, on the fateful day of his homegoing service, I was proud and grateful to stand before the congregation and declare who my dad was to and for me. Heroes never die; their spirits continue to live forever. Without a doubt, all my dad's life lessons and wisdom continue to live on within me to this day.

When I returned to Lansing on the Tuesday following my dad's services, I was still in a somber mood. However, during the Democratic Caucus meeting that was held prior to the start of session, I was quickly reminded of some sobering facts: Democrats got our a**es handed to us in the 2010 general election! What do I mean? For one, where I served in the state House, Republicans outnumbered Democrats, 63-47. By and large, Republicans had seized control of every branch of state government, including the governor's office, the upper chamber of the state Legislature, and the courts. Moreover, the state attorney general and secretary of state offices were also won by the GOP.

With control of the gavel, Republicans made all the rules, set the legislative agenda, and had the authority to decide how the legislative maps would be drawn during redistricting–a process that takes place every 10 years. As Democrats, we had our work cut out for us. In fact, it felt like the "D" in Democrats stood for "defense" because we were constantly on our heels. With an onslaught of "bad" public policy to front load the legislative calendar, sometimes our only and best defense was to challenge

Republicans on the House Rules. Unfortunately, it was not enough to stop or even slow down the most egregious piece of public policy that was introduced, passed, and signed into law in less than 40 days.

Which bill was it and why was it so bad?

I'm talking about the emergency manager legislation that was originally introduced as House Bill 4214 of 2011. It was egregious because it threatened the sanctity of what it meant to have a representative democracy. For example, it allowed the governor to appoint and empower one person who had not been elected by the people to make decisions that impacted their lives, thus making the votes of hundreds of thousands of people in mostly urban cities and struggling school districts across the state null and void. At the same time, the powers normally granted to duly elected mayors and members of city councils were reduced to rubble with one stroke of the governor's pen. Likewise, school districts like Detroit Public Schools, which already had an emergency financial manager for more than a decade, could further see elected board members vacated of their responsibilities as well. In these elected leaders' place, a state-appointed emergency manager would have unilateral authority to sever labor contracts, sell municipal or school district assets, dismantle pension plans, and hire an unlimited number of consultants, all in the name of fiscal management.

To truly understand the severity of this legislation, just do a Google search on "Flint Water Crisis." With wide media attention, the world witnessed second-hand the devastation that happened on the ground in Flint, Michigan, where tens of thousands of residents were exposed to dangerous levels of lead and lives were disrupted because of a single decision made under Emergency Management to change the source of their drinking water. Poor men, women, and children who suffered from lead poisoning, legionnaires disease, and even death paid a hell of a price for what was supposed to create cost savings.[8, 9]

Before it ever reached this degree of devastation, I stood up to fight against the legislation. "The Speaker recognizes Representative Howze," said the gentleman standing behind the rostrum, as I prepared to give my first official speech from the floor of the Michigan House of Representatives. "Mr. Speaker, I rise to speak in opposition to House Bill 4214." As I presented my argument for why the bill should not pass, I asked members who were planning to support the legislation to reconsider their vote. Unfortunately, their minds were already made up, and the bill passed with 63 Republicans voting "Yes," and 47 Democrats voting "No."

When Session adjourned that day, I was in the process of walking out of the chamber when the speaker pro tem tracked me down and said, "Representative! Even though you did not win the argument, you made a good case." From his comment, I learned that there was a space for my public speaking skills in the legislature. In addition, I discovered that although he and I did not see eye-to-eye on the emergency management legislation and several other issues that followed, the door had at least been opened to develop a relationship with someone on the other side of the aisle. It didn't hurt that he was part of leadership, too.

As summer approached, I had barely gotten my seat warm before there was talk about running for re-election. Mentally, I was not ready to give it any serious thought. However, the redistricting process had a way of forcing the issue. During that time, the environment in Lansing was tense. With Republicans in control of drawing the new district lines, the Democratic Caucus was on edge about our chances of winning back enough competitive seats to regain control of the House majority. Meanwhile, Detroit members were preparing to lose two seats in the House given the city's population loss per the 2010 Census. Instead of having 12 House districts represented by a member from Detroit, there would only be 10. As such, the stage was being set for three awful MMA-style matchups in which Detroit members would be forced to run against each other in the 2012 primary.

At first, the maps that I viewed with Republican leadership did not show any signs of my seat being negatively impacted. However, in a strange plot twist, I ended up being drawn into a 3-way race with two other incumbents. What?! How in the heck did that happen? To add insult to injury, a portion of my original district was included as part of a newly drawn open seat where the boundary began only two blocks east of my home. TWO BLOCKS! I don't know about you, but it was blatantly obvious to me that someone did not want me to return to Lansing for a second term. Who could that have been? Think about it. Now answer me this: Who would have benefited most from the lines not being adjusted by two frickin' blocks to allow me to run in the open district? In response, all I can say is, "Payback is a MUTHA!"

Nevertheless, people wanted to know, "What is Rep. Howze going to do?" As it turned out, I had three available choices: 1) Take my chances and run in a 3-way race against fellow colleagues; 2) move into the open district to establish residency and then run, or 3) sit out the 2012 election cycle altogether and wait to run for the Detroit City Council District 3 seat in 2013. In weighing these options, I did not like Option 1 because I was not interested in tearing down my colleagues to advantage myself or vice versa. Although, in hindsight, I probably would have won that race.

CHAPTER 11—LET'S GO HIGHER: MICHIGAN HOUSE OF REPRESENTATIVES

Even though Option 2 had been suggested by some seasoned politicians as a possible solution to my dilemma, it was out of the question for me. I did not want to do anything that I felt was in direct violation of my integrity and personal code of ethics. No matter what they said, the last thing I wanted was a news reporter sticking a camera and microphone in my face, asking, "Representative Howze, where exactly do you live? I see your name on the lease for this new apartment, but our records show that you still own the property at…" Yeah, nah, I did not want to be THAT politician! Sorry!

Option 3 was not a bad idea, but I was not looking to go backwards. I only wanted to move forward.

What else could I do?

For seven whole months between July 2011 and January 2012, I kept my powder dry and did not let a soul know what my plans were—including my own chief of staff, unfortunately. While it appeared I only had three options, there was a fourth option that no one saw coming, except for Erik, of course. Together, we knew the element of surprise would completely catch people off guard. As such, on February 2, 2012, I scheduled an appearance on the popular Local Fox 2 Detroit TV talk show called Let It Rip where I announced my candidacy for Mayor of Detroit. Shut the front door!

After my announcement, more than a dozen local and national news outlets ran the story, including the Huffington Post, Associated Press, and MLive, to name a few. Afterwards, I held one fundraiser for my mayoral campaign in Lansing to capture some early support. I quickly learned how much more difficult it was for me as a sitting representative to raise money because people knew for certain what my intentions were. In addition, many did not want to fully commit to my mayoral campaign because it was just too early, and no one knew for certain who else would throw their names in the ring. For this reason, people outside of my inner circle argued that my announcement to run for mayor came too soon. Had it been anyone else, they would have filed to run for their current position as a state representative. If successful, they would then turn around and put their name on the ballot for the other position, in this case, mayor. There were some politicians who took this path of least resistance where there was minimal risk. If they lost the mayoral bid, they always had their state representative seat to fall back on. I did not choose to follow the ways of a typical politician. I was determined to be different and demonstrate my commitment to the voters of Detroit. My motto is, "You either get all of me or none of me!" Bottom line!

By April 2012, rumors started to spread about a certain CEO of a Detroit hospital system planning to also run for mayor. Speculation grew when this person moved with his family from a nearby suburb to an affluent neighborhood on the westside of Detroit. Although he denied it, when first asked by members of the Detroit media, anyone with half a brain could see what was about to happen. While feeling like he was disturbing my apple cart, I recall meeting him at a Meet & Greet that he hosted at the hospital when I was a candidate for city council three years earlier. By all accounts, this was one powerful man who previously served as Wayne County Prosecutor and a deputy county executive. Without question, he carried a lot of clout. However, I did not let any of that faze me. In fact, when one of my colleagues said, "Lisa, you know Mike Duggan is running, right?" With all due respect, but "F*** HIM!"

Let that sink in for a second. {*Mm-hmm. Yup!*}

Why did I take that attitude?

Believe it or not, my response was less about Mike Duggan and more about the mindset of my colleague. Let me explain through a movie illustration. I don't know if you ever saw the movie "The Great Debaters" starring actors Denzel Washington and Forest Whitaker. There is a scene in which Denzel Washington's character, Mr. Tolson, has his debate team sitting in canoes in the middle of a lake. He then engages their minds through a series of questions. I loved their responses! Here's an excerpt of their exchange:

> *Mr. Tolson:* Who's the judge?
>
> *Team:* The judge is God.
>
> *Mr. Tolson:* Why is He God?
>
> *Team*: Because He decides who wins or loses, not my opponent.
>
> *Mr. Tolson*: Who's your opponent?
>
> *Team*: He doesn't exist.
>
> *Mr. Tolson*: Why does he not exist?
>
> *Team*: Because he is merely a dissenting voice to the truth I speak.

The dissenting voice that these young people referred to in the movie is equivalent to the negative voice that exists in our own heads. Its job is to point out our perceived limitations, present obstacles as being insurmountable and larger than life, to then paralyze us with fear. If we were in the same space right now, I'd tell you to holler back at me if you know I'm telling the truth! When this voice starts to whisper in your ear, don't weaken under the weight of its words. Instead, acknowledge and dismiss it at the same time by saying, "I hear you, but I'm not listening to you today! Now, go somewhere and sit down!"

As far as I was concerned, I did not have any opponents, whether real or perceived, whether present or anticipated. Frankly, the only person who could defeat me was me.

> As far as I was concerned, I did not have any opponents, whether real or perceived, whether present or anticipated. Frankly, the only person who could defeat me was me.

As the legislative year neared a close, I remained the only declared candidate running for mayor of Detroit in the 2013 election. As for Mr. Mike Duggan: Well, he was busy waiting out the clock on the one-year residency requirement to qualify as an eligible candidate.

If I were to assign a theme to the farewell speech that I gave as I prepared to leave the Michigan House of Representatives, it would be, "Effect change where you are for as long as you are." Although my heart was set on becoming Detroit's next mayor, fortunately, I did not have to wait that long to do something major for my city. In fact, it was during the 2012 Lame Duck session that I voted to support three pieces of legislation that were extremely important to the city of Detroit and various local, regional, and national stakeholders. Thanks to my courage to choose policy over politics, Detroit and Detroiters became the beneficiaries of 65,000 new streetlights in the city, a mini transit system called the QLINE that, in its development, served as a catalyst to bring billions of dollars in additional investment, and a billion-dollar commercial, retail, and residential development deal that generated several thousand construction-related jobs. Today, District Detroit is home to Little Caesars Arena where the Detroit Red Wings and Detroit Pistons play.

At one point during my speech, I reminded my colleagues that "These seats do not belong to us. They belong to the voters of the state of Michigan who send each of us here to represent their interests and not our own." By carrying that conviction, it made it easy for me to accept the fact that it was time for me to move on. I completed my assignment, and as someone once told me: "No matter what, you will always and forever be 'The Honorable Lisa Howze.' Your name has a permanent place in the annals of the State of Michigan's history books."

I know my mom and dad would have been proud of me!

CHAPTER 12

LET'S GO EVEN HIGHER: DETROIT MAYORAL RUN

Fifty thousand dollars ($50,000) for a Super Bowl ad! Was it worth the investment or wasteful spending? It depends on who you ask. Before I spill the tea on how I became the first mayoral candidate in Detroit history to have a commercial run during the Super Bowl, let's take a moment to talk about a pattern of behavior and the resulting trend you may have noticed throughout my story thus far. In case you missed it, I have never been afraid to invest in myself.

I have never been afraid to invest in myself.

From the origins of me becoming "The Candy Girl" in high school with a $13 investment in M&Ms, to the college student who invested $100 in an Amway distributorship, to the entrepreneur who walked away from a good-paying job with great benefits to then invest thousands of dollars in personal development, to finally the budding politician whose first $100 investment in political radio ads reached thousands of voters in the race for Detroit city council, I have always believed that, no matter how little or great the sacrifice, my reward would be even greater. As a result, I have been blessed to experience consistent career elevation and advancement. For instance, your girl went from being a student at the "Big House" to serving in the state House. Therefore, based on what I know today, if you were to ask me if the $50,000 Super Bowl ad was worth it, you better believe my answer would be YES! However, if you asked whether we maximized the potential of the ad, sadly, I'd have to say, no.

I have always believed that, no matter how little or great the sacrifice, my reward would be even greater.

Keep reading and you will understand why.

When we released information to the media about the ad, every major news outlet reported on it. Facebook followers were in a frenzy, as supporters and detractors alike offered their opinions. Some foolishly believed I spent "a million dollars" on the ad, while others speculated on where the money came from to afford it. When the TV network aired my commercial right after Beyonce's performance during the Super Bowl XLVII Halftime Show, I could not have asked for a better placement, which made the ad priceless.

According to one news source, "The ad reached an estimated 400,000 people—or more than half of the city's population." If you do the math, the cost per viewer was only 12 ½ cents. The writer continued by stating, "But the value went well beyond a 30-second TV clip: Howze reminded the media that the mayoral race is about more than Duggan and Napoleon, both of whom have generated a disproportionate amount of attention. She showed that she can raise money with the big boys."

CHAPTER 12—LET'S GO EVEN HIGHER: DETROIT MAYORAL RUN

Wait! Duggan and Napoleon? Yes! Based on my earlier characterization of these two gentlemen, I had to do what some may call extreme to get noticed, even though, neither of them had officially declared their candidacy. However, that did not stop the media from keeping their names in the headlines. How else were they going to sell newspapers?

It all began when Mike Duggan moved from the suburbs into Detroit's historic Palmer Woods neighborhood where many of the city's wealthiest professionals lived. Immediately, local newspapers and national media blogs made it a story and started to fan the flame of racial tension in the city by asking, "Is Detroit ready for a white mayor?" The provocative headline suggested that if Detroiters elected Mike Duggan, it would put an end to 40 years of Black leadership that began when Coleman A. Young, a Tuskegee airman and former state legislator, became Detroit's first Black mayor in 1973.

The Black male-dominated clergy in Detroit were not going to sit by and let that happen. So, they along with several labor union leaders rallied their support behind Detroit's native son Benny Napoleon, who they figured would give Duggan the biggest run for his money, should he decide to run. Besides, what did he have to lose? Nothing really, considering he had just been re-elected in the previous year to a four-year term as Wayne County Sheriff.

No matter what they did, I had no plans of backing down–not even for my friend Benny. Can you blame me? Think about it. In the same year that Benny ran for re-election, I chose not to. Rather than doing what was safe and convenient, I was willing to make a sacrifice, when in hindsight, I likely would have won against the other two incumbents in the 2012 District 3 race for state representative. At the time, however, I was more interested in demonstrating my commitment to the citizens of Detroit versus hanging on to my paycheck and elected status. Therefore, when I ran the Super Bowl ad, my goal was to send a strong message to everyone, including my would-be opponents, that I was in it to win it!

Sounds great, but where did things go wrong?

There was nothing wrong with the ad itself. With the theme, "Better for Detroit," my message was, "Detroit cannot get better until life gets better for the residents who live here." Timeless, right? So, what was the problem? Once the ad aired, the campaign failed to make the most of the ad while public interest was at its peak. For instance, when people on social media shared their excitement about the ad, there was no call to action. The world truly was our oyster, and we could have easily capitalized on people's enthusiasm by directing them to my campaign website to make a donation. However, I was advised to not ask for contributions because it would "make it seem like we needed the money." Well, duh! We DID NEED the money to run more ads among other things. In fact, in our initial press release, we committed to run the ad for the entire week following the Super Bowl. Unfortunately, it did not happen. Although the additional investment would have been a fraction of what we paid for the one-time ad, we simply didn't have enough money to make it work.

Money alone was not the problem either. As you know, I never let the lack of money be an excuse to not get results. In this case, it would have cost us nothing to get me out in the community the following week when my name and facial recognition would have been at an all-time high. We could have visited a series of churches,

CHAPTER 12—LET'S GO EVEN HIGHER: DETROIT MAYORAL RUN

beauty and barber salons, and diners to engage with hardworking people across the city. Can you imagine all the photos we could have taken with people holding a football with my name and campaign slogan, "Better for Detroit," printed on it to commemorate the commercial? These same photos could have been posted on social media and used in campaign literature. Unfortunately, we were not organized enough to get those things done either. As the old adage goes, "The fortune is in the follow-through." As a campaign, we made it onto the field, but instead of making a touchdown, we got to the one-yard line and fumbled the damn ball! Sheesh!

You don't have to admit it out loud, but has that ever happened to you, either literally or figuratively speaking? If not, let this example be a lesson to you to plan and execute your play all the way through to completion.

Although Erik and I knew we dropped the ball big time, no one outside the camp was any wiser. They assumed the campaign was flush with cash. Unfortunately, we could only hold that perception for so long. Pretty soon, the fanfare fizzled, people who were attracted to my campaign came and left, and the media went back to covering the "Duggan and Napoleon Show". I could imagine a reporter saying, "Uh, let's keep it moving, Bob. There's nothing to see here!"

The race did not begin to see more balanced coverage in reporting until three months later when nationally syndicated columnist Rochelle Riley wrote a feature story about me in the Detroit Free Press, entitled, "Lisa Howze is unbowed by obstacles to becoming mayor." Although I didn't have a well-oiled political machine or a six- or seven-figure war chest to finance a sophisticated campaign, like my opponents, I refused to let that stop me. As a female candidate in a male-dominated field, I had something those guys did not have: my story.

As much as I talked about the finances of the city, I also spoke about the future of our children. Who would they look up to? Who would help them believe that anything was possible? As I focused on appealing to women and heads of households who were responsible for raising these children, I was excited to see Ms. Riley write about my entrepreneurial endeavors as a youth and teenager. How many kids do you know that either sold candy in high school or had a lemonade stand in front of their homes? From the moment I was exposed to entrepreneurship, it changed my reality forever. As a female candidate for mayor who was unbowed and unbothered by the giants in the race, I wanted to help Detroiters change their reality as well. Therefore, when Ms. Riley's article was shared with readers both near and far, she was helping to spread a message of hope and possibility, which in essence, represented the story that was going untold.

When the story ran, it ignited a fire in me that I was prepared to put on full display during the mayoral "Great Debate" in Mackinac the following week. If there was one place where I thrived the most, it was on the debate stage. I could always rely on my public speaking skills to effectively articulate the issues, make my case, and give Detroiters a reason to vote for me. When compared to my opponents in debate settings, I was as fierce as they come. Just ask Mike Duggan.

For instance, at an earlier candidates forum hosted by the city's largest municipal labor union, one of the questions related to privatization, which is always a major concern for represented employees. After hearing the "happy talk" coming from Duggan

CHAPTER 12—LET'S GO EVEN HIGHER: DETROIT MAYORAL RUN

at the far end of the panel, I looked to the candidates who were seated to my immediate left and right and asked, "Which one of you is going to take him, or do you want me to take him?" When I realized that neither was willing to man up, I took it upon myself to say what needed to be said. As such, I used the privatization question as an opportunity to define my opponent. Guns blazing, I started with, "Let. Me. Tell you. About. Mike. Duggan!"

Anytime you hear someone begin their response in that manner, look out! Based on my opposition research of him, my goal was to poke holes in whatever he said about being a "Turnaround Guy", expose his weaknesses, and demonstrate that he was not infallible as the television commercials made him appear. While I could not see his reaction to my statements, the priceless expressions on the faces of his supporters who were in the audience told me everything I needed to know.

Shortly after the forum ended, someone from Napoleon's camp ran up to me in the most animated way possible and said, "Damnnn, Lisa! Put your weapons away! Don't hurt nobody!" Finally, there was a young lady who lingered near the platform to have a word with me. While wearing a Duggan 4 Detroit t-shirt, she said, "Wow! I wish I had known about your campaign earlier; I'd be with you."

Was she experiencing buyer's remorse? Were there other voters like her who wanted to switch sides after seeing and hearing me speak? What would happen if more Detroit voters had an opportunity to hear my message and see me side-by-side with the two candidates who were favored in the media?

The Great Debate of the 2013 Detroit Mayoral Election on Mackinac Island provided the perfect opportunity for voters at home in Detroit to take a closer look at my candidacy, as they watched the live streamed coverage. In the live audience at the Grand Hotel were business leaders, state and local lawmakers, members of the media, and a host of other interested parties, who each paid $200 for a separate ticket to witness the action up close and in person. By the time everyone was positioned on stage, it was apparent that I was the only female candidate seated among five men, including fellow candidates Mike Duggan, Benny Napoleon, and Fred Durhal, Jr., along with moderators Stephen Henderson and Nolan Finley from the Detroit Free Press and Detroit News, respectively.

Was I uncomfortable?

Not at all. Having grown up with four older brothers, I was used to standing out like a rose among thorns. Just kidding, bros! Seriously though, it would have been extremely awkward if I had to sit on a bar stool, as originally planned, while wearing a skirt with my legs fully exposed and nowhere to comfortably place my feet. My team strongly urged the organizers to change the seating to the plusher leather armchairs. Here's a question: Should I have adapted to the situation and changed into pants instead? Unequivocally, the answer is no. How many times are women forced to adjust to a system that was never designed with us in mind? To some it may seem trivial, but I exercised my voice in that situation. Besides, like I told one of the organizers who happened to be a woman, "I did not pack any pants in my suitcase!"

With legs crossed at my ankles, I was all girl on that stage, but by no means did I hit like a girl. When Nolan Finley kicked off the debate with, "These folks paid for a good scrap. No rules!" he didn't have to tell me twice. I came prepared to be a thorn in

CHAPTER 12—LET'S GO EVEN HIGHER: DETROIT MAYORAL RUN

Mike Duggan's side, picking up where I left off at the candidates' forum. While referencing all the high-profile positions that he had vacated, I asked him if things ever got "hot" at the City of Detroit, "Can Detroiters trust you to stick and stay?" Judging by the visible redness on his face, he did not care for how I positioned my question. Oh, well; my bad! Then, to keep things spicy, I didn't let Benny Napoleon walk away from the debate unscathed. I took a jab at him, too, when I brought up the number of appointees he had on payroll in the Sheriff's department. In return, he hit me back with a great one-liner when he said, "Lisa Howze is always talking about being an accountant, but she can't count!" I admit that stung a bit, but it was a good one.

Beyond that, what more could either of them do or say? Not much. I had a solid platform and neither one of them could come close to debating me on the numbers. In fact, they both agreed with my assessment of the city's finances, as we were all trying to stave off a state-appointed emergency manager.

Once I returned home to Detroit, I was told that my approach during the debate may have been "too aggressive" for certain people's taste, and I should perhaps "soften my appeal." In other words, "act like a lady," I suppose. Here's what I discovered: no matter what you do or say, somebody is not going to be happy. Rather than change my style to appease a few, I preferred to be true to myself and the people I hoped to serve. Evidently, my unabashed willingness to speak truth to power resonated with Detroit voters. Based on a poll taken after the debate, I had improved my standing in the race by nine points.

Where do you think those projected votes came from? The frontrunners no doubt. Therefore, to answer an earlier question, with more exposure, I was bound to win more support. Do you think my opponents understood that as well? Of course, they did. Now, tell me. If you were in their position, would you have wanted to share the debate stage and continue to lose votes to someone who was building momentum? Of course, not.

After a short while, it did not matter because in a span of 17 days, the entire mayoral race was in upheaval. No one felt the effects more than Mike Duggan and his campaign committee. It all began after the May 14 filing deadline when perennial mayoral candidate, let's call him Allen Burrough, challenged the legitimacy of Duggan's candidacy based on language in Detroit's new city charter that questioned whether Duggan met the one-year residency requirement to run for mayor. Therefore, while it appeared there were only five men on stage with me in Mackinac, really there were six. Allen Burrough was the invisible sixth man who, instead of exchanging words in a heated debate, chose to take his fight to the courts to get Duggan kicked off the ballot altogether.

On June 11, which was less than two weeks after the debate in Mackinac, a Wayne County Circuit Court judge ruled that Duggan's name should be removed from the August 6 primary ballot. Then, a week later, the Court of Appeals confirmed that the lower court's ruling would stand. As a result, Duggan, who was guilty of filing his nominating petitions two weeks too soon, held a press conference the day after the ruling and officially withdrew his name from contention. In an interview, he stated, "I just don't think there's a viable path forward for winning."

What a relief! Maybe now, Black folks in Detroit don't have to wake up to another tired news headline, asking if we were ready for a white mayor, as if it were a foregone conclusion!

CHAPTER 12—LET'S GO EVEN HIGHER: DETROIT MAYORAL RUN

With Duggan out the race, Benny Napoleon had a comfortable lead in first place. At the same time, the conversation started to shift in my favor. For good reason, political commentators and analysts started to include my name in their discussions about the mayor's race. According to a poll conducted by Main Street Strategies, I was polling in second place with 15% of the vote. Think about that for a moment. SECOND PLACE! For a hot minute, the race was starting to look like a Napoleon-Howze match-up for the November election. Did the Super Bowl ad from four months earlier help to put me in this position? Or was it the fact that I had presented myself as the "next best option" to help lead the city out of its financial crisis? Whatever the case, I enjoyed the attention and growing interest in my campaign.

Therefore, as my standing increased in the polls, my ability to raise funds became easier. Certain businessmen, who otherwise would not have given me the time of day, were happy to pull out their checkbooks and support my campaign. For example and without blinking an eye, a commercial real estate developer used his American Express black card to make a $1,000 contribution to my campaign. Here's the deal guys: it was not a hard sale! In an election in which the city was under emergency management due to a financial crisis, who would you have supported? Would it have been the career cop who was skilled at fighting crime or the financial expert who understood money and how to leverage it? I'll wait. No, seriously, let's face it. My candidacy just made a whole lot of sense!

What did not make sense, however, was my failure to tie up a loose end as soon as I learned of it. Lisa, what do you mean? When Mike Duggan ended his campaign after being kicked off the ballot, I was advised to meet with him and ask for his endorsement. If he agreed to endorse me, then guess what? His supporters would have no doubt become my supporters.

If it were that simple, why did I not do it? Was it pure naiveté or did I let my pride get in the way? If only I had done as they advised, just maybe I could have prevented what happened next. After receiving a lot of encouragement from his campaign committee, Mike Duggan decided to reenter the race as a write-in candidate, only nine days after his withdrawal. WTF! Just like that, my fifteen minutes of fame fizzled to an unexpected end! I had no choice but to chalk it up as a missed opportunity and lesson learned.

Mike Duggan clearly was the type of person you did not want to underestimate. As he returned to the campaign trail, so did the cloud of attention, both negative and positive. Candidates like Allen Burrough, who was responsible for getting Duggan kicked off the ballot in the first place, continued to hurl flagrant attacks against this man who proved to be unflappable. It was like the more dirt you tried to throw on him, Duggan would just shake it off and keep stepping up and showing up. What was the reward for his resilience? Well, the news media continued to do what they had done best by heaping praise on him for reviving what many of us thought was a dead campaign. However, I reached a point where I could not afford to give him any more attention than he deserved. Instead, I needed to direct my focus on what was happening in my own camp.

Financially, we were struggling. To keep my campaign alive, we needed a significant influx of cash, and we needed it fast! With Duggan back in the race, all the support I had from business leaders went up in smoke. What other options did I have? I was at a crossroads in my political future, and I realized no one was coming

CHAPTER 12—LET'S GO EVEN HIGHER: DETROIT MAYORAL RUN

to rescue me. After much thought and prayer, I decided to pull the funds from my retirement account. Yeah, I know! It probably was not the ideal place to get the money, but again I was willing to do whatever was necessary to stay in the race and be competitive. Too much was at stake to back down this far into the race, especially with the investments already made. As the saying goes, "In for a penny, in for a pound!".

If only I could get members of the team to understand my sacrifice. Prior to meeting with them, Erik was the only person I told about using my retirement funds to support the campaign. I also shared with him my frustrations about how certain members of the team were not pulling their weight. During the meeting, some of them had the nerve to criticize me, saying, "Well, Lisa, on the campaign trail, you need to stop doing this or start doing that!" Why did they fix their lips to utter such nonsense? They must not have known I was in no mood to hear their bullsh*t critiques that were interrupted by a tirade of F-bombs from me.

WARNING: If your eyes are too sensitive to read the next part of the story, I suggest you skip ahead to the following paragraph. However, for those of you who don't mind if I keep it real, here's what I said: "We are five f***in' weeks out from the primary! This campaign has been running on fumes! I've asked some of you to do simple things like organize literature drops in the buildings where you live, and you can't seem to manage that! And, today, you want to tell me what the f*** I'm doing and not doing! I just dropped a sh*tload of money into this campaign from my retirement account! That's what the f*** I'm doin'! How much have any of you given?"

I was heated! It took Erik to calm me down before I truly exploded, and no one wanted to see that side of me. So, they just sat there shocked into silence. I hate that I had to go there, but sometimes a well-placed F-bomb is necessary to communicate your point and get results. After all, we had a campaign to run and a race to win. In those final weeks, team members made an earnest effort to step their game up. As Erik often said, "Playtime is over!"

With only two weeks remaining until the primary Election Day, we ran another television ad that featured Ms. Edith Johnson, Detroit's political influencer that you met in Chapter 10 during my city council run. In addition, we had my all-time favorite little Miss Leah Jeffries, who had a key role in the Fox television show, "Empire." Before she became famous, she first captured my heart when she was in my commercial for the Super Bowl. The only difference was this ad cost considerably less. However, its significance rested in the imagery and copy that we chose. For example, as the voiceover from the announcer says, "There have been many African American women who…" we included flashes of iconic women like Coretta Scott King, Shirley Chisholm, and Rosa Parks. These women come from a long line of ancestors upon whose shoulders I stood and continue to stand. If I could harness a fraction of the strength, courage, and fierce determination that each of them embodied, I would count it an honor. The ad closed with me being surrounded by a community of neighbors, as I humbly asked Detroiters for their vote.

This television ad was perfectly timed and served as a great segue into the final debate of the campaign, which happened to be hosted in the presence of a live hometown audience at the beautiful Charles H. Wright Museum of African American History. With all thirteen mayoral candidates participating, we were told that we had been assigned to one of three panels based on a random drawing. "Random, huh?" I had my doubts. Okay, you tell me. How random was it that the same three candidates—Duggan, Napoleon, and Durhal, Jr.—who shared the debate stage with me in Mackinac were all part of the same panel at this debate? Then, get this. Why didn't Allen Burrough, or anyone else for that matter, serendipitously round out that panel instead of another female candidate who just so happened to enter the race as I was preparing to launch my Super Bowl ad? If you ask me, none of this sh*t was by coincidence. And, if I told you once, I'll tell you again: "Lisa Howze" was not on that panel because they did not want this smoke!

To make matters worse, there was a problem with the sound system that only seemed to impact me. For instance, whenever it was my turn to respond to a question, the microphone would cut in and out, making it difficult to hear or understand me. As a result, the moderators were dumbfounded, I was disappointed, and the viewers at home were demanding fairness. In fact, some of them took to Facebook to express their frustrations and stated, "Lisa's mic keeps going out. You see…they really don't want to hear the truth!" If we're being totally honest or keeping it 100, it was too close to the August 6 primary for those who were considered frontrunners to risk ceding any more votes to me. Therefore, with all the "randomness" that took place that evening at the Museum, none of it was by accident but very much by design.

PRIMARY ELECTION DAY

This was it. The long-awaited primary Election Day had finally come! After voting at my own precinct, my driver took me across town to the Northwest Activities Center, which is a premium polling site in Detroit with multiple precincts and high voter participation. When we arrived, what I saw was enough to make me want to cry, "Game over! Let's just go home!" The only problem was the day was just starting. What did I see? Mike Duggan's write-in campaign had poll workers with sandwich board signs strapped to their bodies, instructing folks on how to write in his name on the ballot and fill-in the oval next to it. These frickin' signs were huge! They had to measure at least 3' x 2' and were printed in full color for everyone to see. I could not believe my eyes!

Curious to learn more, I approached one of the poll workers who then told me that he was not a "true" Duggan supporter but agreed to wear the sign and work the poll since Mike's camp was paying him and others $100 for the day. If you know anything about campaigns in Detroit, $100 is premium pay for a full day at the polls. What did I surmise from all this? First of all, Mike Duggan was not playing! This man was in it to win it, and he was not leaving anything to chance. Second, he had lots of money flowing through his campaign to afford this scale of an election day operation. Finally, it was clear that people can and will work for money without being committed to the candidate or cause. Can you blame them?

I was in no position to judge those people for how they chose to put food on their tables. I just needed to get the hell away from there because the whole scene was robbing me of my zeal to finish the race strong. Therefore, when my new driver pulled up in a chocolate brown Lincoln Town Car with the butter cream-colored leather seats, I had no idea that I was in store for the ride of my life.

The woman behind the wheel had features like a Nubian goddess from Africa, whose mocha-colored skin glistened in the sunlight and created the perfect contrast to the beautiful, bouncy curls of white hair that covered her crown. At least 70 years or more young, this woman had a lead foot like you wouldn't believe! If it normally

CHAPTER 12—LET'S GO EVEN HIGHER: DETROIT MAYORAL RUN

took 25 minutes to get from one end of town to the other, she did it in half the time with me laughing all the way. Not only did she make moves through traffic, but she effectively put a bright spot in my otherwise dreary day! Who was this amazing woman? She was none other than Mrs. E. Moore, whom we affectionately called "Obama-Mama" because of her connection to the White House and passionate support of our nation's 44th president.

At the end of the night, I knew I had given my best effort but did not feel confident about the outcome. Sure enough, Duggan and Napoleon finished in the first and second spots, respectively, which I expected. However, I was more surprised that I had dropped to the fourth-place[10] position behind the other female candidate who must have gained an advantage during the final debate of the campaign when she was paired with Duggan, Napoleon, and Durhal, Jr.–the same bunch that I faced in Mackinac. Nevertheless, I earned approximately 5%[10] of all votes cast.

When I gave my concession speech this time, I reminded my supporters again that we had no reason to hang our heads. We gave it our best shot, and I certainly appreciated everything that everyone had done to get me as far as I had gotten. Sound familiar? My message was consistent with the one I shared after my loss for city council. I am a firm believer that you should never allow your circumstances to change who you are. Therefore, in pure Lisa fashion, I closed with a line that said, "This is not the end of me!" In other words, I may be down, but you should never count me out. As far as I was concerned, the loss was merely a temporary bump in the road. After I finished speaking, we cranked up the music and danced to the Wobble song: "Get in there! Yeah, yeah!"

After leaving the party, I checked in to a nearby hotel that the team reserved for me. I spent the night in quiet reflection.

THE THIRD CALL

The following morning, before checking out of the hotel and after posting a positive affirmation on Facebook, I received a phone call. The person on the other end of the line clearly took me by surprise. When he uttered the words, "Hi Lisa, this is Mike Duggan," I could not believe my ears. He continued, "I wanted to call and congratulate you on a well-run campaign. I'd also like to sit down and talk to you about supporting my candidacy." At that moment, I pulled the phone away from my ear, looked at it, and thought to myself, *Man, don't you remember all the bad things I said about you? Are you sure you are asking the right person?* Returning to the phone, I asked if I could get back to him shortly. He agreed.

I immediately hung up the phone and called Erik. I said to him, "You're not going to believe who just called me!"

"Who?" he asked.

"Mike Duggan!" I replied. "Ooh!" he said. I then told him about how Mike wanted to sit down with me to talk about endorsing his campaign. Erik then told me that I should expect a call from Benny as well. He advised me to, "Call Mike back. Tell him that you will sit down with him and to meet you at the campaign office at 2 p.m. When Benny calls, schedule a meeting with him one hour later." I did as Erik suggested.

With only a couple of hours to spare, I had to stop for a minute to catch my breath. The thought of them seeking MY

ENDORSEMENT after having just contended against them was overwhelming.

In these meetings, I knew I needed to listen more and talk less, as it was my turn to vet them. By asking a series of questions, I could observe the differences in their responses. In the end, I hoped to have enough insights and information from both candidates to comfortably allow myself to answer the following three questions:

1) Does he have a compelling vision for the city?
2) Does he have a plan to support his vision?
3) Does he have access to resources that would make his plan attainable?

If you haven't figured it out by now; no one was getting a free pass from me!

As each meeting concluded, I let both Mike and Benny know that I would not be making a commitment to either one of them anytime soon. Besides, not even 24 hours had passed since my campaign ended. In addition, I needed time to clear my head and think about what was next in my own life. Thankfully, I had a keynote speaking engagement lined up two days later in Indianapolis, Indiana. You're probably wondering, how in the world was I scheduled to speak—out of state no less—when I had just finished running for mayor?

Fortunately, I had always maintained a strong relationship with my friends at the Michigan Association of CPAs. As such, one of my favorite persons there, whom I call my sister from another mister, both recommended and prearranged for me to speak at the 2013 Diversity Summit of the Indiana State Society of CPAs (INCPA) five months earlier. The audience included INCPA high school scholars, college students, aspiring CPAs, young professionals, and accounting firm representatives.

In preparing for this event, I wish I could say that my presentation was completed well in advance. Honestly, one to two days earlier would have sufficed. It certainly would have made my drive to Indianapolis more comfortable and less nerve-racking. However, when I tried to prepare the night before leaving, my mind continued to race with thoughts of the campaign and how it ended. For this reason, I could not focus to save my life. Every time I tried to put pen to paper, I came up empty. The only remedy for this mental block was to pack up the car, get behind the wheel, and tap into my driving-motivation-inspired speech development process. If you are a speaker, you know exactly what I mean when I say, "some of my best speeches were crafted from the road."

The only difference this time was that I had not solidified my speech topic until I reached the parking garage of the venue. With only 30 minutes to spare, I turned off my car's engine, grabbed a notebook, and drew a picture of a table with four legs. Across the top of the page, I wrote: "Diversity Must Always Be on the Table for Discussion." I planned to open my presentation with that statement and then allow the rest of the words to flow from my heart as I shared my personal journey to becoming a CPA and all the unique career moves that I had since made, followed by three points for the audience's consideration. How did that sound to you? It sounded like a great plan to me, so I moved forward with it. By the time I reached the conference ballroom, got mic-ed up, and introduced to the audience, I was fired up and ready to go!

The message that I left the audience with was this: "Diversity is a topic that must remain on the table for discussion. As a nation, we cannot afford to grow complacent and be lulled into believing that we live in a post-racial society[11]," considering that President Barack Obama had just been re-elected to serve a second term in office. "Race still matters." As such, I encouraged the organizations that were represented in the audience "to embrace diversity" if they wanted to be competitive. Finally, in speaking directly to the Black students and young professionals in the room, I reminded them that, "We have not arrived. Don't get it twisted! Hard work, determination, and perseverance are still necessary tools for success."

Afterwards, the great feedback I received made the trip worth its weight in gold. For example, one high school student, who told me she had been inspired by her mentor to become a CPA, added that she "had no idea how being a CPA could open up so many diverse opportunities." After hearing me talk about my bid for mayor, another young lady vowed to someday return to her hometown of Gary, Indiana, to run for mayor. Wow! Who would have known that after coming off a personal loss, I could travel four hours away from home to an entirely different state and help to unlock young people's imagination about what was possible for them? Can you imagine how gratifying that was for me? More than the income I earned from speaking at the event; I was excited to have made an impact as well. When I think about it, impact and income are the fruit of someone who is walking in their purpose. Would you not agree?

Was there other evidence that I was in the right place at the right time doing the right thing?

Absolutely!

When the event ended, I was able to reconnect with my college roommate Raquel, who had moved to Indianapolis with her family after accepting a position with a local law firm. Was it any coincidence that her office was within walking distance of the venue where I had just spoken? I don't think so. As she toured me through the office, I learned that she was the only African American in leadership, which makes the need for diversity a relevant topic within the legal profession as well. Nevertheless, seeing Raquel after nearly a decade apart was like putting frosting on the cake–a true bonus indeed.

Over dinner, Raquel served as the perfect sounding board to help me work through the important decision that I was set to make about which candidate to endorse in the general election. As we talked, I made it clear that I wasn't looking for anything from either candidate, while also not knowing what was next for me. Sensing my deep internal conflict, Raquel said, "Lisa, you can't be a wandering generality." Whoa! She just hit me right between the eyes with that statement. Did she honestly view me as a drifter—someone who lacked direction and was aimless in her pursuits? Perhaps.

Although, in my heart of hearts, I knew that I had been under divine guidance from the moment I quit my corporate job seven years earlier. For that matter, my internal compass had led me to this critical place in my life where time had caught up to an earlier declaration that I made to Raquel some 20 years prior. Do you remember the summer between our freshman and sophomore year when Raquel asked me why I wanted to stay in Detroit after graduation? My reply was, "Because Detroit is coming back, and I'm going to be part of it!" No truer words had ever been spoken by me as a young woman who knew very little about politics.

Therefore, after spending what turned out to be the entire weekend with Raquel and her family, I returned to Detroit feeling energized

CHAPTER 12—LET'S GO EVEN HIGHER: DETROIT MAYORAL RUN

and ready to meet with the two candidates for the second time as promised.

To remind you of my choices, let me paint a picture of who these gentlemen were:

- **Benny Napoleon** was Detroit's native son. He spent his career in law enforcement, and at one time served as Chief of the Detroit Police Department. As Wayne County Sheriff, Benny was well known, well-liked, and had great influence in the community along with religious leaders and organized labor. To know Benny was to love Benny. The way he engaged people of all ages, races, and backgrounds was magical. When he spoke, it was as if words touched their souls. Like me and more than 80% of Detroit residents, Benny was Black.

- In contrast, **Mike Duggan** was a lawyer by trade who spent his entire professional career working in the city of Detroit as a deputy county executive, county prosecutor, and CEO of a hospital system. Despite that, some simply viewed him as the "White dude" who moved into the city from the suburbs just to run for mayor. However, his willingness to sit in hundreds of living rooms and listen to the concerns of everyday Detroit citizens earned him a great deal of respect, not to mention write-in votes during the primary. Apparently, those individuals bought into his reputation as "The Turnaround Guy," and believed he could transform Detroit, starting with the neighborhoods.

To kick off the second round of conversations, Benny was first to share with me his outlook for the election and what he saw as strengths to help him remain competitive down the stretch.

When Mike and I met, we talked about the need to promote entrepreneurship and economic development, which were two important pillars of my campaign's platform. Whereas I had originally been the one asking all the questions, at a pivotal moment in our exchange of ideas, Mike turned the tables and asked, "Lisa, do you want to change the world?" Whoa! I was not expecting that question. How would you have responded? While changing the world is no small feat, something about the significance of the question gave me goosebumps. As such, I enthusiastically responded, "Absolutely! Sign me up for that any day!"

Next, I asked him, "So, what would endorsing you look like exactly?" He gave me three options, saying, "You could:

1) Make a public endorsement.
2) Make a public endorsement and decide to come into the office every day and work on the campaign; or
3) Make a public endorsement, come into the office every day and work on the campaign, and serve as a surrogate who goes out and speaks on my behalf."

While I liked what I heard from Mike, I was not ready to make a commitment.

At the conclusion of both meetings, I walked each candidate to the door and said, "I'll be in touch."

Afterwards, I had some serious soul searching to do. Initially, I asked for input from Erik and one other advisor who both sat quietly and observed each of my conversations with the candidates. First, the advisor made it clear that the expectation from "the streets" was that I would go with Benny. Erik, on the other hand, said, "Ew, Lisa, this is a tough one! You know Benny is my boy, but honestly, it's your call." I respected what they had to say and knew there were other members within the camp who wanted to meet to weigh in as well. However, I kindly refused to entertain such a meeting because I knew in my heart of hearts that I would need to reach that decision on my own.

Whereas my team agreed to respect my wishes, nothing stopped the flood of phone calls, text messages, Facebook posts, and private messages that I received from folks outside of my camp. They either wanted to know who I was going to support or outright suggested that I team up with Benny. In addition, I was forewarned by a couple of individuals that if I indeed had plans to support Mike, it would be "illegal" for him to offer me something in exchange for my endorsement. *No sh*t, Sherlock!* Can you not see the problem with the positioning of that statement? For one, it was presumptive and one-sided, as it could easily apply to Benny as well. Furthermore, it was insulting to my character and intelligence. Did they not believe I was more than capable of making a clear-cut decision without having my judgement clouded by the prospect of personal gain?

In any event, neither candidate offered me anything, and honestly, I did not enter any of those meetings with an expectation of what I might receive in return. I simply wanted to do what I felt was best for the city of Detroit. Therefore, in exercising my own due diligence, I evaluated both candidates on the same criteria that I looked for in my first conversations with them. If you recall, the person I planned to support with confidence had to have a compelling vision for the city, a plan to support that vision, and the ability to make it happen. At the end of the day, Mike Duggan gave me that assurance.

Two days later, I called Mike to let him know that I would indeed endorse him for the Office of Mayor of Detroit in the 2013 general election. He was thrilled. As such, we planned to hold a press conference to make my intentions known to the world six days later. However, I was not going to officially pull the trigger until I had talked to Benny. I wanted him to hear the news from me first.

If you think for a second that making that phone call was easy, think again! In fact, my palms were sweating as I nervously dialed his number. With every ring, I felt my heart pounding against my chest, as I thought about how this one phone call would impact our friendship and his trust. You gotta remember that this was a man whose unwavering endorsement of me in my bid for city council—just four years earlier—had helped to catapult my political career. When I came up short in that race, he was the first one to call and encourage me to run for state representative and did everything he could to ensure I won. So, is there any question why I had to pick up the phone and personally tell him what my plans were?

When he answered, it felt like my heart took up residency in my throat, but I managed to utter the following statement: "Hi Benny. This is Lisa. I just wanted to call and let you know that I will be endorsing Mike Duggan tomorrow during a press conference. I wanted you to hear it from me before you heard it anywhere else." As I waited for his response, the ear-piercing silence that permeated through the phone was even more unnerving. The brevity of his response was enough to let me know he was not happy with my choice, to say the least. However, my decision was so much bigger than an individual or my personal relationship with them. This election was about the future of Detroit.

CHAPTER 12—LET'S GO EVEN HIGHER: DETROIT MAYORAL RUN

Once I agreed to endorse Mike, I was prepared to follow through with all aspects of support that he shared with me in our second conversation, including holding the press conference, participating in radio interviews, working in the campaign office, and serving as a surrogate at various community functions. To sum it up nicely, I was ALL IN!

To put things in motion, we held the press conference at Leddy's Wholesale Candy Store. Why there? For sentimental reasons, of course; it was where I began my entrepreneurial journey as "The Candy Girl." Therefore, Mike and his team had no problem honoring my request. Surrounded by boxes of sugary sweets, just like I remembered, I told the press why I had chosen Mike Duggan as the candidate I believed was best suited to lead the city of Detroit as its next mayor.

The press conference went over without a hitch. However, during my ride home, a breaking news story reported that approximately 18,000 votes that went to Mike Duggan in the primary could potentially be disqualified based on a technicality. If this projection held up, essentially nothing would change, except that Benny Napoleon would be declared the top vote getter in the primary with momentum potentially shifting in his direction going into the general election. At first, I was naturally concerned, given that I had just endorsed Mike. After several attempts to reach him by phone, I became anxious, wondering what all this meant. Eventually, he called me back and assured me that everything was going to be alright. "This is just another bump in the road," he said. "We're going to get through this just like we've gotten through everything else." His words were reassuring.

When I made it home that afternoon, I tried to rest, but I couldn't. My adrenaline levels were still running high. To pass the time, I lay across my bed talking on the phone to friends well into the evening. Around 9 p.m., I received a call from one of my sources in the media who wanted to get a statement about my endorsement of Mike Duggan and the contested election results. While speaking with this person, I heard a noise coming from the lower level of my house. It was a deep thumping sound that made me stop mid-sentence and say, "Wait a minute; I hear something!"

BOOM! BOOM!

Startled by the persistent pounding, I rhetorically asked, "What is that?" It continued.

BOOM! BOOM! BOOM!

"It sounds like somebody's trying to break into my house!" Once I heard the disturbing sound for the third time, I was completely convinced that someone was indeed breaking into my house. I told the reporter, "I got to go!" and hung up the phone. I then called Mother Edith and told her what was happening and frantically asked her to call the police and send them to my address, which I quickly gave her.

I guess I could have called the police first, but I was too busy thinking about where to hide. I looked toward the closet, but then remembered that in the movies, the criminals always checked the closets first. My next thought was to hide underneath my bed since there was plenty of clearance. With the commotion still happening downstairs, I could not help but think, "They're coming to get me!" The hysterical thought occurred to me based on an episode from the TV show Scandal that I had recently watched. The situation involved an assassin who was attempting to break into Olivia Pope's apartment to kill her, but with one shot to the forehead,

CHAPTER 12—LET'S GO EVEN HIGHER: DETROIT MAYORAL RUN

Jake Ballard was there to save the day. If you are a Scandal fan, do you remember that episode? In my case, I needed someone to step in and save the day for me. While underneath the bed, I finally called 9-1-1. When the operator answered the phone, I frantically said, "This is Lisa Howze! I was a candidate for mayor! Today, I just endorsed Mike Duggan, and now *they're* breaking into my house! Please send the cops right away!"

Afterwards, I called my next-door neighbor to ask if she could look out her window and tell me what was going on. When I learned that she was out of town, she suggested that I call her husband on their home phone. No answer! In a panic, I called her back and asked for the phone number of her next-door neighbor who lived two doors down from me. While dialing my neighbor's number, I could hear voices outside of my home. When she picked up and realized it was me on the line, she said, "We're here, Lisa. Where are you?" I told her that I was still upstairs hiding underneath my bed. She assured me that it was safe to stop hiding and come downstairs, while also warning me that my back door has been kicked in.

When I reached the bedroom that served as my home office, I saw the damage that had been done. As I looked around the space, nothing was missing, except some money that I had sitting on top of the printer on my desk. While waiting for the police to arrive, I learned that my next-door neighbor's husband was responsible for scaring off the five punks who not only tried to break into my house but were successful. While waving his pistol at them, he said, "Hey! What are you doin' over there? Get away from that house!" That explains why he didn't answer the phone when I called. He was too busy being a hero and possibly saving my life. Thank God for GOOD "nosy" neighbors! When the police finally arrived, I told them what happened, as they assessed the crime scene and dusted for fingerprints. After the police left, Donovan and another neighbor worked together to secure my back door until I could get it replaced and repaired.

I then took to Twitter and Facebook and posted the following statement: "While everybody on Facebook has been frantic all-day Tuesday about my endorsement of Mike Duggan, five men kicked in my back door while I was home. I was not harmed. The only thing taken was $53 I had on my desk. Do you think this was a coincidence?" I asked. By no means did I think so.

As a result of my tweet, word got back to my godmother that my house had been broken into. In a panic, she called me to see if I was okay, especially since we had just spoken earlier that evening. I told her that I was a bit more ticked off than I was shaken. To put her mind at ease, I assured her that I would be staying the night at a friend's house until I felt safe to return home.

Around 4 a.m., my sleep was interrupted by the sound of Twitter notifications. Who was pinging me at that hour? I discovered that two news reporters who read my earlier tweet were asking if I'd be willing to have an on-camera interview at 7:30 a.m. to talk about the break-in. As sleep deprived as I was, I managed to pull myself together and met them in front of the building where my campaign office was located. When asked if I thought the break-in was politically motivated, I unequivocally said, "Yes!" Judging by all the negativity that was posted on Facebook that day from people who were not happy with my decision to support Mike, what else was I to believe?

In a follow-up question, they asked if I had a firearm to protect myself. I told them I'd be getting a shotgun, signaling to anyone who was watching, "Try me again, if you want to!"

CHAPTER 12—LET'S GO EVEN HIGHER: DETROIT MAYORAL RUN

After wrapping up my interviews with the TV stations, I received a call from Mike's communications director. He heard about the break-in and wondered if I felt comfortable proceeding with the radio interview that we had pre-arranged. "Absolutely!" I replied. "I'll see you there soon." In the face of extreme vitriol coming from people in the community who called me everything but a child of God, I refused to back down. Even when someone who had been inside my campaign quarters sent a scathing email to my campaign director exclaiming, "If Lisa Howze was on fire, I wouldn't even p*ss on her to put out the flames!" I did not relent. No form of intimidation or name-calling would dissuade me from keeping my commitment. If anything, the critics only forced me to become more tenacious in my support of Mike. My mindset was, "If you push me, I'll show you just how far I will go!"

As Mike and I tag-teamed questions from callers who dialed into the radio program, it was clear that he and I had a good rhythm and flow. Afterwards, some supporters within the Duggan for Detroit ("D4D") campaign commented that we sounded good together on the radio. Once again, I felt affirmed in my choice and was ready for the next steps.

My first visit to the campaign office was eye-opening. There was a noticeable difference between his campaign operations and mine. First, there was dedicated space and private offices organized by functional area: campaign management, field operations, communications, volunteer coordination, senior and faith-based outreach, and phone bank operations. The leadership team met consistently at 8:30 a.m. every morning, Monday through Friday. The meetings were well-organized, professionally run, and lasted no more than an hour. The primary objective was to report activity from the previous day, assign tasks for the current day, and note any special intel gathered from the field. When I witnessed all of this, I thought to myself, "Wow! So, this is what a real campaign looks like, huh?"

Originally, I was assigned to work on Mike's economic development platform given my interest in entrepreneurship and small business ownership. However, he switched gears on me one day when he asked me to work with him on debate prep. "Okay, but I've never done that before." To which, he replied, "That's okay. I'll have Rick brief you on what you need to know and do." He was referring to Rick Wiener, an attorney and former lobbyist who once served as chief of staff to former Michigan Governor Jennifer Granholm after leading her transition team. Between Rick's experience leading debate prep for candidates and my fierce ability to debate Mike during the primary, he trusted that we would work well together. After Rick and I initially met, I was still a little nervous about what to expect, but I took on the challenge all the same.

My first objective was to research my candidate's opponent. Instinctively I gathered video footage of Benny Napoleon speaking at the candidate forums and debates held during the primary. I studied his mannerisms and speech patterns. I even examined how he engaged people on an emotional level, which was an advantage that I knew he would have over Mike. Therefore, I wanted to see Mike adopt a new approach to his delivery. By no means did I expect him to copy Benny's style, but I wanted him to recognize what he had to overcome. To appeal to a broader base of Detroit voters, he had to bring it! As the "Turnaround Guy," everyone already knew that he was competent and could answer all the questions with his eyes closed and hands tied behind his

CHAPTER 12—LET'S GO EVEN HIGHER: DETROIT MAYORAL RUN

back. However, in our first two-hour prep session, I told him, "I don't need you to just answer the questions. I need you to connect with the people. I need you to speak to their hearts not just their heads."

I need you to connect with the people. I need you to speak to their hearts not just their heads.

In the first of three scheduled debates, the D4D camp was confident that Mike came away with the win, and then, the media confirmed it. Personally, I was delighted to see how he incorporated my coaching throughout the debate. After recalibrating his own message, the sheriff walked away from the second debate on top. Detroiters loved it when he talked about "strapping on his Glock" to defend the community against criminals who perpetrated crimes on innocent women and children. The third and final debate was ruled a tie. Based on an exit poll of audience members, neither candidate convinced his opponent's supporters to switch sides. Therefore, the key was to win over undecided voters.

With less than one week to Election Day, I was asked to represent the Duggan campaign as a guest on Let It Rip. The Napoleon camp sent a representative as well. Rather than discussing the merits of Benny's candidacy, his rep yielded her time to make defaming accusations against my candidate, while also taking a potshot at me. Too smart to take the bait, I kept my cool and chose instead to use my time for its intended purpose: advocate for Mike Duggan and appeal to undecided voters.

While addressing the show's hosts, I said, "Mike Duggan is the best candidate to become mayor of the city of Detroit. No one is going to outwork him. The field team is out knocking on doors every single day and engaging voters in every neighborhood across this city." Then, turning to the cameras to speak directly to Detroit voters, I said, "On November 5th, vote Mike Duggan for Mayor of Detroit."

The text message Mike sent me afterwards made it safe to say that he was pleased with my representation. The next day, I also received a call from a respected business leader in the community who said, "You were great at maintaining your composure. I see why Mike has you on his team."

So, what impact did the **"Lisa Howze Effect"** have on the outcome of the 2013 Detroit Mayoral Election? Let's go back for a second. Do you remember when I asked you to keep in mind the percentage of votes I received in the primary? It was 5%, right? What some short-sighted folks may have classified as "not a whole lot of votes," let me show you how significant the 4,000 plus votes that I received really were.

On election night, hundreds of Team Duggan supporters gathered in a hotel ballroom in downtown Detroit to celebrate the campaign and anxiously await the final election results. It didn't take long for the media to declare Mike Duggan the winner with 55% of the vote. FIFTY-FIVE PERCENT! Think about that. What if 5% of the vote had gone the other way? Instead of Mike Duggan having a clear and decisive victory over Benny Napoleon, the election could have come down to the wire with a nail-biting finish. Since it did not, need I say more?

Amid all the cheers and fanfare, Mayor-elect Mike Duggan made his way to the stage to greet and thank his supporters. To memorialize the historic election, the local newspapers captured photos from that night, and in them, you could see me standing

CHAPTER 12—LET'S GO EVEN HIGHER: DETROIT MAYORAL RUN

by the mayor-elect's side. It was a very proud moment for me and all who were in attendance. WE DID IT, DETROIT! WE DID IT!

The following day, I received a text message asking, "Where are you?" I thought to myself, *oh, shoot, where am I supposed to be?* Apparently, a meeting had been scheduled at the campaign office. When I arrived, it seemed like everybody was there, from campaign supporters, team leaders, and members of the inner circle. The mayor-elect called everyone together so he could name the leaders of his transition team. When the media learned about it, one news outlet reported, "Detroit Mayor-elect Mike Duggan has announced the appointment of former Michigan state representative Lisa Howze and former Detroit Police Chief Ike McKinnon co-leaders of his transition team." While my appointment was totally unexpected, it explained why he made a point to text me that morning.

The Transition Detroit team had less than six weeks to develop an organizational chart and operations plan that the mayor-elect could implement upon taking office. My primary focus was on the city's finances and business operations, while Mr. McKinnon focused on public safety operations within police, fire, and EMS. Meanwhile, Mayor-elect Duggan had been working hard to secure a power sharing agreement with Emergency Manager Kevyn Orr that outlined his authority to control city operations while the emergency manager focused on the bankruptcy. With assurances to move forward, Mike returned to the transition office, asked to meet with me, and then said, "I want you to serve as my chief of staff."

Surprised once again, my first thought was, *why me?* I was sure there were other experienced people on the team who would have loved to fill that role. However, Mike had already developed a pattern of consistently asking me to step up, from endorsing his candidacy to serving as his debate prep partner to co-chairing his transition team to now becoming his chief of staff.

Here's the thing: I never sought any of those roles. When I eventually accepted the responsibility, it was simply to contribute and offer my support. Obviously, the unselfish commitment that I continued to exhibit while co-leading the transition team was the exact quality he was looking for in the person that would serve in the number two seat of the city. Unsure exactly what the role of chief of staff entailed, I was reminded of a quote by Virgin Airlines CEO Richard Branson, who said, "If someone presents you with an opportunity and you're not sure, just say yes and figure it out as you go."

When the news became public, Crain's Detroit Business reported: "Former State Representative Howze, who represented Detroit's second district, ran against Duggan in the 2013 mayoral primary. She lost, but he tapped the certified public accountant to co-chair his transition team and then elevated her to chief of staff. Howze previously worked as an analyst for DTE Energy and had an unsuccessful bid for Detroit City Council in 2009."

Did you catch that? In case you missed it, the write-up from Crain's is chock-full of lessons on turning losses into wins, setbacks into bounce-backs, and tests into testimonies. In a matter of seven years, I had gone "from a place of obscurity to public notoriety," as my friend Danielle Avis once put it. Based on my consistent acts of faith, I had been rewarded above and beyond anything I could ask, think, or imagine.

Little did I know, this period of joy and jubilation would take on a new meaning on the other side of the new year. Indeed, it was the calm before the storm.

CHAPTER 13

IN OVER YOUR HEAD

"Lisa, I need business cards and a new desk and chair for my office."

"I don't like this office. I'd prefer one closer to the mayor."

"Lisa, please be sure to assign a space on the executive parking lot to this list of individuals."

"Oh, by the way, they also need key fobs to access the back elevator."

(Wait a minute! {Head turning slowly.} Who da f**k gave that person a badge, let alone authority to make promises to people that I had not agreed to?)

"Lisa, when are we going to be hired (into the administration)? We see certain other people from the transition team have started working already. When is our turn?" *(Referring to Erik and a few others.)*

"Lisa, I'd like to hire this person, but they are only willing to come on board if we pay them X!" *(The nerve!)*

"This person hasn't been paid at all. When are you going to get them on payroll?" (*I'm trying. There are such things as processes and procedures that we must follow. Sheesh!*)

"Lisa, the consultants want to meet at 2 p.m. to discuss the bankruptcy and plan of adjustment. Don't be late!" (*What? Don't be late? Who in the hot h*ll did they think they were talking to?*)

"I know your hands are full, but the mayor needs his computer set up and emails synced to his iPhone."

"Ms. Howze, Sorry to bother you. I have another resident on the line who asked to speak with you. I'll transfer them now."

(*F*****K! Give me a break!*)

Have you ever felt like you were being pulled in "*fifty-eleven*" directions—all at the same time? If so, welcome to my world! If not, it's okay. As the old folks used to say, "Just keep living!" For now, let me give you a behind-the-scenes view of what my life was like as chief of staff from the very beginning. It was a classic case of "that was then vs. this now." Emotionally, I had been transported from a place of calm and self-assurance to total chaos and mind-crippling anxiety. What do I mean? One minute, I felt like I was on top of the world. The next minute, I felt the bone-crushing weight of the world on my shoulders. To truly appreciate the contrast, let's take a step back for a moment to recapture a sliver of time nestled between the announcement of my appointment to chief of staff and when I officially started in the Duggan administration.

CHAPTER 13—IN OVER YOUR HEAD

It was during the 2013 Christmas holiday break that I found myself walking barefoot along a sparsely populated beach in Ft. Lauderdale, Florida. Although the sky was overcast with a blanket of clouds, I could not resist making my way to the ocean before returning home to Detroit. With the dampened sand squishing between my toes, my body instantly relaxed as I deeply inhaled and exhaled the moist, cool air. After campaigning in high-heel shoes for over a year, my tired, aching feet playfully danced with the ripples of waves that gently crashed against the shore before retreating to the ocean again. In between each rhythmic cycle of nature's aquatic ebbs and flows, I was gifted with a fresh canvas of sand in which I wrote, "DUGGAN 4 DETROIT" and "DETROIT COS WAS HERE!" I know. Sounds a little corny, right? I didn't care. I was filled with so much gratitude and thanksgiving that it just felt like the right thing to do at the time. Meanwhile, before the rolling surf could wash the words away again, I snapped a quick photo to remind myself of the peace and tranquility that I felt in that fleeting moment.

Fast-forward to January 1, 2014, when Mike Duggan was sworn in as Detroit's 75th mayor. In a small interoffice ceremony, he was surrounded by family and key members of the team. The occasion was somewhat bittersweet since the city's fate was still in the hands of a bankruptcy court judge and an emergency manager. Despite being under state control, Mayor Duggan was not going to let anything stop him from rolling up his sleeves and getting to work right away. In fact, by the time the local news aired at 6 o'clock that evening, Detroiters had a chance to witness their new mayor behind the wheel of a city-operated snowplow. *What?* Yes, you read that correctly! If you think that's unusual behavior for a mayor, you're probably right. However, Mike Duggan is different.

For instance, when Mother Nature decided to blanket the city of Detroit with six or more inches of heavy, wet snow on New Year's Day, Mayor Duggan was ready to jump into action. Without hesitation, he and the director of the public works department came together to develop a snow removal plan to ensure residents could safely move in and out of their neighborhoods. To make matters worse, however, the winter storm brought with it below-freezing temperatures, broken water mains, and sinkholes large enough to swallow a 6,000-pound SUV. In fact, one unsightly sinkhole happened to be located within 100 yards of city hall and served as a terrible reminder to the mayor of how far the city's crumbling infrastructure had fallen into disrepair.

As the stubborn, blizzard-like snow refused to let up, frustrations from angry citizens continued to mount. Likewise, the phones at the front desk of the mayor's office continued to ring off the hook. When residents demanded to speak with the mayor, their calls were redirected to me instead. One woman told me how her car had been blocked in the driveway by the heavy snow that had been pushed to the curb by the snowplows. Understandably, she was furious about not being able to take her elderly mother to the doctor or pick up medicine from the pharmacy. Another woman complained that the snow was piled so high at the bus stops that she did not feel safe while waiting for the bus that was routinely late. Story after heartbreaking story, I listened to Detroiters share their hardships related to basic city services. For a moment, I was reminded of the struggles my mother faced during my childhood when we regularly rode the bus from one end of town to the next, as it was our only form of transportation.

Some thirty plus years later, as chief of staff, I was responsible for holding department heads accountable to right any wrongs and deliver quality services to the citizens of Detroit. For some issues, one phone call was all it took. Other matters were not as easy and could only be cured with time. Unfortunately, time was a luxury I did not have. With no opportunity to catch my breath, I had been thrust into a fast-paced, constantly evolving environment, where things needed to be done quick, fast, and in a hurry. Without question, I had pressures coming from every side. When I was not addressing constituent concerns, I was either attending a series of meetings, checking items off a long list of requests from the mayor, on-boarding new staff, while working tirelessly with the emergency manager's office (EMO) to approve the Mayor's Office budget. In fact, the level of scrutiny and oversight from the EMO made the approval process extremely stressful and time consuming.

To illustrate how intense things had become, one dreary January afternoon, while barricaded in my office, I posted a sign outside my door that read, "PLEASE DO NOT DISTURB. I AM WORKING ON YOUR DEPARTMENT'S BUDGET. THANK YOU!" As I crunched the numbers and submitted various budget scenarios for approval, at a snail's pace, I slowly started to rack up victories for the executive leaders. The heaviest lift of them all, however, was getting the EMO to approve the formation of a new city department called the Department of Neighborhoods (DON). This was no easy feat since it ultimately increased the budget by over $1 million for 16 new political appointees. Even so, the investment was essential to Mayor Duggan's ability to make good on a campaign promise that said, "Every neighborhood has a future!" With the green light to move forward with hiring, it meant I had a future as well. *Lord, Have Mercy!*

As a leader, it is one thing to deal with stress that comes from outside pressure, but the pressure that comes from within creates a different kind of stress. What do I mean? First, let's examine the dynamics of the group I was given to lead. For all intents and purposes, I was the new kid on the block. Prior to my appointment to chief of staff, I had only been part of #TeamDuggan for about five months. It might as well have been five minutes when compared to other members of the team, including those in the executive ranks and certain administrative support staff.

Collectively, they were a mix of veteran politicians, long-time Duggan loyalists, and folks who had either worked on or supported the mayor's campaign from the very beginning, including the period when I was his "not so nice" opponent. As a unit, they had an established circle of trust which allowed them to work well together. Furthermore, their experience with "Mike Duggan, the man" and "Mike Duggan, the candidate" gave them another advantage I did not have. What was it? They had a better understanding of "Mike Duggan, the mayor"—his style, the nature of his demands, and the rapid pace at which he operated. I, on the other hand, was just beginning to learn those things. While going and growing through the process, I guess you can say I got baptized by fire!

With the problems in the city being as vast as they were, the mayor wanted to move quickly at solving them–seemingly, all at once. Every unique demand felt like a fresh log of wood tossed into the fiery baptism pool that only intensified the heat. I worked late nights and sometimes into the wee hours of the morning to keep up and catch up, but it was near impossible. Delegation was not my strong suit. Therefore, if the completion of certain tasks got delayed because I mistakenly believed that I was the one who needed to personally do them, the mayor had no problem finding someone else who could get it done sooner. Can you blame him? As the chief executive of the city, he had every right to do what

CHAPTER 13—IN OVER YOUR HEAD

he felt needed to be done to advance the mission. However, it did not soften the blow to my confidence that was gradually replaced by anxiety and insecurity. Instead of growing in my role, I found myself shrinking on the inside, yet reserving enough room for impostor syndrome to have a seat at the table.

Did anybody else know how I felt? Yes, if you include Erik. Otherwise, the nature of politics can make it difficult to share your innermost thoughts, concerns, and fears with others when trust has not fully been established. However, when I confided in Erik, he always told me, "Lisa, you worry too much! Everything is going to be just fine." I always trusted his judgment, but some days it was tough.

Six weeks into the new administration, in mid-February, the mayor called me into his office to get a pulse check. "How are you doing?" he asked. I got a sense that he genuinely cared about my well-being. He knew that I was carrying a lot of responsibility on my shoulders. At least at this point, all the heavy lifting of assembling the core team was complete, except for one position–director of government affairs. Given my experience as a former state representative, the mayor figured I would be ideal to fill the role and lead his legislative policy agenda in Lansing. Quite naturally, I was concerned about how this new responsibility would change my role as chief of staff. According to him, nothing would change. Therefore, as I accepted the new assignment to work with old friends in the Michigan Legislature, I continued to represent myself as the mayor's chief of staff, only with added legislative duties.

Unfortunately, the more time I spent in Lansing, the more people outside of City Hall started to question and even spread rumors about my status within the administration. Can you imagine receiving a phone call from a reporter asking you to verify something that someone else posted concerning you on social media? It did not feel good to respond to speculations about my career. As far as I was concerned, if it did not come from the mayor himself, it was pure gossip.

Nearly ninety days after our initial meeting, the mayor recognized that I had become increasingly more effective serving in the government affairs role. As such, he decided to make a permanent change in which I went from being his chief of staff to becoming his chief government affairs officer. After informing me, the plan was to update cabinet members the following day.

As the mayor began to make his announcement about the changing of the guard, he noticed that I was seated in the back row of the conference room. While gesturing for me to take a seat at the table, he said with conviction, "As long as I am mayor, Lisa Howze will always have a place at this table!" To this day, I have never forgotten those words, as I felt valued and appreciated. In addition, his statement sent a clear message to anyone who may have had doubts or lingering concerns about what the change truly meant. For me, it was about serving the citizens of the city of Detroit no matter which hat I wore. When the meeting concluded, I congratulated the new chief of staff and offered to assist with her transition.

In the grand scheme of things, Mayor Duggan was not wrong to make the switch. Here's why. Lansing was familiar territory; I did not need a road map. I knew who all the key players were. I had earned people's respect on both sides of the aisle in the House and Senate and in the governor's office. Furthermore, I understood the legislative process and how to leverage relationships to get things

CHAPTER 13—IN OVER YOUR HEAD

done. Not to mention, I was partnered with the incomparable Ken Cole, the city's long-time lobbyist who was a wealth of knowledge and strong advocate for the city of Detroit and her people. In that first year, we were able to get five critical pieces of legislation through the Legislature and signed into law by the governor.

Besides legislation that helped the city crack down on copper theft and emerge from bankruptcy in record time, I am most proud of the three laws that helped the city create jobs for Detroit residents, keep families in their homes who were otherwise delinquent on their property taxes, and remove blight caused by abandoned, fire-damaged homes. In each case, I worked closely with the bill sponsors, their staff, and subject matter experts within city government to prep the bills for passage. In addition, my relationship with the speaker pro tem was key because of the instrumental role he played in helping to get the bills across the finish line.

I'll never forget the final hours of the 2014 legislative session when he called and said, "The Detroit bills are up next!" With excitement, I rushed to the 3rd floor of the Capitol to watch the action play out from the gallery. One by one, each bill passed with bi-partisan support. It was such an awesome feeling; I could not stop smiling! My next phone call was from Mayor Duggan, who said, "Good job!" Sometimes that's all you need to make it worth the long hours and sacrifice, right? After the late-night session officially closed around 6 a.m. the following morning, I did as the mayor advised and went home to get some much-needed rest. It was safe to conclude that my first year back in Lansing was a huge success!

To put icing on the cake, while introducing members of his cabinet at the 2015 State of the City address, the mayor gave me the most glowing public endorsement when he said, "And to the woman who is getting things done in Lansing, our chief government affairs officer, Lisa Howze!" I stood and gave my best Miss America impersonation as I waved hello to the audience. In all seriousness, those words of affirmation were enough to energize me for the legislative year ahead.

> Before I continue, can I give you a word of caution? As you rack up similar wins on your job, please take your victory lap. Just know that not everyone is going to celebrate you or your success. I know that sounds disheartening, but I would rather you be prepared than surprised. Then, when it happens, you won't need to make a fuss. Just make a mental note, smile, and keep it pushing! Got it? Good. Let's go!

As we rolled into the new legislative session, momentum was certainly on our side. The city was winning, the mayor was winning, and I was winning, too! The question is, what happened? At what point did I lose my mojo? We've all been there, right? To help illustrate my point, let's put this in the context of a romantic relationship. Everything is going along smoothly. You feel amazing, and your partner (a.k.a "Bae") feels amazing to you. Then, suddenly, a shift occurs, and something feels off. You can't quite put your finger on it, but in the words of R&B singer Keith Sweat, you know "something, something, something, something just ain't right!" Then, what's the first thing you do? Blame yourself, right? You start wondering if you did something wrong, as you replay different scenarios in your mind. When that gets old, you look to find fault in the other person. Rather than communicating with your partner, you turn to your best friend for advice when all you really want is validation for your feelings.

Does this pattern sound familiar? If you said yes, then please understand that a similar chain of events can occur in work situations and relationships as well. In my case, I knew something was off when I noticed a growing number of proverbial cooks in my "legislative kitchen" and folks crossing over into my legislative lane. When coupled with certain other changes that were obvious to me, if no one else, I can assure you that I began to enjoy my job less and less. Whereas Lansing had been my escape from the undercurrent of day-to-day politics at City Hall, I found myself in need of a more enchanting type of escape.

By fall of that year, my prayer was answered when a trusted friend invited me to a gathering at his mom's house. I was not quite sure what to expect when I arrived, but I soon learned that it was "one of those things." You know what I mean, right? If Amway, Avon, Mary Kay, or even Tupperware registered in your mind, you are correct. However, the direct sales presentation I saw on that night was different. Instead of talking about soap, cosmetics, or food storage containers, the featured product this time was TRAVEL. Who in their right mind would not want to leave the cold winter weather in Michigan to enjoy a warmer climate with sunny skies and oceanfront views?

As such, when the presenter asked, "If you could be anywhere in the world right now, where would it be?" people started shouting out places like Hawaii, Miami, and Cancun. Inspired by our responses, the 34-year-old marketing and public relations expert with the most infectious personality then asked, "So, how many of you love to travel?" My hand only went up partially. Why? While I had been to various cities for conferences, I really did not have many travel experiences that were strictly for vacation purposes, with the exception of visiting Orlando, Los Angeles, and Las Vegas. As for international travel, my passport had not been stamped in over 15 years. As this young woman continued to show images of alluring beach resorts with breathtaking views at some of the most coveted travel destinations in the U.S. and abroad, it did not take a whole lot of convincing for me to say yes. The rates were amazing, and the timing was perfect, considering I had recently renewed my passport. I was determined to not let another 10 years go by without using it.

Therefore, on November 1, 2015, I became a member of DreamTrips, the number one travel club in the world. By far, it was one of the best decisions I ever made in my life. I say that with conviction because it literally saved my life. I went from traveling once or twice per year to eight to ten times per year. While that may sound excessive, it really had become a necessity for me. Between family members once again leaning on me heavily and the ever-changing winds of politics, I needed a healthy distraction. As such, every quarter, I had somewhere to look forward to going–whether for a weekend getaway or an extended stay. I don't know about you, but travel had become that deal for me! And the bonus for the City of Detroit was that I usually came back to work reenergized and ready to serve. In fact, one of my greatest aha moments related to my service in the mayor's office occurred while on the beach in the Caribbean.

> Indulge me, if you will, as I take you on a trip down memory lane. Oh, don't forget to bring your Rum Punch! I think you're going to enjoy what is up ahead.

CHAPTER 13—IN OVER YOUR HEAD

During the first half of 2016, there was not much activity happening in Lansing. Frankly, lawmakers on both sides of the aisle started to experience what was called, "Detroit fatigue." The city had so many heavy-lift policy issues the previous two years that newer items—while important, moved at a much slower pace. It was fine by me because the legislative lull created the perfect opportunity for me to get good and lost–on vacation, that is!

Thankfully, I had already booked a trip to Punta Cana, Dominican Republic for five nights at the beautiful Hard Rock Hotel Casino and Resort. One of my high school classmates, Zara Matthews, decided to join me on this trip. Besides the price being right, she wanted to know what had caused a noticeable change in my attitude since her last visit home when I was serving as the mayor's chief of staff. At that time, she said my "spirit seemed weighed down." However, in preparation for our trip to the D.R., she saw "a whole new side of Lisa emerge—happy, vibrant, and full of life."

On our first day at the beach, I was relaxing and soaking up the sun while Zara was playing along the edge of the water, which was a magical blend of the Atlantic Ocean and Caribbean Sea. When she gestured for me to join her, you would think that I would have delighted myself in this rare opportunity. However, I was reluctant. Even though Zara was not technically asking me to swim, I still approached the water with extreme trepidation. I mean, once the water reached my kneecap, I was anxious to turn back. Zara, on the other hand, wanted to enjoy the serenity of the bluish-green water a while longer.

As she reached for my hand to go out a little farther, you might as well have heard the theme song from Jaws, the horror movie about the big white shark, playing softly in the background. This was not a good idea! Without warning, a gigantic wave came along and knocked me to my knees. In the process, my favorite Coach sunglasses, which I forgot I was still wearing, were snatched off my face and swept away by the current. Still bent over, I started to panic as the water washed over my head. Flailing my arms like a mad woman, I cried out for help! In pure Zara fashion, she calmly said, "Lisa, just stand up."

In my distress, it did not occur to me that my friend, who under normal circumstances is shorter than me, was still standing in the same water that I THOUGHT I was drowning in. Isn't that interesting? After regaining my sense of awareness, I could feel the sand beneath my feet again. At that moment, I realized that I did not need anyone else to save me. Why? Because I could literally save myself by simply standing up.

So, what does this story have to do with my job or your job, for that matter?

Just as the title of this chapter suggests, as an accomplished professional, there will be times in your career when you feel like you are "in over your head." With that said, can I just talk directly to my sister-friends for a moment? For the gentlemen, who are reading this book, continue to follow along, as I am sure there will be some gems that you can share with the boss women in your lives.

Ladies, I would like you to take a moment to think about that time when something unexpected happened at work that negatively impacted you. Did you feel like you had been toppled by a powerful wave? While it may not have killed you, it may have robbed you of your confidence–an important characteristic that helped you reach your elevated position in the first place. Depending on how

CHAPTER 13—IN OVER YOUR HEAD

many times you were hit by that wave, chances are you lacked the strength to fight back. Worst yet, you probably submitted to its force, thinking you had no other options. Well, I am here to tell you that you always have options. ALWAYS!

In my example from the beach, like most of us, I cried out for help, hoping somebody else would come rescue me. Thankfully, Zara was not having it! She simply said, "Stand up!" In other words, *shut up, calm down, and assess your surroundings, Lisa!* Once I listened and followed her command, I was able to regain my footing and move forward in my own power. The same is possible for you. In certain situations, you will not need to ask for outside help. As a matter of fact, no one is coming to save you anyway! Here is why: you don't need saving. Everything you need has already been provided. Therefore, the next time you feel like you are "In Over Your Head," listen for the still small voice inside, telling you to stand up and then walk in your own power.

No one is coming to save you anyway! Here is why: you don't need saving.

As for me, once I stopped drowning in my own insecurities, I began to focus only on those things in the administration that were within my control. Therefore, when the perfect opportunity presented itself, I was prepared to take advantage of it. In fact, the project was so awesome that you would think it had been delivered to me on a silver platter. In the end, not only did the project help to restore my confidence, but it also put a pep in my step and helped to revive my career.

Quickly, what was the "perfect project" that I keep referring to? It was Mayor Duggan's Expanded Earned Income Tax Credit

(EITC) Initiative. WHAT?! I know it may not sound sexy but remember government's job is to serve the people, not ourselves. With Detroit having the highest concentration of poor people living below the poverty line, ironically, Mayor Duggan recognized that Detroiters were leaving more than $70 million on the table every year in unclaimed tax refunds, in the form of these credits. Based on the success the City of New York had in helping its residents maximize their refunds, the mayor wanted to duplicate that success in Detroit. Upon hearing him share this information during a cabinet meeting, a light bulb immediately went off in my head. <<DING!!>> I knew I was a uniquely qualified member of the team who could add value in this area.

After 10 months of coordination, collaboration, and planning, in June 2017, I presented the results of the initiative to the mayor and my colleagues during cabinet. The first slide in my presentation included an image of a beautiful African American family of four that had been featured throughout the campaign on printed literature, banners, and billboards. I used this image as a reminder to my colleagues of the families that "depend on us to help improve the quality of their lives."

As a result of our efforts to increase awareness and expand access, everyone was proud to learn that approximately $315 million in federal and state tax credits went back into the pockets of more than 92,000 Detroit tax filers. That was huge! As it related to closing the gap on the amount of money left on the table each year, we saw EITC refunds increase by $74 million compared to the previous year, thanks to approximately 18,000 more Detroiters filing a return. Therefore, we more than exceeded the mayor's minimum target of $70 million. Break out the bubbly! This was worthy of celebration, right? Wait, not so fast!

CHAPTER 13—IN OVER YOUR HEAD

At the conclusion of my presentation, my colleagues' applause and cheerful faces affirmed something for me personally: I had regained my voice. In fact, one of my colleagues, who watched me go from trial to triumph, said to me afterwards, "Lisa, you have always had it in you." Wow! If anyone needed to be convinced, it was me. For some reason, I had been looking for the affirmation of others when all along, I should have been affirming myself. I'm reminded, therefore, of a quote by Marianne Williamson that says, "Your playing small does not serve the world. There is nothing enlightened about shrinking so that other people will not feel insecure around you." Then, I love the way it continues with, "... as we let our light shine, we unconsciously give others permission to do the same."

> Have you been playing small? Do you repeatedly doubt yourself or your abilities? If you have ever had a problem trusting your own voice, this next part of the story will show you how to get it back.

With the cabinet meeting presentation behind me, my focus was on the press conference scheduled the following day. Mayor Duggan and I along with our partners at the Accounting Aid Society, United Way of Southeastern Michigan and Bloomberg Associates were planning to update the media and public on the impact of our efforts. When I arrived in the office early that morning, I was greeted in the hall by the mayor's chief of staff, who informed me that he would not be participating in the press conference after all. My heart immediately sank with great disappointment. "Wait! What? How is it possible that the press conference is canceled after...?" She interrupted, "The press conference is not canceled. It's still going to happen, Lisa. You're going to lead it." *Huh?*

That changed everything. As I tried to maintain my composure, I walked back to my office to have a closed-door conversation with myself. In the beginning, I was like, *OMG! OMG! This is not happening! How could he?* For a moment, I felt like I was drowning again, except there was no one nearby to tell me to stand up. I had to be that person for myself. I took a few deep breaths and with each exhale my anxiety slowly melted away. I told myself, "Girl, get it together! Stop trippin'! You are more than ready. You were made for this moment. In fact, this moment was made for you. Now, go stand in front of the media and deliver like you have done time and time again!"

So, that is exactly what I did. While there were charts and figures to help quantify the financial impact we had made through the initiative, nothing was more impressive than having a real-life example of how this program was helping to transform the lives of families in Detroit. For example, I'll never forget the young woman who also participated in our first press conference. At that time, she was expecting her third child and had aspirations to use her anticipated tax refund to make a down payment on a new home. In her update, she shared how she was able to buy a used car and fund her unpaid maternity leave. Through it all, she never lost sight of her dream to become a homeowner. So, what did she do? She enrolled in a credit repair program to put herself in the best position to qualify for a mortgage. Impressive, right? Just like the first time, this young woman's story—her poise and her presence— warmed my heart and the hearts of everyone listening once again. Her testimony alone was enough reason for me to stand up and speak up in the first place.

CHAPTER 13—IN OVER YOUR HEAD

When the press conference was over, I was relieved and felt a sense of accomplishment. My first inclination was to return to my office and kick off my heels to give my calves and feet some relief of their own. With toes wiggling freely underneath my desk, I reflected on the day's events. I thought about how the morning started. What first appeared to be a disappointing change in plans developed into a defining moment in my career. Was it happenstance that the mayor could not participate in the presser? A last-minute change with no warning? I'd say not. Why? Say it with me: **"Everything happens for a reason!"**

The more I thought about it, the more I got a sneaky suspicion that the mayor's bailing out on me on such short notice was a setup—and I don't mean to fail. Based on a prior conversation in which we discussed what was next for me, I sincerely believed the press conference was a setup for me to win! As a result, I sent him a text message saying, "If I were a betting woman, I'd say you did that on purpose." He texted back this smiley face: 😊 *BOOM!* My suspicions were correct!

In closing, I want to leave you with seven (7) keys that will help you stand up and catapult your success using my experience with the EITC initiative as an example:

- **Be an active listener**: I listened for opportunity when I heard Mayor Duggan discuss the problem during cabinet.

- **Do your homework**: Immediately following the cabinet meeting, I researched additional facts about the federal EITC.

- **Position yourself as a subject matter expert**: My credentials included being a CPA and member of the Board of Directors for Accounting Aid Society, the

Detroit-based agency that had been providing free tax preparation assistance to eligible taxpayers for nearly 45 years. Not to mention, I was a former state representative who worked on EITC-related issues at the state level.

- **Follow-up:** I sent an email to the mayor and his chief of staff to share my findings and offer my assistance.

- **Begin with the end in mind:** Once it was confirmed that I would lead the initiative, I immediately started to strategize the media campaign that resulted in interviews with television, radio, digital, and print media outlets.

- **Leverage your authority:** I had no problem using the power of the mayor's office to win the support of stakeholders inside and outside of city government.

- **Have fun:** Whatever you do, do it with joy, as if you were working for a greater purpose and not simply for the approval of man.

Through my example, you should see that standing up is not a choice that you make one time, but a choice you must make time and again. Therefore, remember this always: each time you stand up, you are not just standing up for yourself; you are standing to help others stand as well.

Each time you stand up, you are not just standing up for yourself; you are standing to help others stand as well.

SECTION III
WISDOM

The discernment to maximize the meantime

CHAPTER 14

MAXIMIZE THE MEANTIME

"Hey Lisa! Are you still in the mayor's office?"

The person asking was not someone whose name would regularly be mentioned in the ivory towers of Detroit politics. However, I had known them to have strong connections to grassroots organizations in the community. As I had been serving in the administration for about two and half years at this point, my response was, "Of course, what makes you ask?" They replied, "Well, it's just that we haven't seen or heard anything from you in a while. Is everything alright?" Sadly, it was not the first time someone had raised the question. I ain't gonna lie; it made me feel some kind of way. Had I gotten lost in the shuffle? Had my political career reached its plateau? If so, how could I experience a breakthrough and change the public's perception that "something must be wrong"?

Surely, I am not the only one who has ever asked these kinds of soul-searching questions. Perhaps you have asked similar questions of your own. Based on what you read in the previous chapter, it was clear that the mayor's earned income tax credit (EITC) initiative gave me an opportunity to not only stand up but stand out. In fact, it was the catalyst that helped to breathe life back into me as well as my career. Notwithstanding all that, I later discovered how much of a blessing it was to be "hidden" and not always in the public's eye. How so?

Let's face it. We can all name a few politicians or political appointees who have made the news for all the wrong reasons, right? With my legacy intact, it dawned on me that during those periods of darkness when I appeared to be hidden and silenced that the invisible hand had been working a miracle on my behalf. Not only was it protecting me from political booby traps, but it was also rebuilding my character—teaching me patience and understanding and increasing my faith. All were necessary to prepare me for my next career move and life after politics.

That's right! Six months after I completed the first year of the EITC initiative, I was blessed with an opportunity to transition out of local government and politics and begin a new career in higher education. In my role as vice president of a leading non-profit, private university, I was responsible for student success, strategic partnerships, and market expansion in the Detroit region. Not too shabby for a woman who thought she was "drowning" nearly two years earlier. Ha! All jokes aside, nothing about this blessing would have been possible if, in the period leading up to it, I had not learned to "Maximize the Meantime," as the title of this chapter suggests.

To understand what I mean, let's first identify examples of when you might be experiencing a "meantime moment." Meantime moments can generally be described as the pregnant pause between where you are and where you desire to be. When I counsel professional women who feel stuck in their careers, they all are in search of what's next or how to advance in their present place of employment.

CHAPTER 14—MAXIMIZE THE MEANTIME

Who are these women? They typically are well-compensated but overworked and under-fulfilled. Others feel underpaid while being overworked and underappreciated. Both groups, if you ask me, are living below their potential. Many times, they ask, "Why am I here?" Then, in times of frustration, some have gone as far as to say, "I can't wait to get the **** up outta here!"

Whether you are a manager of a fast-food restaurant or an advertising executive who leads creative campaigns for major brands, when career stagnation turns into extreme frustration, you are 100% experiencing a meantime moment. Don't worry! My job is to help you get through it by sharing an example of what it looked and felt like for me to maximize the meantime during my last seven months of service in the mayor's office.

Let's rewind the clock back to June 2017 when Mayor Duggan and I met for lunch at a quaint downtown diner that was within walking distance of the office. With his executive protection unit standing nearby, the waitress directed us to the second floor where we were seated at a table reserved especially for the mayor. The purpose of our meeting was to discuss the preliminary results of the successful EITC initiative prior to my formal presentation to cabinet and members of the media that would follow five days later.

When he asked me what I wanted to do next, instead of giving a direct answer, I asked, "Where do you see me?" He then talked about how he wanted to reestablish the human services department in the city and saw me as the ideal person to lead it. Grateful for the consideration, I responded, "Well, to be honest, I was thinking I would really like to seek opportunities outside of city government." In a somewhat surprised yet supportive tone, he asked, "What did you have in mind?" I told him about an opening for an executive position at an organization that was integral to quality of life in downtown Detroit. I had been studying the position for a few weeks and believed in many ways that I met the qualifications. The mayor agreed that I'd be great in the role and offered to make a phone call on my behalf to the leader of that organization.

Lo and behold, when we returned to the office, we noticed that the very leader we had just talked about was walking into the mayor's executive office suite. Coincidence? Of course, not. You should know by now—there are no coincidences in life, only divine appointments. Indeed, this one was playing out before our very own eyes. In his quick wittedness, the mayor said, "Oh, there he is now! You go that way while I go this way!" *Good idea*, I thought, as I walked in the opposite direction to avoid crossing paths with the person. An hour later, the mayor sent a text message strongly urging me to submit my resume ASAP! This was great news, except for one problem. Aside from the resume I put on file when joining the Duggan administration, I really had not updated my resume in over a decade. I had some work to do, quickly!

Rather than struggle to make the updates on my own, I knew I needed professional help. Therefore, I reached out to a friend who is an HR expert that specializes in transforming outdated resumes into eye-catching career magnets to attract recruiters. Given the urgency of the situation, I told her that I was willing to pay top dollar to expedite the process, which normally takes a week to finish. Forty-eight hours later, I had a refreshed two-page resume that was replete with industry buzzwords and a progressive format. My friend did not disappoint. In fact, she exceeded expectations when she also provided a template to help me draft a stellar cover letter. After a few small tweaks, I was proud to submit my application, resume, and cover letter to the agency responsible for

CHAPTER 14—MAXIMIZE THE MEANTIME

handling the search. That was the easy part. The hard part was waiting to hear from the recruiter about next steps.

After successfully making it past the phone interview with the recruiter, I was invited to meet with the CFO and CEO for an in-person interview. I thought it went well but waiting to hear if I made it to the second round was a long, agonizing process. In the meantime, one of my colleagues had gotten permission from the mayor to tap me to lead another unique initiative in the city called Project Clean Slate (PCS). Because I was waiting for feedback from my job interview, it was difficult for me to commit to my colleague. In fact, for a long time, I purposely avoided having a real conversation with him about the initiative because as far as I was concerned, I had one foot out the door and the other one on a banana peel.

However, my hopes were shattered when the CEO called at the end of July 2017 to inform me that he and his team decided to move forward with a different candidate. Although it was not the news I wanted to hear, I was grateful for the process. Before ending the call, the CEO said, "Lisa, prior to you coming in for the interview, I did not know much about you. I am glad I had an opportunity to meet and get to know you. If another position comes across my radar that I believe would be a great match for you, I will be sure to mention your name." I thanked him and expressed my appreciation for his time and consideration.

There was one other opportunity that I pursued that summer, but I did not get it either. As I shared my frustrations with Mayor Duggan, it became apparent to him that I really wanted to leave the administration. When he offered to have another member of the team help me "find something," I quickly declined. "No. No. Mr.

Mayor!" I exclaimed. "I am here...at your service." In other words, I did not want him to involve others. I preferred to keep it a private matter between him and me. Besides, if I were going to leave, I wanted to do it on my own terms. As such, those two setbacks were the catalyst for setting my meantime moment into motion.

During such time, I decided to reengage and fully devote my attention to the mayor's vision to reestablish the human services aspect of the Detroit Health Department that had been discontinued under a previous administration. In this capacity, I would continue to lead the EITC initiative, while adding the PCS initiative to the mix. For the record, PCS was an effort that originated in the city's law department to assist Detroit residents whose criminal background was making it difficult for them to find employment, housing, or aid to further their education. The goal was to help them access legal representation to expunge their criminal records and become productive citizens within our society. Both initiatives were worthy causes to commit my efforts, so that's where I focused my attention "in the meantime."

Fast-forward to September 2017 when I received an unsolicited email from a human resources executive with the university. In the message, the gentleman, who we will call Jim, informed me that the university was looking for a site in Detroit to locate their new campus and a leader to help with the expansion. I nearly dismissed the message altogether because I did not recognize the person's name who suggested that Jim contact me. In fact, four days had gone by before I eventually responded. Crazy, right? I think my mind was just preoccupied with other stuff. When I finally called him, I apologized for the delay and asked how I could help. We ended up scheduling a late afternoon lunch meeting the following week. For some reason, I added that I had a "hard stop" after one

CHAPTER 14—MAXIMIZE THE MEANTIME

hour. Mind you, I had never told anyone that in my whole life; he had become the first. I guess you could say, I was "on one" that day!

When I arrived at Pho Lucky restaurant around 2 p.m., the place was nearly empty. Jim was already seated at a table near the window, overlooking Woodward Avenue. Before joining him, my mind was made up that I was not there for me. At best, I would gather information and pass it along to someone in my network. At least, that's what I thought.

After ordering duplicate servings of the Pho Chicken with bone marrow, Jim began to share the university's plans and the qualities they were looking for in the campus leader. I listened intently and then asked a series of questions to better understand their goals and assess their existing business activities. The more he talked; the more questions I had. What was supposed to be a one-hour conversation lasted over two hours. So much for my "hard stop," right? Noting the lateness of the hour, we agreed to wrap up, so I could get back to the office.

The next day, Jim sent an email thanking me for my time and stating how he thought I had a "strategic mind." In turn, I thanked him for the opportunity to discuss the university's plans and agreed to meet again two weeks later. In the meantime, I visited the university's website and was blown away by its vision statement. In part, it stated how the university "aspires to be renowned as a quality institution of higher education that understands the market better than any other institution." However, the part that resonated with me most spoke to exceeding employer expectations, transforming communities, and get this—"**changing lives by believing that every person can achieve his or her dream.**" I had to put my hand over my heart after reading that last line. I thought to myself: *Gee, that sounds like me! If I can come to work every day and feel inspired about inspiring others, then that is the place for me!*

When Jim and I met again, we exchanged small talk before he cut to the chase and asked, "So, are you going to apply or what?" *Oh, shoot! Okay.* It had not occurred to me that he had been "recruiting me" for the position the whole time. There I was thinking that I was just having lunch and being "helpful." When I submitted the online application, I noticed the position required a master's degree. I thought to myself, *YES! It finally paid off!* By it, I was referring to my master's degree in finance from Walsh College. If you recall, I graduated in 2004 and then left corporate life in 2006. So, well over 13 years had passed before I could finally put my advance degree to work. Sounds like a long time to wait, right? As it has been said, "I'd rather be prepared for an opportunity and not have one than to have an opportunity and not be prepared." Therefore, I highly encourage you to pursue an advanced degree, especially if your employer is willing to pay for it like mine did.

"I'd rather be prepared for an opportunity and not have one than to have an opportunity and not be prepared."

In addition to meeting the graduate degree requirement, I was grateful that my resume and cover letter were ready to submit, making the application process virtually seamless. Thankfully, I had put in the work ahead of time when I pursued the two opportunities earlier that summer. Neither of them worked out in my favor, but they did work to my advantage.

Think about it. If I had not attempted to stretch outside my comfort zone and apply for a chief development officer and executive

CHAPTER 14—MAXIMIZE THE MEANTIME

director position, I would not have been as prepared to apply for a vice president's position at the university. Instead of being intense and aggressively pursuing one opportunity after the next, I did what most coaches may tell their star athlete, "Play loose and let the game come to you." Therefore, when I least expected it, the university opportunity presented itself to me. I did not go looking for it.

After submitting my application, things seemed to move quickly. They wanted to schedule my interview before the end of October, which was less than two weeks away. Even though I'd just be returning home on a Monday after a weekend trip to Las Vegas, I had no other choice but to schedule the interview for the Tuesday morning after my return.

When I arrived at one of the university's regional campuses, Jim greeted me in the hallway and directed me to the interview room. As each person introduced themselves, I made mental notes, connecting their faces and names with many of the profiles that I had studied the previous night. Among the 12, there were two women who served on the executive leadership team. I knew that I would need to impress them, given the amount of influence they carried. I was ready!

After the introductions, I was asked to take a seat at the head of the table which allowed me to see everyone's faces. Jim sat in the center seat at the far end of the horseshoe-shaped table, just opposite me.

He opened the interview with the following:

"Lisa. Again, welcome. Now that you have met all of us, would you mind spending the first five minutes telling us about yourself and why you believe you are best suited for this position?"

"Jim, that is an excellent question," I replied. "The best way to get to know me is to understand what I believe. Therefore, I have three fundamental beliefs:

1) In life, there are no such things as mistakes, accidents, or coincidences. Everything happens for a reason.
2) People and organizations do not suffer from a lack of money. Instead, they suffer from a lack of imagination and creativity.
3. If you want to become significant in life, you must first attach yourself to a cause that is much bigger than you." In other words, it's not about me because it's much bigger than me.

Sound familiar?

In wrapping up the interview, Jim explained, if successful, the next steps would include an invitation to visit the main campus, where I would also meet with the university president. When we debriefed in the hallway afterwards, Jim surprised me when he said, "Well, as I stated, the next step is to have YOU come to Grand Rapids." My mind was like: *Wait! What are you saying? Am I going to meet the president?* But how? *You have not even talked it over yet with the other members of the panel!* Instead of uttering my thoughts out loud, I just nodded my head and smiled, while my insides were doing cartwheels and backflips. Ha! Obviously, the fix was in! Jim and his team had already decided that the job was mine. I just needed to keep showing up and putting my best foot forward.

CHAPTER 14—MAXIMIZE THE MEANTIME

Can I tell you something? Life has a funny way of coming full circle. You see, I had forgotten that I had already met the president. In fact, it was two years earlier when I was part of a meeting that I arranged between the university president and Mayor Duggan. At that time, the president wanted to inform the mayor about the university's plans to locate its new campus in Detroit. Coincidence? You know better! Sometimes when you are going through your meantime moments, it is possible to experience a defining moment as well. Many times, you will not recognize it until well after that moment has passed.

Without going into further detail, you can already see where this story is leading, right? When it was all said and done, the university made me an offer that I could not refuse. However, before I get too far ahead of myself, there were three commitments that I needed to fulfill before moving on from the administration to take on the new leadership role. I like to think of them as parting gifts to the mayor and the citizens of Detroit that helped to round out my legacy of service at the City.

First up was the mayor's re-election. In February 2017, I helped to jumpstart the conversation when Mayor Duggan asked me to represent him on Fox 2 Detroit's LET It RIP. Dressed in a crimson red blazer that overlaid a sheath, navy-blue dress with white polka dots, my long, straight, black hair, which was parted on the left, hung at least four inches below my shoulders with soft curls on the ends. Seated in the center chair on the panel, I was flanked on my left by the late great political mastermind Steve Hood, and on my right was political consultant Adolf Mongo, who was representing state Senator Coleman A. Young II. At the time,

Senator Young, whom I also served with in the state legislature, had not formally announced his candidacy for mayor, but we all knew that it was coming.

My job on the show was to articulate why Mayor Duggan deserved a second term. In an even and deliberate tone, I ran down a list of the mayor's accomplishments, quoting facts and figures from the city's balance scorecard. I was untouchable when it came to numbers, and the mayor trusted me to play to my strengths. By the end of the night, I knew I had done my job based on the affirming message I received from him. In addition, my friends and family had a knack for hyping me up with the classic "I see you!" text message. What more could I ask?

Fast forward six months later to August 2017, when Mayor Duggan won the primary election with 67.7 percent[12] of the vote compared to his opponent, Senator Young, who placed second with 26.7 percent[12] of the vote. The crowd that gathered at the Historic St. Regis Hotel to celebrate the mayor's sizable victory looked quite different than those who supported him four years earlier. How so? Labor union leaders and members of the Detroit clergy had joined in celebrating Mike Duggan alongside members of the business community and neighborhood block clubs from across the city like never before. Most notable among the elected officials who participated in the festivities was none other than Sheriff Benny Napoleon, who had publicly endorsed Mayor Duggan's reelection campaign earlier in the year.

Personally, I did not linger for too long at the reception because I had a flight to Jamaica to catch the next morning. It was time for the annual girls' trip during my birthday month. Not to mention, the timing of this trip also allowed me to be a bridesmaid in

CHAPTER 14—MAXIMIZE THE MEANTIME

Danielle Avis's wedding. Woot, woot! While packing, I received a text message from the mayor letting me know that I should plan on being his debate prep partner again. All I could think was, "This is going to be fun!"

We planned for two debate prep sessions in mid-October. Ironically, they ran parallel with the timing of my conversations with the university. Since there was only going to be one televised debate between the candidates, I had to bring my A-game to our mock debate sessions. To prepare, I pored through pages of opposition research provided by the campaign team. I reviewed YouTube videos of Senator Young speaking in public settings and from the Senate floor in Lansing. I studied his mannerisms, the inflection in his voice, the tone of his message, and thus, his anticipated method of attack.

Unlike the 2013 campaign, Mayor Duggan was not going up against the charismatic and beloved Sheriff Benny Napoleon. Instead, he needed to defend his record against a younger, mostly bombastic, yet awkwardly brilliant state senator who carried his father's "million-dollar name," as one political insider put it. Yes, Coleman A. Young II is the son of the late Mayor Coleman Alexander Young who served as Detroit's first African American mayor from 1974 to 1994. The question that the younger Coleman had to answer was, "Could he successfully uphold his father's legacy?"

The mayor's campaign committee projected that the central themes of the debate would include race, poverty, and the condition of Detroit neighborhoods. With an advanced copy of the sample questions, I had time to craft responses that reflected what I thought Coleman might say. While getting into character, I fully committed to adopting the senator's persona and position on the issues. As a result of letting my imagination run wild, I wrote some extremely outlandish stuff. When I tell you it was bad, believe me, it was baaad! I said to myself, "Ooh, he (the mayor) gonna be mad at me!" Oh, well. I had a role to play, and anything less would have been a disservice to my candidate. So, let's go!

Once the first mock debate got underway, my goal was to bring the heat early and often. I even asked myself, "What would Coleman do?" To make this simulated debate feel real, I had to think like him, speak like him, and act like him. As part of my debate strategy, I anticipated that the senator would seek to do three things: 1) define the mayor as being for downtown business leaders and not the people in the neighborhoods; 2) appeal to poverty-stricken Detroiters, many of whom had been ravaged by water shutoffs across the city; and 3) show how Detroiters were no better off under the present administration than they were four years earlier. Each area of focus was carefully curated to force the mayor to respond to the growing characterization of Detroit as the "Tale of Two Cities."

With fewer than a dozen other individuals hand-selected to be in the room, we all agreed that the mayor should be prepared for a question about downtown and Midtown versus the neighborhoods. Unlike my colleagues, however, my advice to the mayor was, "Don't run from the attack when it comes. Instead, turn and face it." While standing firm, "acknowledge that there is a difference, and then share your vision for how you plan to close the gap by making sure opportunity is available for everyone." For some, my approach seemed risky. However, I truly believed that if you want someone to stop chasing you; you first must stop running! Have courage to face life's harsh realities and deal with them accordingly.

CHAPTER 14—MAXIMIZE THE MEANTIME

By our second session, the mayor had become stronger in his responses. He had even developed an offense of his own. Notwithstanding, I continued to launch attacks, with every statement becoming more and more derisive. My goal was not to be nice nor placate the mayor. Instead, I wanted to unnerve and push him to the point where he got so pissed off that his head felt like it could explode. Why? Because that is what his opponent was prepared to do.

While many of the things I said were over the top and biting, they were necessary. At one point, my partner in crime—Rick Wiener, who was also in the room, wondered if I still had a job. The mayor and I both knew better. In fact, he understood that I was preparing him for the worst-case scenario. For example, if he showed anger or too much aggression toward his opponent, he would surely lose the debate. While it may not have affected the overall outcome of the election, we could not risk giving his opponent any momentum going into the final days of the campaign.

When the actual debate took place on October 26, 2017, Mayor Duggan was poised and prepared. Surprisingly, Senator Young was more controlled and focused with his remarks at the start of the debate than I certainly anticipated. Even so, he managed to get a few digs in early, but the mayor was unbothered. As the debate progressed, I proudly sat and watched how everything that the mayor and I had practiced played out on the television screen. The mayor stayed on message, remained calm, and delivered as the CEO of a major city should. In reading some of the comments posted on social media that night, someone said, "It appears to me

If you want someone to stop chasing you; you first must stop running! Have courage to face life's harsh realities and deal with them accordingly.

that the incumbent is winning." To which, my college roommate replied, "Yes and the person who prepared him went to school with us." Ha!

After the debate ended, the mayor left the TV studio to join his supporters where we had all gathered at a nearby watch party. When he saw me among the crowd, he said, "I knew I needed to have you in the room." Once again, I had done my job. However, we still needed to get him across the finish line on election day before I could declare that my commitment was complete. Fast-forward 12 days to November 7, 2017, when I found myself among hundreds of people packed into a hotel ballroom, chanting, "Four more years! Four more years!" Mike Duggan had been reelected mayor of the city of Detroit.

As for Senator Young, he went back to the Michigan legislature to finish the last year in his second term as a state senator. He spent the next three years as a political consultant, while getting healthy and transforming his physical appearance. In rebranding himself as a statesman who still carried his father's million-dollar name, Coleman positioned himself to run and win an at-large seat on Detroit City Council in the 2021 election. Then Senator Young and now Councilmember Young is a shining example of someone who successfully maximized the meantime. It would not surprise me if he tossed his hat in the ring to run for mayor again in 2025 or 2029.

As I bring this chapter to a close, let's recap. There were three commitments that I made to the city in 2017. With the Mayor's reelection out of the way, I could turn my attention to Project Clean Slate. Based on my assessment of the program, only a fraction of Detroit residents, who petitioned to have their criminal records set aside, were successful in doing so compared to the mass of

CHAPTER 14—MAXIMIZE THE MEANTIME

people who needed an expungement but did not qualify. Because state law narrowly defined eligibility, I formed a coalition with the assistance of Bloomberg & Associates to redirect the city's efforts from expungement fairs to changing the state law. Ultimately, the city partnered with the state attorney general's office, and the Michigan legislature to expand the law and increase eligibility. In 2021, Governor Gretchen Whitmer signed legislation into law that made hundreds of thousands of Michigan residents eligible for expungement for the first time. Although the change did not occur on my watch, I am proud of the role I played four years earlier in helping Detroiters start a new chapter in their lives, while opening doors of opportunity that had previously been closed.

In rounding out my three commitments, I led another press conference for the kickoff of the 2nd Annual Expanded Earned Income Tax Credit Initiative, days before my departure from city government in January 2018. The EITC Initiative has been going strong ever since, as the city continues to partner with Accounting Aid Society and United Way of Southeastern Michigan. Over the years, I have seen the campaign billboards and thought to myself, "That's my legacy right there!"

Finally, I share these stories as a continuation of what you learned about me in the previous chapter when I felt like I was in over my head. It just goes to show you that the greatest lessons in life teach us that it is not about how or where you start but how and where you finish. To finish strong and finish well, you must learn to "Maximize the Meantime!" In fact, it is the only way to successfully go to the next level.

CHAPTER 15

NO SETBACK... GIRL, BOUNCE BACK!

What started out as my presentation topic for a women's leadership conference in May 2019, "No Setback... Girl, Bounce Back!" has since become a clarion call to empower girls and women across the globe. In that presentation, I talked about my life and career in ways that I had never done before in public. For example, I shared the disappointment of not passing the CPA exam on my first two attempts and then not getting promoted to senior auditor on schedule with my peers. In chilling detail, I spoke about the day my mom suffered a stroke and how the pain of losing her pushed me toward my purpose. Regarding my political years, I talked about running for office three times: first losing, then winning, then losing again in my bid for Detroit mayor. Ultimately, I ended up winning, as I was given one opportunity after another to lead and then become an executive member of Detroit Mayor Mike Duggan's administration.

When plotted over a 20-year timeline, the audience could see how my life and career had been filled with ups and downs or what some may call peaks and valleys. Peak times are wonderful but being in the valley is no fun. Like meantime moments, valleys and periods of setback are uncomfortable spaces to navigate. Why? Because frustration is in the valley. Disappointment is in the valley. Unmet expectations are also in the valley. I get it; no one wants to go through the valley. No one wants to be patient in the meantime either. And, while no one wants to experience a setback, I have found those moments create the greatest opportunities for growth.

Therefore, when I submitted the title for my presentation to the conference organizer, I thought about how I had persevered through one of the most tenuous times in my career, when I felt like I had been in over my head. However, when I stood before this group of women as a recently appointed vice president of a university, my achievement was a testament to how a setback is not a setback for a woman who bounces back. Hence, the mantra, "No Setback… Girl, Bounce Back!" was born.

When I think about the other women in that room, they were human resources executives, public relations representatives, and leaders in industry. While they may not have shared my exact experiences, their responses signaled that they could feel my pain. Why? Because they had unspoken pains of their own. No matter your walk of life, pain is a great equalizer. Hence, no one's pain is greater or less than the next person's. The simple truth is hurt hurts. However, society would have you believe that "successful people" with college degrees, executive titles, fancy homes and cars, and a few nickels in the bank do not have problems. That could not be further from the truth. Unfortunately, the very people that need to be liberated from this perception of perfection are the ones who feel compelled to keep up the charade. How? Either consciously or subconsciously, women do this by wearing the mask.

CHAPTER 15 — NO SETBACK... GIRL, BOUNCE BACK!

Before the pandemic in 2020, Black women in corporate America have been wearing a mask to hide their pain for decades. The fear of being "found out" is always present. *What if they knew you had a family member who was incarcerated? What if they knew you were in an abusive relationship? What if they learned your son or daughter was gay?* What if...? I could go on and on and list several truths about our authentic lives that we hope to keep secret, as we hide our faces in shame. Then there are the plaudits, awards, and accolades that act as accessories—or shall I say, accomplices, that help to keep the mask in place.

In the late '70s, '80s, and early '90s, I grew up watching cartoons on Saturday mornings with my four older brothers. The Looney Tunes® franchise was our favorite—as it was a literal blast to see what shenanigans Bugs Bunny and the rest of the gang got into each week. In the afternoons, our eyes were glued to the television screen when the World Wrestling Federation came on and featured matchups between Hulk Hogan and Andre the Giant or Jake the Snake Roberts and Macho Man Randy Savage. During the week, we reserved our special seat on the couch or floor, as we gazed at the following shows: The Six Million Dollar Man, The Bionic Woman, The Incredible Hulk, and Wonder Woman. In each of those programs, the main character had a mix of superhuman strength, speed, vision, hearing, or ability to jump long distances. Of them all, only Wonder Woman wore a cape, as a symbol of confidence, elegance, strength, and power. For Black women today, the cape is a close cousin to the mask.

Let's put this theory to the test. Shall we? On weekdays, she wears the mask to insulate herself from the inquisitive stares that come from individuals who sit outside her very small circle of trust. However, during the evening and weekends, she exchanges this mask for a different mask that gets accompanied by a matching cape. Instantly, she shifts into superhero mode, in which she tries to save those around her, including family members and friends. Naturally, she allows their problems to become her problems while they remain oblivious to the fact she has struggles of her own. Besides, she's done such a great job suppressing her pain, how could they notice? While the "Black Girl Magic" show continues, the cape and her acts of s-heroism help to brand her as everyone else's "go-to." A sister-friend of mine stated it best when she asked, "Who does the 'go-to' go to?"

Right!

Who is there for her when she cries herself to sleep at night? When sex and alcohol seem to bring more emotional distress and heartache than relief, where else can she turn? Sure, there is church on Sunday, but remember, there too, she wears the mask. It becomes a vicious cycle that repeats itself when the 6 o'clock alarm sounds on Monday morning.

Sis-sss! I see you! With every muffled tear you cry, I hear you, and I feel you. You have been through so much, and I commend you for holding it together all these years. However, you have been carrying the weight of the world on your shoulders for way too long. It is time you let it go. Remove the mask and take off the cape. I know you mean well, but it is no longer your responsibility, duty, or obligation to save everybody else at the risk of losing yourself. You may be strong, but some things were never meant for you to carry. Instead, leave that weight to a Higher Power that is much stronger than you.

C'mon, sis! It's time to transform. It's time to evolve. If you want to elevate your life and career—if you want to go from strength to courage to wisdom, you must let go of things that weigh you down. You can start with your incessant need to be in control. Ahh! I bet you didn't know I was going to go there, did you? The fact is that it took me a long time to learn this lesson. For example, whenever one or more of my family members found themselves between a rock and a hard place, they automatically turned to me for financial help. Each time I extended my hand and wallet, life for them was good—temporarily—until another need arose.

For years, I guilted myself into believing that if I did not help when I had the means to do so, then I was not being a good sister, aunt, or niece. This same issue is highlighted in pop culture through LeBron James' cable television series called *Survivor's Remorse*, in which million-dollar star basketball player Cam Calloway finds himself emotionally conflicted about "making it out" while balancing his family's demands on his time, resources, and lifestyle. Like Cam, minus the million-dollar contract, no less, I had become the fallback option for many in my family who habitually looked to me to cushion their fall whenever they got into financial trouble. For some, I realized that I had been doing more harm than good. Let's face it, I had become their enabler and desperately needed to break away from that pattern.

The first shift occurred in April 2018, when I received an urgent text message that read, "Send money A.S.A.P." I finally said, "NO MORE!" Why was I so emphatic this time? First, this sh*t had been going on for at least seven years! Secondly, if I had not taken a stance, neither my family member nor I would have known what they could achieve. As a result, I am proud to say I have not had to send a money transfer through Western Union® in the last four years. Why? Because this family member is fully employed and now able to take care of their own responsibilities. What a relief!

Clearly, this was a real-life example of what it means to, "Let go and let God!" It turns out that's who was in control the whole time—not me.

After you release control, the next thing you must do is cut ties with negative emotions like regret, guilt, and blame. However, the greatest culprit of all to separate from is unforgiveness. Why? Unforgiveness hijacks your joy, fractures your focus, and holds your hopes and dreams hostage, with no plans to let them loose. When you choose to carry unforgiveness on your payroll, there is a high price to pay. It never takes a break. It does not know when to quit. Except when you go on vacation, unforgiveness packs a bag and says, "I'm coming with you! Don't worry; no one will see me." Unforgiveness is quite a manipulative character that will have you believing you've got it all under control. At least that is what I thought until my true self got exposed during a conversation with a friend.

I use the term "friend" loosely because Kareem and I were more like long-time acquaintances. We originally met at a party through his cousin who attended Walsh with me. Some years had passed before we randomly reconnected because of a social media post I made that drew him to the restaurant and lounge where I happened to be celebrating my birthday. After a few failed attempts to date, we decided to just let things be. Later, when my career transitioned into higher education, our paths crossed again. He asked me out, and this time I decided to get out of my comfort zone (a.k.a. "my head") and meet him for drinks. After all, a bearded Black man, blues, and bourbon seemed to go well together. Just saying. 😊

As we sat, sipped, and talked, Kareem eventually made a comment about my vacation photos on Instagram. As I had been traveling extensively for at least three years, my images captured memories of some amazing experiences in various parts of the world. Whether I was visiting the Isle of Capri in southern Italy, standing in front of the Eiffel Tower, wearing a kimono in Tokyo, or riding a camel across the Sahara Desert, you name it: I was living the life. However, Kareem suggested that although I appeared to be happy in those photos, "To me Lisa, it just looks like you are running away from life." WHAT?! *Who in the hot h*ll did he think he was talking to?* His words would not have stung as badly had they not been true.

He had no way of knowing that I had maintained a pattern of escape for as long as I could remember. For instance, during my college years, visits home on the weekends or during the summers were synonymous with grief, as my mother continued to wallow in despair over my one brother's incarceration. I did my best to avoid the sight of her pain by indulging myself in work and outside ventures like Amway. While attempting to grow my Amway business, I ended up getting involved in a relationship with an older man, whom I originally only planned to make my business partner. While he treated me well and bought me gifts, I was not with him for his money because I was not without money of my own.

So, what was it then? He gave me something more valuable—a sense of peace, love, and security. All the things I felt I was missing at home. Do you see in this instance how family dysfunction can lead to a young girl to make decisions that she may not have otherwise made? My uncle tried to warn and tell me to "date a young man your age…with **muscles**," no less. Did I listen? Of course, not. I was young and naïve, but I thought I knew it all. Besides, my nose was so wide open that I thought my old dude's muscles were just fine. Ha! (*Silly me.*)

In getting back to my conversation with Kareem, who was able to see through my veil of protection, I finally let down my guard and openly talked about aspects of my personal life. As my emotions lay naked before him, I felt vulnerable. Outside of those in my inner circle, few people ever got to witness that side of me. More than answers, Kareem gave me a chance to take a closer look at the role I played in my family that frankly kept me frustrated, disappointed, and borderline bitter.

In search for answers to my dilemma that was not limited to dollars but others' behavior, I came across a sermonic message on YouTube by Dr. Dharius Daniels who said, "There are five (5) types of people you cannot help." As a self-proclaimed enabler, this message opened my eyes and helped me understand that my ability to help someone else is not solely up to me. The other person needs to be an active participant in their own rescue. If they are not open to receiving the help, "What *is* we talkin' about, really?" The truth of the matter is that it is painful to sit on the sidelines and watch them repeat the same mistakes and suffer unnecessarily simply because they refuse to listen. However, you and I cannot worry ourselves to death while our loved one is content living "their" best life versus the life that we would hope for them.

The problem is that when we try to mold other grown folks into our image and after our likeness, we are the ones who end up hurt. For example, I assumed when I offered my "expert advice" that my family member would follow it and move forward in life. However, when that did not happen, I was left holding a bag full of disappointment that in turn was delaying my own advancement.

As an enabler, when you fail to put boundaries in place, timelines get prolonged, and you end up putting your life on hold while waiting for someone else to "get it together." In addition, without setting limitations on what you will and will not do, it is easy to second-guess whether you should have done more when truly you have done more than enough. Since I was guilty on both counts, I had in essence created an uncomfortable existence for myself—in my own home, no less. Therefore, to avoid dealing with the issue head on, I overindulged myself in work and used travel as another means of escape. Perhaps it was this behavior that Kareem noticed when he suggested that I had been "running away from life."

Less than a year after my conversation with Kareem, the pandemic hit, my travels stopped, and my stress level went through the roof! It was way past time for me to stop running. As such, the pandemic forced me to slow down and see how the weight of carrying someone else's burden was not only breaking my back but nearly driving me insane. I couldn't take it any longer! I needed space to think, time to focus, and courage to regain control of my life! If I had continued to put my happiness in someone else's hands, do you know I'd still be waiting? Instead, I decided my peace of mind was too precious to subject to someone else's invisible timeline. Therefore, if I was going to be in harmony with myself, I had to put on my big girl panties and reclaim peace and quiet for myself. If you feel where I'm coming from, please write " I FEEL YOU!" on the line below:

_____

Thank you.

Now that we are on the same page, what is my advice to you?

"Girl, go to bed!"

I wish someone had said those words to me at least five gray hairs ago. Nevertheless, here is what my newfound wisdom has taught me. When you try to help someone and they refuse to listen, do not take it personally. Furthermore, do not allow that person's actions or inactions rule your thoughts, feelings, or emotions. If you do, you in essence give them complete control over your life. In fact, you render yourself powerless–not by force but by choice. Always remember, it is you who does that—not them!

The good news is that you can go from being an enabler to someone who is empowered to get aggressive about your own happiness, align with your purpose, and accept other people for who they are instead of who you want them to be. When you fight for your happiness like your life depends on it, you will discover that being happy requires a bit of selfishness. Why not? You've always shown up for everyone else. Isn't it time you started showing up for yourself? As you get in alignment with the plans that were created for your life, you will see how much more peaceful your life can be when you are following your path as opposed to crossing into someone else's lane. With acceptance, not only are you able to show compassion, but you can also show grace by giving your loved ones the time and space they need to find their own way. Acceptance is so huge because it is another means to take the internal pain that you have so expertly hidden behind the mask and replace it with inner peace. When your soul is at peace, you can and will sleep better at night. Trust me!

Furthermore, the journey to peace is a process that can only be achieved when you cross the bridge between unforgiveness and forgiveness. Start by forgiving yourself for taking so long to get this revelation. Trust me, you are not alone. While we will never be able to recapture the time we've lost to the past, we can rejoice about the gift we have called the present that when used wisely can prepare us for a brighter future.

> To help you on your journey, I have designed an exercise that has three parts that I believe will change your life if you decide to take it on. Just like in the opening pages of this book when I wrote a letter to my younger self, I want to give you permission to write not one but three letters of your own—one to forgive yourself, the second one to thank yourself, and the final one to forgive others who hurt you.

Letter #1: Forgive Yourself

In the first letter, forgive your younger self for past mistakes. Keep in mind, the so-called mistake or mistakes did not have to occur over 20 or 30 years ago. In fact, you may want to forgive yourself for a decision that you made in the last 5 years. I always say, "Where you are today is based on the decisions you made five years ago. Where you will be in the next five years will be determined by the decisions you make today." No matter the circumstances or when the event occurred, make peace with your past by accepting responsibility for the role you played. Therefore, write the letter, free yourself from the past, and move forward in faith toward your future.

Letter #2: Thank Yourself

In the second letter, imagine yourself 5, 10, or even 15 years from now. To be clear, the person that you hope to become in the future is writing to the person you are today. In other words, Lisa in 2027 is writing a letter to Lisa in 2022. Got it? Great!

What does your future self say to you? Are the words "THANK YOU" included anywhere in the letter? In the spirit of iconic rapper Snoop Dogg, who thanked himself after receiving a Hollywood star, make a list of all the things you would like to thank yourself for. To become the best version of yourself, I believe there are some key characteristics that you must develop. For example, the seven character-building statements that follow will give you an idea of what I mean:

- Be coachable
- Be consistent
- Be patient
- Be persistent
- Be responsible
- Be thorough
- Be unstoppable

In addition to these seven, there are more than 70 other character-building statements that I have created outside of this book to assist you with this development exercise. Next, think about the actions you can and will take to become your ideal self. Remember, this is the person who is writing you the letter today. For example, will you study a foreign language, start a business, establish a nonprofit organization to champion a worthy cause, go back to school, buy a new home, start a family, end a bad relationship, jump out of an airplane, or start a new career? As you can see, there are no limits here. Let your imagination run wild!

Letter #3: Forgive Others

The third part to this exercise is even more critical because it involves forgiveness of others. We often make the mistake of believing that if we forgive someone else, somehow, we are letting them off the hook for their inconsiderate behavior. Newsflash, forgiveness is not for them; it is for you! Instead of waiting for the other party to apologize, explain what happened, or provide closure, own your power by treating their offense as a bad debt that can never be repaid. In other words, they owe you nothing. In fact, there is nothing they can do to give you back the sleepless nights or the time or money you lost. In summary, forgiveness gives you and me the freedom to move forward, which is always our best option. Therefore, in the third letter, decide who you NEED to forgive. I stress the word "need" because forgiveness is like a daily vitamin; it is essential to your overall mental, emotional, and spiritual well-being.

The other party could be someone from your past who hurt or disappointed you or betrayed your trust. After you identify them, think about who you were at the time. How old were you when it happened? How did you respond as the events unfolded? Did you feel powerless? Did you confront the person? Did you keep it to yourself or tell someone else? Did they do anything about it, or did they sweep it under the rug as if nothing happened?

There are a variety of relationships between child and parent, subordinate and supervisor, student and teacher, siblings and friends, in which some type of offense occurs. Whatever the case may be, here is your chance to get your power back. Whether you decide to give this letter to the intended party is completely up to you. The most important thing is that you complete the exercise and free yourself to let go of any negative emotions attached to that bottled-up unforgiveness. With each stroke of the pen or keyboard, you give yourself permission to release the pain and lift the burden of guilt, regret, and blame off your life. Are you ready?

Even if you are not, I get it. I just asked a lot from you. It would not surprise me if you were reluctant to complete this writing exercise altogether. Remember, I told you in the beginning how I hate doing exercises at the end of each chapter in a book. As promised, I did not burden you with such an onerous task. Go ahead and say, "Thank you, Lisa!" You will thank me even more five years from now after you have completed the writing exercise. Why? Because I not only believe, but I **know** it will change your life! How can I speak with such confidence? This entire book writing experience has been life-changing for me–cathartic even. In many ways, sharing my story has allowed me to think about things I have not thought about in a very long time. It has also allowed me to reexamine my life based on the people, places, and events that have influenced who I am at my core.

For example, I had to forgive myself for all the times I wished I had been born into a different family. No matter what drama or trauma I may have been exposed to as a child, or dysfunction I may have experienced as an adult, I now realize that there is no such thing as a "perfect" family. Every family has its issues, and the people in that family unit experience various levels of their own hidden pain, which is reason enough for you and me to forgive them.

CHAPTER 15—NO SETBACK... GIRL, BOUNCE BACK!

Before I started writing this book, I thought I was the only woman whose little girl inside was still dealing with pent-up resentment toward her mother. That may surprise you, considering how much I have praised my mom throughout this book. Nothing about the above statement changes how incredible she was in making sure I had the necessary tools to succeed in life. However, I cannot deny there were times when my feelings got hurt, or I felt emotionally distant from her. To prove that I am not alone, I have since encountered other women and girls of all ages who have talked to me about the emotional scars they suffered in their relationships with their moms. In some cases, there are adult women who sadly have not spoken to their mothers in years.

What I would not give to hold my mother's hand again! If only I could speak to her and let her know, "I see you, Mom!" it would be such a relief. Considering that I cannot with mine, perhaps you can with yours. But what if you choose not to? The stain of the pain remains no matter how much you try to suppress it or pretend that it is not there. I know you have done everything in your power to avoid it, but now may be the time to face it. No more running. No more hiding. Give yourself permission to deal with it–whatever "it" may be. The thing is, I can't tell you what "it" is–only you know. As such, only you can do the work to help free yourself from it.

Why is this so important, Lisa?

Doing the work for me started a long time ago. With *Candy Girl Mentality*, I am merely picking up where I left off. More importantly, I know that the quality of my life and the health of my future largely depend on how well I heal

I know that the quality of my life and the health of my future largely depend on how well I heal from events in my past.

from events in my past. Besides, unaddressed hurt and unprocessed pain are too heavy a load to carry into my future. Therefore, I am making a conscious decision to keep the line free so I can be ready to answer the next call. With a clear mind, I can carry out my next assignment.

Guess what? I want the same for you. In fact, when I think about my journey thus far and the obstacles I have had to overcome, my ability to bounce back from life's setbacks was never meant for me to say, "Hey, look at me and what I have done!" Rather, it is to say to you, "If I can do it, you can do it too! And when you do it, I hope you do it even better!"

Now, c'mon! We've got work to do.

CHAPTER 16

EACH ONE, TEACH ONE!

*A*re you ready to land this plane?

On a flight to Los Angeles from Detroit in December 2019, I was seated in Delta Comfort next to a young man who was tall, White, and low-key handsome. Incidentally, his bladder was working overtime from all the complimentary beer he had consumed. "I'm so sorry!" he said, after his third roundtrip to the lavatory in the sky. Under different circumstances, I would have been annoyed by the constant interruption, but in this case, I did not have a care in the world. I was content to get away from the routine of life in the "D" to spend two glorious nights in LA with family, followed by five days of oceanfront vacationing in Hawaii with friends.

Once settled into his window seat again, this young man introduced himself as Payton Miller, a 25-year-old audit senior associate who worked for one of the Big 4 accounting firms in Detroit. In addition to us both being CPAs, I learned that Payton and I shared a connection with Junior Achievement (JA). He served as a member of the Junior Achievement of Southeastern Michigan Board of Directors, and I credited the organization for helping me launch my candy business in high school. Because Junior Achievement changed my life, I admired Payton for his commitment to give back and expose elementary school students to concepts in financial literacy, economics, and entrepreneurship.

While saddened that his busy work schedule had kept him out of the classroom, he told me about an experience at a school where the predominant student population was Latinx. In preparing to teach the class about debit and credit cards, the classroom teacher cautioned him to not bother, stating, "These children's parents do not have those (debit and credit cards). Therefore, they will never have them." What kind of cockeyed bull was that coming from an educator?! No student should have to live down to the limiting beliefs or low expectations set by adults whose responsibility is to lead, guide, and prepare them for the future without bias. Thank goodness for organizations like Junior Achievement that help fill in the gap with volunteers like Payton who play a critical role in teaching children and youth about financial concepts that they otherwise may have never known existed.

As our conversation shifted, Payton confided in me about his career aspirations. I listened intently as he sought my advice on whether he should remain on his current career path or pursue different opportunities either inside or outside his firm. While the choice was totally up to him, I shared insights about relevant experiences that I had at various stages of my career, which he found beneficial. After our flight landed, we connected our LinkedIn profiles, and then I turned him onto my favorite restaurant in the Orange County area where he said he was headed. As I described the amazing food, the breathtaking views, and the alluring drive to the top of the hill where the Orange Hill Restaurant sits, Payton promised me that he would be sure to book a dinner reservation;

if not then, certainly on a future visit. Overall, our exchange was profound because it transcended race, age, and gender. Instead of letting our differences create a barrier to communication, we were able to make a genuine connection and add value to each other's lives based on our common interests. It was then that I fully appreciated my role, not only as an ambassador for the accounting profession, but as someone who enjoys sharing my life experiences.

Why did I share this story with you?

In the introduction to this book, I stressed the importance of mentorship. Just like I was able to support Payton, I have benefited over the years from people who took time to share their knowledge and experiences with me. In many ways, their support and guidance have shaped me into the woman and professional I am today. As such, I wholeheartedly believe, "To whom much is given, much is required." In other words, when you reach a certain level of success, acquire expert knowledge and skills, and collect a combination of unique experiences, you have a special obligation to give back and uphold the African proverb that suggests, "Each one, teach one." In case you were not aware, this idea of passing on your know-how originated during American slavery. When an enslaved African who had been treated as property and denied an education, learned to read or write, they were obligated to teach the next person and so on. Therefore, the ability to read and write (and teach others) had become their superpower.

What is your unique superpower ("USP")?

Before you say, "I don't know," or "I don't have one," I want you to think about that thing you do so well that no one else living, dead, or yet to be born can say they did it better. That's right! For all I know, you could bake the best pound cake in town with just the right amount of lemon zest. Perhaps your outgoing nature and spirit of hospitality allow you to plan an unforgettable experience time and time again for guests during special occasions. Maybe you have a knack for creating content on social media that goes viral. No matter how big or small, your unique superpower is not only worthy of celebration, but it is also worth sharing with the world.

While it is important to understand your gifts and talents, it is equally important to know what you don't do so well. For instance, if my best friend were to have a potluck dinner at her house, and I decided on a whim to make and bring a tray of macaroni and cheese or potato salad, what do you think would happen to it? I'll tell you! It would just sit there, as other guests would be inclined to ask, "Who made this?" I'm sure you have asked that question a time or two in your travels. Well, guess what? My sister-friend whom I've known since I was 10 years old said that she might try it but would be hesitant if it didn't look right. Ouch! My feelings were hurt. Really, but not really. The truth is I know my limitations. While I may not make the most desirable mac n' cheese, I have had friends fight over my vegetarian-style collard greens, which Zara affectionately calls, "LiLi Greens!" How about that!

Seriously, I may not be best known for my culinary skills. However, if you have a question or concern about your career or finances, then I'm your girl! For instance, my friends and family frequently call me for advice about how to handle certain situations at work or make financial choices that give them the best bang for their buck. Why me? Over the course of my life, they have watched me have success with money, which has been well-documented throughout this book along with my career advancement. Therefore, in the spirit of "Each one, teach one," I will spend the balance of this chapter, and thus conclude *Candy Girl Mentality,* talking about something that is even more important than money. You may ask, "What could be more important than money?" Your money mindset. To drive home my point, I will use two illustrations. The first one involves a person who directly sought my advice, and the second illustration describes a type of person who could benefit from applying the financial principles that I teach.

For some of you, these principles may seem simple on the surface, but I promise they can have a profound impact when put into practice. However, before we go there, let me paint a picture of what I mean by money mindset by first introducing you to my friends, "Just" and "Only."

When I first ran for public office, I met people from all walks of life, representing various occupations–from schoolteachers and bus drivers to sanitation and hospitality workers to business owners and CEOs of publicly traded companies. Neither was more or less important to me than the other. Whereas some could write larger campaign checks, others could cast a vote for me at the ballot box. As such, I valued them equally. However, it always broke my heart whenever someone who earned money at the lower end of the pay scale said to me, "I'm just a cashier;" or "I'm just a bus driver;" or "I'm just a security guard." **JUST**!? What do you mean, *just*?

Then there were those who said things like, "I only make $13 an hour," or "If only I made more money, I could..." Hold up! No matter what you do for a living, if it is legal, moral, and ethical, your title or wages should never be used to define who you are or determine the value you bring to the world. Besides, there are some six-figure earners who live paycheck to paycheck. Better yet, think about your favorite celebrity who once had a multimillion-dollar contract but later ended up going broke. No matter how much money you make, "You cannot out-earn bad spending habits," as I once saw on an Instagram meme.

With that said, let's meet Jasmine King whose profile and money situation are included below.

Illustration No. 1: Onward and Upward

Name:	Jasmine King
Age:	26
Gender:	Female
Education:	Master's degree in criminal justice
Occupation:	Public safety personnel
Base Salary/Hourly Wage:	$65,000 annual salary, plus O/T
Situation:	

Jasmine is a young, single woman with no children. She has a mortgage, car note, and $40,000 in student loan debt. After tithes and paying all her household bills, including insurances, Jasmine has approximately $1,500 in disposable income left over each month.

Jasmine does not see an opportunity to move up in her organization since promotions are based on seniority. As such, Jasmine does not plan to stay with her employer for long.

One Sunday after church, she shared all this with me and then asked, "Lisa, what should I be doing with my finances at this stage of my career?"

In many ways, Jasmine reminded me of myself, especially since I, too, became a homeowner at age 27. Instead of having a new car note, I drove a used 1991 Mercury Cougar that was completely paid for, and fortunately I had little to no student loan debt. Although I was earning a similar salary, I told Jasmine, "It's not about how much you make, but how much you keep." To be financially "F.I.T.,"

CHAPTER 16—EACH ONE, TEACH ONE!

I recommended that she avoid or at least minimize the following: fees, interest expense, and taxes. See the table below for details.

Fees (and Penalties)	Interest Expense	Taxes
✓ Pay bills on time ✓ Avoid late fees ✓ Avoid negative comments on credit report	✓ Pay additional money each month toward mortgage principal (e.g., $100 or whatever is affordable) ✓ Shorten the life of the loan ✓ Save dollars paid in interest ✓ Same concept applies to student loans ✓ Pay credit card balances in full each month	✓ Participate in employer's (401k, 403b, or 457) savings plan ✓ Contribute up to the maximum allowed ✓ Invest in a Roth IRA ✓ Start a home-based business ✓ Other tax planning strategies

On a scale of 1-10 using the information above, how financially F.I.T. are you? _____

While you are giving that some thought, you should absolutely commit the next two points to memory. In fact, write them on sticky notes that you can post on your refrigerator or bathroom mirror. *Is it that serious, Lisa?* Yes! The first one is, **"Idle money is easily lost."** In other words, money that does not have a specific assignment, purpose, or goal attached to it can easily disappear without a trace. Case in point, how many times have you gotten paid on a Friday, but by Monday morning, you wondered where all your money went? If you don't have a plan for your money,

Idle money is easily lost.

trust and believe that someone or something else will make plans for you and it.

My second point is, **"Always expect the unexpected."** Like Jasmine, you may be interested in leaving your job someday. What happens if your job leaves you first? I know we don't like to talk about losing our jobs, but job loss is real! Just ask the record 3.3 million[13] American people who, in one week at the start of the pandemic, found themselves applying for unemployment benefits. Not to put you on the spot, but how long could you go without a paycheck before you were unable to pay your bills? Do yourself a favor and ponder that question for a second.

Always expect the unexpected.

According to a 2019 wealth survey conducted by The Charles Schwab Corporation, a discount brokerage services company, 59% of Americans live paycheck to paycheck[14], while only 38% have an emergency fund.

> Do you have an emergency fund? If not, are you preparing to have one?

I highly recommend that you make it your business to set aside a minimum of $1,000 for an emergency within the next year, if possible. As I always say, **"It is better to be prepared for an emergency and not have one**

It is better to be prepared for an emergency and not have one than to have an emergency and not be prepared.

than to have an emergency and not be prepared." Just as I shared with Jasmine, if you concentrate on becoming financially F.I.T. and give your money an assignment, being ready for the unexpected will take care of itself.

Illustration No. 2: Pitfalls and Pain

Next, meet Justin Case, a gentleman whose persona I created from a combination of people whom I personally know, or I have been exposed to their stories in some form or fashion. The Justins of the world do not subscribe to the wealth philosophy of "the more you make, the more you should keep." Instead, they follow a more impulsive practice that says, "The more I make and keep for myself, the more I will have to spend on things that bring me pleasure." In other words, they constantly do the two-step with their money, which is: Earn then burn. Let's take a closer look.

Name:	Justin Case
Age:	52
Gender:	Male
Education:	High school diploma
Occupation:	Laborer
Base Salary/Hourly Wage:	$17.25 per hour plus O/T
Situation:	
For much of his adult life, Justin Case has been underemployed and living at home with his mother. However, since successfully completing one of the city's workforce development programs, Justin has been fully employed by the local factory for the past six years. While he agrees that his job has added structure and stability to his life, Justin still believes that he does not make enough money. Even after his regular hourly pay increased from $13.00 per hour to $17.25 per hour (almost a 33% increase), Justin unfortunately finds himself repeating old money habits that prevent him from getting ahead financially and living comfortably on his own. It seems that no matter how much money he makes, Justin has a hard time holding on to it long enough to make it count.	

Before I discuss the money pitfalls that can lead to a world of financial pain, can you join me in celebrating older adults like Justin for their courage to enroll in training programs that result in them re-entering the mainstream workforce? For many, this is no easy feat, as they work to better their lives. However, without proper financial guidance to go along with their job training, it is very possible that an individual in Justin's position can find themselves in worse financial shape than they were prior to getting the job. What do I mean? Simply put, more money means more responsibility. In fact, it only takes a few missteps at the beginning of their new money-earning journey to turn their financial world upside down. As such, it pains my soul to see people make mistakes that could have otherwise been avoided in the areas of taxes, credit management, and savings. See the table below for a few common examples:

Simply put, more money means more responsibility.

Taxes	Credit	Savings Plan
✓ Not having enough taxes withheld from your paycheck	✓ Responding to too many credit card offers to open new accounts ✓ Financing large purchases like a used car before repairing your credit, which results in paying higher interest rates	✓ Not setting up automatic savings to pay yourself first before there's a chance to miss the money ✓ Not participating in employer's retirement savings plan ✓ Not creating an emergency savings fund

Not to belabor the point, but you do not want to mess with the IRS. Owing a family member is one thing, but owing the federal government is never a good idea if you are not able to pay. The same is true for creditors. They want their money plus interest. If you are not accustomed to paying your balances in full, those purchases can become quite expensive over time. While credit cards can be a powerful tool to help you build positive credit, they can also be dangerous weapons in the hands of an unskilled and undisciplined spender.

As the debt mounts and the financial pressure builds, the person is vulnerable to every negative event that could possibly impact their financial situation. Without a solid plan on how to dig themselves out of debt, they resort to their default statement that says, "I don't make enough money," or "If only I made more money, I could…" It is this type of thinking that believes more money alone will solve all your problems. It simply is not true. Remember, you cannot out-earn bad spending habits.

Anytime I hear someone complain about how "little" they earn, it tells me that they are not appreciative of the "little money" they make, nor do they understand that more is reserved for those who can be trusted with a little. Therefore, gratitude is as much a part of the principle of financial stewardship as any other value.

Case in point, when I started my candy business in high school, I "ONLY" had $13, which was $2 short of the $15 it took to purchase a full case of M & M's. What if I had let that stop me? What if I had not convinced the store owner to remove a few boxes so I could buy what I could afford? First and foremost, I would have never been able to double my money, not once but several times over and again. With consistent effort and a growth mindset, I was able to take as little as thirteen dollars and turn it into thousands of dollars. What originally was not enough soon became more than enough. Therefore, through this simple example, I strongly encourage you to **never underestimate the power of your ONLY!**

Never underestimate the power of your ONLY!

As a matter of fact, being "the only" has worked to my advantage. For example, during my first political campaign, my battle cry was, "I am the ONLY certified public accountant running for Detroit city council." In that case, I used my "oniness" to set myself apart from the rest of the pack. Although I came up short in the general election, that loss led me to the state House, and ultimately the mayor's office, before I was elevated into a leadership position in higher education. Hence, the trajectory of my career would have never reached various levels of success had I not distinguished myself as "the only."

While some people may feel isolated in their oniness, I have always felt empowered. Nevertheless, it is not lost on me that there is an enormous responsibility that comes with being the only anything. Whether you are the only child, the only African American, the only woman, the only Black woman, the only one willing to take a stand, or the only one in your family to go to college, it takes a lot of strength and courage to fill any one of these amazing roles. As my oniness has granted me the good fortune to access certain rooms and sit at exclusive tables with government officials, corporate CEOs, university presidents, and other "BAD ASS" boss women leaders, it is wisdom that teaches me that I am not put there *just* for me. Indeed, my purpose for being anywhere that I am blessed to sit—or stand—is to inspire little girls and young women who look like me to see and know what is possible. After all, representation matters.

Therefore, as I bring *Candy Girl Mentality* to a close—but never our relationship— I want to remind you of my three fundamental beliefs:

1) In life, there are no such things as mistakes, accidents, or coincidences. Everything happens for a reason.
2) People and organizations do not suffer from a lack of money. Instead, they suffer from a lack of imagination, (appreciation), and creativity.
3) If you want to become significant in life, you must first attach yourself to a cause that is much bigger than you." In other words, it's not about me because this thing is so much bigger than me.

By pulling back the curtain on my life, sharing my story, and taking you on an adventuresome ride through my ups and downs, it is my hope that you have been touched, moved, and inspired to practice the principles promoted throughout *Candy Girl Mentality* for yourself. As you adopt an entrepreneurial mindset, commit to being unstoppable, and recognize that life is happening for you and not to you, please be sure to pass your good fortune on to somebody else. Then, and only then, will you be upholding the principle of the African Proverb that encourages *each one to teach one*.

CITATIONS

[1] National Society of Black Certified Public Accountants, Inc. "First 100." NSBCPA.org. https://nsbcpa.org/first100 (accessed September 14, 2022).

[2] National Association of State Boards of Accountancy. "How Many CPAs Are There?" NASBA.org. https://nasba.org/licensure/howmanycpas/ (accessed September 14, 2022).

[3] City of Detroit. "Election Summary Report. Primary Election – August 4, 2009. Wayne County, Michigan. Official Results." DetroitMI.gov. https://detroitmi.gov/sites/detroitmi.localhost/files/2018-05/official_summary_total_report_08-04-09.pdf (accessed on September 15, 2022).

[4] Wayne County Campaign Finance Information System. "August 24, 2009, Post-Election Primary Campaign Statement. Committee Name: Committee to Elect Lisa Howze for Change." Wccampaignfinance.com. https://wccampaignfinance.com/Public/ViewFiledReports (accessed on September 22, 2022).

[5] Wayne County Campaign Finance Information System. "August 24, 2009, Post-Election Primary Campaign Statement. Committee Name: Friends of Ken Cockrel, Jr." Wccampaignfinance.com. https://wccampaignfinance.com/Public/ViewFiledReports (accessed on September 22, 2022).

6 Wayne County Campaign Finance Information System. "August 24, 2009, Post-Election Primary Campaign Statement. Committee Name: Committee to Elect Frederick Elliott Hall." Wccampaignfinance.com. https://wccampaignfinance.com/Public/ViewFiledReports (accessed on September 22, 2022).

7 City of Detroit. "Summary Report-Group Detail. City of Detroit, Michigan. Official City General Election. November 3, 2009." DetroitMI.gov. https://detroitmi.gov/sites/detroitmi.localhost/files/2018-05/official_nov_gen_09_summary_reports_combined.pdf (accessed on September 15, 2022).

8 Natural Resources Defense Council. "Flint Water Crisis: Everything You Need to Know." NRDC.org. https://www.nrdc.org/stories/flint-water-crisis-everything-you-need-know (accessed September 15, 2022).

9 Britannica. "Flint Water Crisis." Britannica.com. https://www.britannica.com/event/Flint-water-crisis (accessed September 15, 2022).

10 City of Detroit. "Election Certification. August 6, 2013, Primary. Mayor, City of Detroit." DetroitMI.gov. https://detroitmi.gov/sites/detroitmi.localhost/files/2018-05/election_certification_-_august6_2013_city_of_detroit_mayor.pdf (accessed on September 15, 2022).

11 Diverse Education. "The Obama Era: A Post-racial Society?" DiverseEducation.com. https://www.diverseeducation.com/home/article/15088210/the-obama-era-a-post-racial-society (accessed September 15, 2022).

CITATIONS

12 City of Detroit. "Election Summary Report. Primary Election – August 08, 2017. Wayne County, Michigan. Official Results." DetroitMI.gov. https://detroitmi.gov/sites/detroitmi.localhost/files/2018-05/election_results_aug_2017_primary.pdf (accessed September 15, 2022).

13 Business Insider. "3.3 million Americans Filed for Unemployment – and an Economist Predicts It Could Be Far Worse Than the Great Recession." BusinessInsider.com. https://www.businessinsider.com/unemployment-numbers-coronavirus-economy-layoffs-2020-3 (accessed September 15, 2022).

14 USA Today. "Most Americans Are Living Paycheck to Paycheck, Survey Shows." USAToday.com. https://www.usatoday.com/story/money/2019/08/14/paycheck-to-paycheck-most-americans-struggle-financially-survey-says/39940123/ (accessed September 15, 2022).

ACKNOWLEDGEMENTS

"With the Creator, all things are possible."

Matthew 19:26

None of what I have accomplished in life would be possible without the loving kindness and faithfulness of my Heavenly Father. It is through HIM that I live, move, and have my being.

While there are several people to thank for their contributions in helping this book become a reality, I would like to express special appreciation for the following individuals:

- **Shawn T. Blanchard**: You are an amazing mentor, friend, and inspiration for writing books. Thank you for creating the blueprint and consistently coaching me through my book writing journey, along with providing the Author Secrets Empire strategies to successfully bring the book to market. I could not have done this without your expert guidance and the support of your team of graphic designers, web developers, illustrators, editors, and administrators at the University of Moguls Publishing Company. You guys are the best!
- **Ma'at Zachary**: To my dear friend and confidante, I owe you a debt of gratitude for how you blessed this project with your brilliance. Once you helped me nail the book

title, the writing process flowed with ease. Finally, the book cover is as "fire" as it is because of your expertise, keen sense of style, and eye for what is visually appealing.

- **Neeyn Bland:** You were the perfect sounding board for me to bounce ideas about story content and the order of the closing chapters. Your insights and perspectives are much appreciated and carefully weaved into the fabric and flow of this book. Thank you, Sis!
- **Aaron Alfaro:** What can I say? Whenever we join forces, the outcome is always pure magic. In reading the first draft while sipping on your favorite "syzurp," you commented that the book was already a page turner. However, you challenged me to go the extra mile in the editing process to slow down the pace and give the readers a chance to ride every emotional wave of the story with me. As a result of following your expert counsel, the reader's experience will be even greater, as I was intentional about every morsel of value added to each chapter.
- **Leonila P. Centeno:** As my editor, I want to thank you for helping to ease my anxiety about the overall editing process. When I was growing concerned about meeting my "original" deadlines and projected release date, you helped me to understand that I can only create with a clear mind and focused attention. I then grew patient with myself and the process, and now here we are.

Other acknowledgements of individuals or organizations that have had a significant influence in my life and career and the shaping of this project are as follows: Akindele Akinyemi, Kathleen Aro, Sara Azu, Kathleen Alessandro, Jeremy Anderson, Jeff Bergeron, Stephanie Bergeron, Apryl "The Word Stylistz"

ACKNOWLEDGEMENTS

Beverly, Rev. Steve Bland, Jr., Brad Butler II, Allia Carter, Marc Chennault, Helen Clay-Spotser, Marquetta Clements, Katrina Crawley, Bob Doyle, Michael E. Duggan, Hadiatu Dumbuya, Peggy Dzierzawski, Anita Edgar, Crisette Ellis, DeLance Farrell, Bridgett Durrough Wilcher, Nolan Finley, Linda Forte, Rose Gill, Denise Hall-Green, Arica Harris, Stephen Henderson, Jamar Holloway, Jean Jernigan, Edith Johnson, Myrtle "Grandma" Jones, Randy Lane, Jeanne Leonard, Gail Perry Mason, Maureen McDonald, David E. Meador, Dr. Lee Meadows, Edna Moore, Mike Muchortow, Leslie Murphy, Terry Murphy, Binita Naylor, Steve Neavling, Cathy Need, Jerry Norcia, Rochelle Riley, Reginald Pelzer, Sahara Peterson, Desma Reid-Coleman, Shaun Robinson, Lucy Ross, Rachel Rouse-Dawson, Tyrone Sanders, Jr., Edward Shelton, Mark Shows, Dubrece Smith, Dr. Kecia Williams Smith, Mark Smith, Rev. Reginald E. Smith, Cornelia Smoot, Harvey Stiger, Chuck Stokes, Gregory Terrell, Davina Thomas, Gabrielle Thomas, LaShanda Thomas, Terence Thomas, Bankole Thompson, Dave Veneklase, John Walsh, Jon Weirda, Rick Wiener, Chrisalle Williams, Warren Williams, Alan C. Young, Various Staff at the Detroit Athletic Club, Junior Achievement of Southeastern Michigan, and the Michigan Association of Certified Public Accountants.

In Memoriam: I would like to acknowledge the late Angelo B. Henderson, The Honorable Benny N. Napoleon, The Honorable Jewel Ware, The Honorable Woodrow Stanley, and my Leo brother Mr. Kenneth A. Cole for their contributions to my experiences in local and state politics. Each of you left earth way too soon, but your impact in and on my life will forever remain etched in my memory.

ACKNOWLEDGEMENTS

Book Cover Contributors:

Photographer:	Shawn Lee - IG: @shawnleestudios
Hair Stylist:	Randi Alexander - IG: @coco_mercedes_
Make-up Artist:	Antonio Amon Beauty - IG: @antonioamonbeauty
Creative Director/ Wardrobe Stylist:	Ma'at Zachary - IG: @talktomaat
Graphic Designers:	University of Moguls Publishing - universityofmoguls.com
Back Cover Copy:	WordStylistz.com

THE LIFE EXPERIENCE ELEVATION PYRAMID is designed to illustrate the three different qualities needed to overcome life's challenges along your journey to success. Strength, courage, and wisdom are essential to bouncing back from life's setbacks and major disappointments.

NOTE: While wisdom is the principal goal, it can only be obtained through patience and your ability to "Maximize the Meantime." Then, once you reach "The Top," you must share your knowledge and experiences with others to help multiply wisdom throughout the world.

#ITSTIMETOBOUNCEBACK

#ITSTIMETOELEVATE

#ITSTIMETOLEEP

MISSION

CANDY GIRL MENTALITY IS MISSION-DRIVEN

Through individual book sales and bulk book orders, you are helping Lisa to create a clear pathway to success for youth and young leaders across the nation.

CLEAR PATHWAY TO SUCCESS
A CAREER & LIFE READINESS (CLR) YOUTH PROGRAM

Help Lisa impact the lives of students and young leaders nationwide this academic school year and beyond.

Every 150 books purchased provides a school with:

- 15 books

- A supplemental teaching guide based on the principles shared in the chapter entitled, "The Making of Candy Girl"

- 15 Young Leaders will receive a "Clear Pathway to Success" rite of passage experience focused on:
    - Entrepreneurship
    - Financial Competency
    - Career Awareness/ Workforce Readiness
    - Communication Skills
    - Character Development

SCAN TO DONATE
A DOZEN BOOKS

ABOUT THE AUTHOR

*W*ho is Lisa L. Howze?

Lisa Howze is an author, speaker, CPA, and professional strategist, who has well-positioned herself as a venerable leader and ambassador for the accounting profession. As the founder and CEO of The Lisa Howze Experience, LLC – a professional development and educational consulting firm, Lisa is committed to helping students and career professionals bounce back from setbacks using time-tested principles and proven strategies that produce next-level results.

Although she has received accolades as an *Outstanding CPA in Government, Woman to Watch – Experienced Leader, and Notable Woman in Education Leadership*, Lisa is no stranger to struggle. In her flagship book, *Candy Girl Mentality*, she captivates the hearts and minds of her audiences by compelling them to live life on purpose and appreciate how, "Everything happens for a reason!"

To partner with this powerhouse or invite her to speak to your students or at your next professional development conference, scan the QR code to complete an inquiry form.